JOSEPH AKEROYD:
rediscovering a prison reformer

JOSEPH AKEROYD:
rediscovering a prison reformer

RON WILSON

Library of Congress Control Number:		2021914130
ISBN:	Hardcover	978-1-6641-0649-9
	Softcover	978-1-6641-0650-5
	eBook	978-1-6641-0648-2

Print information available on the last page.

Rev. date: 07/14/2021

To order additional copies of this book, contact:
Xlibris
AU TFN: 1 800 844 927 (Toll Free inside Australia)
AU Local: 0283 108 187 (+61 2 8310 8187 from outside Australia)
www.Xlibris.com.au
Orders@Xlibris.com.au
831097

It seems as one becomes older,

That the past has another pattern, and ceases to be a mere

Sequence—

Or even development: the latter a partial fallacy

Encouraged by superficial notions of evolution,

Which becomes, in popular mind, a means of disowning the past.

The moments of happiness – not the sense of well-being,

Fruition, fulfillment, security or affection,

Or a very good dinner, but sudden illumination –

We had the experience but missed the meaning,

And approach to the meaning restores the experience

In a different form, beyond any meaning

We can assign to happiness. I have said before

That the past experience revived in the meaning

Is not the experience of one life only

But of many generations – not forgetting

Something that is probably quite ineffable . . .[1]

– T. S. Eliot, 'The Dry Salvages', Part 3

---

[1] My bolding.

CONTENTS

ACKNOWLEDGEMENTS

There are many people I wish to acknowledge for their assistance and support through this long journey to bring Joseph Akeroyd's story to readers around the world. This work started as an academic thesis and, proud as I am of completing a PhD, I felt it was important to share Akeroyd's story with a much wider audience.

I thank Associate Professor (retired) Sandra Martin (former head of the School of Management at RMIT University) and Dr David Hodges (Program Director in the School of Management and Senior Research Supervisor working with candidates undertaking Research By Project) for your support, guidance, and expertise over the course of my research on the achievements and challenges of Joseph Akeroyd. Both of you challenged me to clarify, extend and communicate my learning with others. I am overwhelmed by the generosity of your commitment to assist me in this quest.

Thank you to Anne Gleeson (GAPS writing and lecturer in professional writing at RMIT), Emman Villaran (Xlibris) and Stuart Kells (author and friend) for providing guidance, editing and proof reading services to clarify meaning, improve flow and smooth language. Stuart, I particularly appreciate your guidance in converting academic speak into a wider audience accessibility. Thankyou Jane Cole and your team at Xlibris helping to bring this text to print and distribution.

I acknowledge the support from the Victorian Department of Justice Correctional Services Division. I appreciate the assistance of former Victorian Corrections Commissioner, Kelvin Anderson for his support for me undertaking this research and helping me gain Ministerial approval the processes to access Joseph Akeroyd's papers from closed holding at the Public Records of Victoria. I especially thank Malcolm Feiner (Correctional Services library resources) for his continuing support to access archived and contemporary prisoner education articles and resources.

I also want to publicly acknowledge the great support from Joseph Akeroyd's family, particularly his granddaughter Margaret Mace for bring to light many aspects of Joseph Akeroyd's life that the research into his private and public papers may not have unearthed. I thank you for the access to your family records, the insightful stories of Joseph the father and grandfather and for the photo of Joseph which emblazons the cover of this book.

I dedicate this research to the many prisoner education colleagues I have worked with both directly and indirectly in Victoria, across Australia and overseas. So many of you have provided the inspiration for me to want to express how important this field of education is to our respective communities. Prisoner education has both actively and unwittingly lead revolution in approaches to teaching and these revolutions have benefitted the field of education in the broadest sense. Prisoner education practitioners are unsung heroes. They have been and will be provided with the greatest education challenge and that is to work with some of the most marginalised people in the world. These are people at the lowest ebb of their lives and often look to their educators to help scale the almost impenetrable barriers to regain their place in their community.

Finally thank you to my wife Louise Wilson and my children Jacob, Samuel and Julia for your amazing forbearance in supporting me through my indulgence committing time and energy to this book.

Ron Wilson

INTRODUCTION

We had the experience but missed the meaning,
And approach to the meaning restores the experience
In a different form, beyond any meaning . . .

This excerpt from T. S. Eliot's 'The Dry Salvages' presents the challenge before all of us – the challenge of gleaning the meaning from the myriad of experiences intersecting throughout our daily lives. Sometimes we draw the meanings from our capacity to stand back and view our experiences considering those who travelled similar paths in the far and distant times. Sometimes the experiences jolt the assumptions we have embedded in our psyche to look at events using different perspectives. Sometimes our experiences lead us into completely revolutionary ways of making sense of the world around us. All too often we just tick the bucket list to record and accumulate the experiences without taking the time to draw out the deeper understanding of what just happened to us.

Schoolteacher Joseph Akeroyd was appointed inspector general of Victoria's prison system in 1924. He held this role until 1947, becoming the longest-serving inspector general in Victoria's history. Drawing on his education background, Akeroyd revolutionised the ways prisons and prisoners in Victoria were managed to current times. However, Akeroyd's reform and legacies were recognised only in part at the time and in reflection from current days. Examination of his private papers within the context of popular criminological theories demonstrated that Akeroyd single-mindedly pursued a positivist agenda to reform approaches to prison and prisoner management. Akeroyd fought private and public battles in his drive to reform in the areas of education in prisons, prisoner classification, sentencing, and punishment.

This book provides a fresh insight into the nature of reform in prison and prisoner management in Victoria in the period 1924–1947 under Akeroyd's education-inspired leadership and reflects on the legacy of those reforms in modern-day penology. Through access to his personal diaries, letters, official reports, and other private documentation, Akeroyd's role in establishing Victoria's unique relationship between education and prison management can now be recognised and acknowledged.

Throughout this book, Eliot's challenge has been taken up to examine the experiences of an educator reforming Victoria's prison system and draw out the meaning of these experiences as in relation to policy and practice reform. This book is not a traditional biography. It takes on Eliot's challenge to look at my recent and past experiences as an educator in the prison system and examine these experiences with those insights which challenged Joseph Akeroyd, an unheralded prison reformer and educationalist.

Finally, this book sets a challenge to all involved in prisoner education whether you are forming policy, advising policy and practice, delivering programs, supporting those undertaking studies, managing those who teach, and/or preparing to teach in these unique environments to reflect on your own learnings and how to adequately prepare for those undertaking this vocation in the future.

Accordingly, I dedicate this to all those who commit themselves to be effective prisoner educators.

CHAPTER 1

My Story: First Days As a Prison Educator

From the very first time I stepped into HM Prison Pentridge in autumn 1977, I knew that I was stepping into a world which I could best described as a parallel universe sited within an easy reach of the central business district of Melbourne.

For many years I, like thousands of other Melbourne residents, travelled past the imposing bluestone wall which encased the entire prison complex. At each corner that we could see stood a rounded turret rising above the wall, and within each turret stood or paced an armed officer, his rifle slung over his shoulder and his gaze inward. Just visible from the road above along the wall was a hint of rolls of barbed wire. On sunny days, the blue-grey walls absorbed the sunlight, casting shadows across the ground; on wintry days, the walls added to the overall bleakness. At night, the walls were silhouetted by the strange orange light emanating from within the compound.

When I was much younger, my father used to drive our family past Pentridge on the way to visit our extended family. I was always told, 'That's where they put bad people.' There was no elaboration, just a statement of uncontested fact – bad people were kept behind these walls.

The walls, hewn from bluestone mined from a nearby quarry (now a lake) and masterfully put together by convict labour, met at the front entrance providing the support to the castle like turrets and yawning mouth of the famous (or is it infamous) Pentridge Front Gate. Sited in the towers was the Pentridge clock tower with the faces of clocks facing each of the four key directions – each telling a different time!

Sometimes as we drove past the front entrance during daylight hours, a few men in overalls would be out the front tending to the neatly manicured lawns and shrubs. A uniformed officer would be stationed nearby. These men would not acknowledge anyone, their heads down and focused on the garden beds and the paths. Everything was neat and tidy.

As a youngster, I often wondered what went on behind those walls. In autumn 1977, I was given my first opportunity to find out. This journey took me through the main entrance to witness the world inside the walls. This was the start of my connection with Victoria's prison system – a connection which has lasted through to this very day.

On that first day, I presented at the front gate as a teacher on placement to the Pentridge Education Centre, a special school registered with the Education Department of Victoria.[2] After three years teaching in primary school settings, I undertook postgraduate studies in special education, and this was one of the placements I experienced in that year.[3]

As I approached the front gate on that day, I vividly recall an older gent standing outside on the pavement next to Champ Street, a small street which served as the roadway connection between Murray

---

[2]   Each Victorian prison and juvenile justice facility was a registered school and had been so since 1954 (i.e. registered with the Victorian Department of Education and resourced and staffed by education-funded teachers and admin staff). I will explain the uniqueness of this arrangement later in this book.

[3]   My interest in special education was piqued through the recognition there are many children in schools who were not coping with the expectations of the curriculum of the time and needed some compensatory support either in the classroom or in supportive environments. I worked in a one-teacher country school and became aware of the limited support for those students with learning difficulties in remote settings. I was so impressed with the tireless work of one educator, Brian O'Halloran, who travelled from one remote school to another to provide support that I resolved at that point to extend my skills into special education.

Road and the terribly busy Sydney Road, Coburg. This gent wore a broad-brimmed hat reminiscent of the 1950s, an ill-fitting heavy brown woollen suit with broad shoulder pads inserted. Under his left arm, he was cradling a cardboard box, tied up with string, to his hip. He was just standing there – motionless, waiting.

Inside the front gate, I went through the routine that I was to become accustomed to for many years. My name was checked against a list of visitors, my ID was checked to ensure I was that person named on the gate list, and my bag and books were checked to ensure I was not bringing any contraband into the prison. When the prison officers were satisfied that I was the person on the list and that I would not contribute a security risk, a phone call was made to the education centre and an escort called for. The experience of this morning laid the foundation for the regular experiences of working in a prison – the experiences of being checked out at every post, the experience of being viewed as a potential security risk, and above all the experience of having to wait. Everyone waits in a prison.

I was escorted through a labyrinth of alleyways and checking points known as posts all the way to the education centre before meeting the school principal, receiving a brief induction, and then being escorted again to another part of the prison where I was to be based for this four-week placement experience.

This escort took me back through the main gate and then travelled to another entrance in the prison via a small gate embedded in the west-facing wall. Before exiting the front gate, the officer on the front door opened the peephole and mentioned to someone behind me, 'He's still there. He cannot get across the road. He'll be back here in no time.' 'Typical' was the response from behind me. Sure enough, after almost two hours of my travelling, meeting with the principal and key staff, and waiting inside the prison, the man standing out front had not moved, still clutching his cardboard box to his hip.

This image is burned into my memory and, upon reflection, became the significant symbolic representation of travel between the parallel universes of prisons and community and prisons within community – me entering a prison in a professional capacity as a teacher for the first time and this man leaving the prison, obviously returning to the community after completion of his sentence.

My awakening on this day did not cease here. My first placement was within G Division, the area where prisoners diagnosed with psychiatric illnesses were housed. Either these prisoners were diagnosed in connection with the conduct of their crime, or they became ill throughout the period of their sentence. The classroom in G Division was something akin to a *One Flew Over the Cuckoo's Nest* experience. There was one man standing at a window inside the room looking over a small courtyard sited at the back of the building. There was another man in an obviously agitated state on the other side of the window yelling at the guy inside. The prisoner inside was peeling pages from a small Bible, holding the torn pages up to the view of the fellow in the courtyard then scrunching the sheet, letting it fall to the floor. After each one, the prisoner outside became more and more agitated. 'Don't worry,' came from a voice behind the desk, 'he [the fellow outside] thinks he is St Peter. He won't come in.' I turned to the person speaking and, assuming he was the teacher to which I was being partnered with, introduced myself. 'I am not *the* teacher,' replied 'Brian' (with a subtle emphasis on the word 'the'), a quietly spoken and clearly articulate person who I soon learnt was a university lecturer now serving a lengthy sentence.[4] 'The

---

[4]   'Brian' was one of the only prisoners I knew who served his full sentence. He was denied parole on a number of occasions. I later crossed paths with Brian

teacher is over there,' said Brian with an air of authority, pointing to a third person with his head buried in a book in the corner of the room. Everyone appeared to respect Brian as the lead educator in this centre!

Whilst I could not articulate this at that time, these initial experiences provided the contextual challenge to understand the feeling that I was now in another world and invoked in me the need to seek an understanding of what my role as a teacher was to be within this most unusual environment. More critically I wanted to make sense of these experiences and seek to understand what my role (i.e. the role of a teacher) would be within the context of education in a contemporary prison environment. The seeds of enquiry were embedded within me to seek to understand the situation the recently released prisoner at the front gate found himself having to face after a seemingly long incarceration and what systems are in place to support those prisoners (particularly those in G Division) when they take their steps through the gate to face the world outside prison walls.

The quest to address these questions led me to observe many tortuous threads of argument and positioning held by observers, researchers, practitioners, and theorists trying to address the critical challenges of making sense of the reasons that particular person is in prison at that point in time. The questions led to the challenges of understanding the role of the prison and how the prison is dealing with those in custody with the full knowledge that most, if not all, prisoners will take the same journey through the gate to return to their community. More so, the questions directly challenged me to

---

again as he regained a non-face-to-face teaching role in a post-secondary education provider. Brian became an amazing source of advice on innovative delivery of distance education programs to those in custody.

understand my role as an educator within the prison and the prison system.

In my early days of teaching in the prison system, I felt education was an outsider and just tolerated by some prison management regimes. Others saw it as a critical component of maintaining 'good order, security and management'[5] by keeping prisoners occupied therefore not engaging in disruptive behaviours. Prisoners viewed education as the one link to keep in touch with the outside world and as holding one of the important keys for starting afresh. Prisoner education was seen by the state education services and allied health services as an important means of supporting the rehabilitative role that many people in the community appeared to expect as a function of prisons.

My feeling at the time was that the relationship between education providers and prison management was always tenuous. As long as the provision of education programs fitted in with the prison management regime and did not create a disturbance to the good order, security, and management of the prison, it (i.e. education) was tolerated. However, in Victoria, the role of education was considered unique. For many years in Victoria, the provision of education services was the responsibility of the relevant state education authority. In other states in Australia, the provision of education services was managed through the respective corrective services agencies.

Also, in Victoria, the 1986 Corrections Act specified prisoners' rights. S 47 (o) specified that the prisoner had 'the right to take part in educational programs in the prison'.[2] This right is not legislated

---

[5]   *Corrections Act 1986* section 21 (1) determined that the governor of the prison is responsible for the management, good order, and security of the prison and the safe custody and welfare of the prisoners (2) ibid.

in any other state of Australia nor, I believe, is it enshrined in any other country.

For me, the questions arose: How did education in Victorian prisons hold such a unique position that it was regarded so strongly to be considered a right for prisoners to access? How did prison education centres operate under the auspices of the Victorian Education Department as registered schools of that department? What were the antecedents leading this unique relationship between education and prison management in Victoria?

It was at a meeting in Pentridge's Northern Prison governor's office one morning in the mid–1980s (I do not recall the exact date!) that the next pivotal moment occurred. Apart from the Pentridge governor and the chief prison officer (CPO) for A Division, I was introduced to an older fellow by the name of Eric Shade. Unlike the governor and the CPO who were formally dressed in their uniform, Mr Shade was dressed in suit and tie complemented with a trench overcoat. Mr Shade was introduced as someone who worked in the prison in the past and was dropping in to catch up on how the prison was working. He expressed an interest in knowing about what was happening in the field of prisoner education. The meeting was an informal discussion about the provision of education services to prisoners in Pentridge's A, J, and H Divisions. There was no agenda for this meeting. Whilst I did not know Eric at that time, I was taken aback somewhat at the warmth of his greeting and his sincere interest in the latest developments in prisoner education.

It was only sometime after that it dawned on me that Eric Shade was a former director of prisons and that he came into that role following service as a prison educator. As it turned out, Eric was the third educationalist to be appointed to the role of inspector general / director of prisons after Joseph Akeroyd and Alex Whatmore.

He was the third link in the trio of inspectors general who were educationalists prior to undertaking their prison management roles. I know now that Eric was a senior teacher at Yarraville Primary School before being appointed chief education and training officer for the Department of Prisons (with a focus on staff training) later to be appointed director of prisons. He was the last of the education-linked prison management dynasty which spanned over 70 years, rendering Victoria as a leading state in the management and delivery of prisoner education not only in Australia but, arguably, in the world at the time. Of those 70 years, Joseph Akeroyd, the first of the education dynasty, held the inspector general portfolio for 24 years. This is a record for the longest-serving most senior prison bureaucrat in Victoria until this current day.

Through my ignorance at the time, I realise now I missed a significant opportunity to learn more about the evolution of the close relationship between education and prison management in Victoria. Whilst I missed the opportunity to access the wisdom and learning from key leaders of the time, I knew I needed to gain greater understanding of the motivations, challenges faced within, and legacies left from this extraordinary period where prison and prisoner management reform in Victoria was influenced by educationalists.

When I learnt that Joseph Akeroyd's personal diary and his personal papers were held in the Victorian Records Office but were accessible only through ministerial approval, I believed these papers may give me some insights into the motivations and processes leading to this period of education-inspired reform in Victoria's penal system. Access to these papers not only provided me some connectedness of historical reforms, but it also helped me reflect on the function and importance of education provision in prison and related custodial settings. Through this experience, coupled with my own experience of working in and managing prison education services for nearly 30 years, I gained deeper insights into how our community works. I challenge every person teaching in prisons to ask themselves to strive to understand of their students what led to this person being here (in custody) at this point in time, and what can I, as a prison educator, do to best support those persons toward their release?

CHAPTER 2
Who Was Joseph Akeroyd?

2.1   Akeroyd the Educator

Prior to his appointment as inspector general, Joseph Akeroyd led a distinguished career as a teacher and then inspector of schools in the Department of Education in Victoria. Akeroyd's private papers and the Department of Education historical records showed he studied education at the Melbourne Teachers' College gaining his diploma of education in 1907 before undertaking teaching duties in Melbourne's northern suburbs.[6]

At the age of 33, Akeroyd enlisted in the Australian Infantry Forces earning the rank of captain prior to being deployed for overseas service. Joseph Akeroyd was appointed captain in the 38th Battalion of the Australian Infantry Forces on 1 May 1916 after serving in the army reserve and cadet corps in the early 1900s. He left Melbourne on 20 June 1916 before disembarking at Plymouth on 10 August 1916. Leaving for France on 22 November 1916, he saw active service until he was wounded in action on 27 February 2017 before being evacuated to England on the same day.

Upon notification of the injuries he sustained, Mr Tate, the director of the Victorian Department of Education, wrote to Akeroyd's wife, Ellen, on 18 June 1917. In part the letter stated,

---

[6]   Akeroyd's private papers (VPRS 6604); Blake, 1973.

I had a long letter from Brig. Gen. McNicoll and there is a paragraph in it I know you will be interested in. I quote it to you: -

'Akeroyd has quite justified our confidence in him. His coy (company) attacked with three others in a big raid recently. One of the first enemy shells got him but he stayed at the front-line directing operations as well as he could until the show was over. His right arm is badly smashed between elbow and shoulder. His left leg torn about considerably, 3 fingers are paralysed, and his face is slightly decorated ('improved' I told him). The Doc took 6 shrapnel pellets out of him in various places. He is now in my old ward Y at Wandsworth.'

It is bad to know one's dear ones are suffering, but it must make you proud to know his comrades speak so highly of him.[7]

He remained in hospital in England being treated for a broken leg and bullet wounds to his arm, shoulder, and face until he returned to Australia on 27 July 2017. He was declared unfit to return to action, and his commission was terminated effective from 9 April 1918. He was issued with the 1914–1915 Military Star, the British War Medal, and the Victory Medal.

One in five enlisted Victorian teachers did not return from the Great War. Captain Joseph Akeroyd was one of those soldiers returning from the Great War to resume his teaching career. Like many of those returning, Akeroyd bore the scars of war. He not only carried the impact of physical injury on his body, but also carried some psychological trauma. Triolo[8] shared the stories of

---

[7]   VPRS 6604.

[8]   Triolo, R. (2012), *Our Schools and the War: Victoria's Education Department and the Great War, 1914–18*, Australian Scholarly Publishing, North Melbourne, Vic., 2012.

many of those returning teachers and the difficulties they endured to contribute to the education of Victorian students. Of Akeroyd, Triolo wrote,

> *Even though he could not write properly as a result of a serious wound to his arm, Joseph Akeroyd resumed the role of inspector in the Bendigo district although sometimes he felt ill and rapidly departed schools. A woman later told Inspector Holloway that the smell from the local soap factory affected him in ome way related to the war.*

Despite these injuries and their enduring legacies, Akeroyd drew on inspiration from his wartime experiences to shape his determination to be an active and positive contributor to his community.

Akeroyd kept a poem within his personal papers, and this poem seemed to epitomise his drive for achieving the best he can for his community.

> *Lieut – Colonel L. F. Clarke, D. S. C. a very gallant officer, killed at Gallipoli, always carried this poem with him.*

> *Did you tackle the trouble that came to you*
> *With a resolute heart and cheerful?*
> *Or hide your head from the light of day*
> *With a craven heart and fearful?*

> *Ah: a trouble's a ton or a trouble's an ounce,*
> *Or a trouble is what you make of it;*
> *And it isn't the fact that you're hurt that counts,*
> *But only, How did you take it?*

> *You're beaten to earth? Well what of that?*
> *Come up with a smiling face;*

It's nothing against you to fall down flat,
But to lie there — that's the disgrace

The harder you're thrown the higher you'll bounce,
Be proud of your blackened eye;
It isn't the fact that you're licked that counts,
But how did you fight and why?

What though you be done to death, what then?
If you battled the best you could?
If you played your part in the world of men,
Why the critic will call it good.

Death comes with a crawl or comes with a pounce,
But whether he's slow or spry,
It isn't the fact you're dead that counts,
But only, how did you die? (VPRS 6604, undated)

It is within the words of this poem which provide insights into the tenacity and persistency Akeroyd armed himself for his venture into serving his community as inspector general of Victoria's penal system.

Despite suffering significant injuries whilst serving, Akeroyd returned to Australia in 1917 and resumed his teaching career where he was promoted to the position of inspector of schools in the regional areas of East Gippsland and Bendigo before taking a dramatic career change to head Victoria's penal system.[9] On his

---

[9]   In 1919, the electoral rolls recorded Joseph Akeroyd and his wife, Ethel, as residents of Bendigo until 1924 when they moved to suburban Pascoe Vale. The move coincided with him commencing his duties as inspector general of prisons in Victoria (becoming Victoria's longest-serving inspector general to this very day). Building on his passion for and extensive knowledge of education, Akeroyd led monumental reforms in prison and prisoner management in Victoria.

return from the European conflicts, Akeroyd's initial appointment was in the Gippsland region and later in the Bendigo region. Beyond his military management experience, it was in his Bendigo role where Akeroyd was first publicly recognised via letters of commendation from the secretary of the Department of Education and the chief secretary for his capacity to organise and harness teachers in Bendigo to support those suffering from the Spanish flu epidemic.[10]

In his diary, Akeroyd noted that teachers were keen to volunteer their skills to help citizens throughout the region during debilitating events. He wrote to the chief secretary extolling the attributes of staff who expressed a willingness to volunteer their services over and above their professional duties. Akeroyd called a meeting of all interested and proceeded to organise the teachers accordingly:

> *The happenings of the past week have brought very vividly to light the sterling qualities of our teachers and I think it truly fitting I should bring them under your notice.*[11]

He outlined how the 'ladies'[12] offered their first aid and cooking skills as well as worked as ward maids alongside the Red Cross, whilst the male sloyd[13] teachers made screens, lockers, and bed rests

---

[10]   VPRS 6604.

[11]   VPRS 6604, 15 February 1919.

[12]   His term.

[13]   'Sloyd work is used in the schools in a disciplinary way as an integral part of general education; the children, generally boys, are employed for a certain number of hours a week in making articles of common household use. It is maintained that work of this kind is especially invaluable in supplementing the ordinary school education of the three R's. It fulfils the injunction "to put the whole boy to school;" it develops faculties which would otherwise lie dormant, while at the same time it trains the eye and does away with clumsy fingers.' http://ebooks.adelaide.edu.au/m/muskett/philip/art/Section8.html (last updated on Monday, 27 December 2004 09:40:53).

or worked as ambulance drivers and stretcher bearers or distributed information around the region. Akeroyd wrote,

> *I would request that the above (report) be shown to the Director as it forms one of the finest examples of citizen service I have known.*[14]

Whilst Akeroyd was strong in his praise for the volunteering teachers, he was scathing in his remarks about others who refused to contribute to the relief effort. Akeroyd wrote in his diary, and in a letter to the chief secretary, that those teachers who did not volunteer 'were branded as shirkers by their comrades during the war'.[15] These early recordings of his thoughts provided insight into Akeroyd's capacity for workforce management as well as his high expectations for professional behaviour in how staff members performed their roles.

Akeroyd demonstrated remarkable empathy towards disadvantaged students facing challenges. His commitment to engage such students provided an important insight into a similar approach he later adapted to engaging prison inmates. Prior to his military interlude, Akeroyd's diary recorded his concern about the effectiveness of school curriculum and its application to marginalised groups within the community. In June 1915, Akeroyd wrote a report on the effectiveness of schools in the East Gippsland region, particularly in relation to schooling Aboriginal children at Lake Tyers. Akeroyd argued that traditional curriculum failed to address the needs of the young indigenous students. Accordingly, he argued that the students remained disengaged from the school process. His diary noted he strongly advocated to the chief secretary via the director of education

---

[14] VPRS 6604, 15 February 1919.

[15] VPRS 6604, 15 February 1919,

to implement trade / work training programs at the earliest possible age for indigenous students. He also referred to the importance of considering training-related programs for students not regularly attending school. Akeroyd wrote of the difficulty some students faced travelling long distances from remote properties to attend school amid a strong demand for children to work on the family farm. He weighed legal pressure to compel student attendance but realised no effective apparatus existed at the time. He also recognised the pragmatic requirements of farming families that needed all available people to work on their small country properties. Again, Akeroyd recommended the importance of supporting requisite skill requirements of rural families by connecting the students with an appropriate training curriculum rather than the prescribed academic curriculum.[16]

Whatever philosophical principles underpinned Akeroyd's thinking at the time, the essential matter is that Akeroyd, a schoolteacher and inspector of schools, became inspector general of Victoria's penal system on 24 January 1924. His role was subsequently expanded on 23 October 1932 to become inspector general of Victoria's penal establishments and reformatory schools.

---

[16]   VPRS 6604, 5 June 1915.

CHAPTER 3

Joseph Akeroyd's Appointment as Inspector General of Victoria's Penal System

3.1 Melbourne in the 1920s

Like many cities in the Western world, Melbourne (Victoria, Australia) faced challenges of fluctuating fortunes in that tumultuous period between World Wars I and II. Recovering from the loss of 16,000 killed in the Great War and many more of the 112,000 enlisted returning with physical injuries and traumatic mental health conditions, Melbourne was hit with further tragedy in 1918. It was commonly thought the returning soldiers brought an additional and unwelcome legacy from the European battlefields. Between 1918 and 1920, Victoria suffered with the onslaught of the Spanish flu which claimed over 4000 lives. Not unlike the recent COVID-19 restrictions, in 1919, the state of Victoria was placed in quarantine. Borders to New South Wales were closed, public meetings were banned, public buildings were shut, and train travel was limited. For a time, Victoria was isolated from the rest of Australia even though it still housed the national parliament (and remained national capital until 1927).

Throughout this period, Victoria was riding a mild oscillation of economic prosperity and recession. Its industry capabilities were challenged by trying to place returning soldiers into work whilst supporting those unable to work through injury or mental illness. Relying on British industry for its manufacturing needs, Victoria's mining capacity was declining, and effort to resettle soldiers in agricultural areas was yet to take hold. Even though these times appeared economically and socially unsettling, Victoria's crime rate was steadily declining. Despite the lessening crime rate (evidenced in falling arrest rates and falling imprisonment numbers), criminal activity centred on gambling, sly grog, cocaine, fraud, and an increasing number of vehicle-related offences.[17] Whilst the number of property theft and personal harm offences committed was relatively low compared to current times, there was a significant mass murder event in the Melbourne Botanical Gardens. In January 1924, one man, Norman List, shot and killed five people before leaving the scene.[18] He turned the gun on himself two days later.

> One of the most sensational tragedies ever known in Melbourne occurred about half-past 6 o'clock last evening. A madman, armed with a rifle, shot 5 persons who were walking or sitting in the Botanic Gardens near Anderson street.[19]

Surprisingly, the press coverage of this incident was not as extensive as the focus on the antics of some of Melbourne's underworld characters of the time, particularly Squizzy Taylor, Long Harry Taylor, and Henry Stokes. Whilst the notoriety of these characters captured Melbourne's interest and piqued readers' focus on underworld activity, there was another aspect of crime

---

[17] Chris McConville (2013), 'Melbourne Crime: From War to Depression, 1919–1929', Australian Dictionary of Biography, National Centre of Biography, Australian National University, http://adb.anu.edu.au/essay/6/text28416, originally published 23 May 2013, accessed 14 November 2017.

[18] This was the first recorded massacre of non-indigenous people in Victoria. Until this time, there were six reported or known massacres of indigenous people by non-indigenous people since 1838.

[19] *Argus*, 24 January 1924.

and criminality that did not register the same level of interest in Melbourne or Victoria or Australia or, for that matter, the rest of the world.

3.2   Akeroyd's Appointment

In January 1924, days before Norman List carried out the carnage in the Melbourne Botanical Gardens, Joseph Akeroyd resigned as an inspector of schools in the Victorian Education Department and commenced his appointment as inspector general of Victoria's penal system. In terms of Victoria's penal history, this appointment marked the start of the Akeroyd era, so called not only because Joseph Akeroyd became the longest-serving inspector general[20] in Victoria's penal history but because the legacies of and prisoner management reforms were driven through his education–inspired philosophies.[21] It was through this education lens he strived to understand the nature of crime and criminality and attempt to use these learnings to reform those punitive prison and prisoner management practices of the past regimes. As an educator, not only did Akeroyd try to influence the practices of his peers and prison workers, he also shared his insights and learnings with the Victorian community to broaden community members' insights into the complex challenges faced within the state's justice system dealing with crime, criminality, and community cohesion.

Prior to commencing in the inspector general role, Joseph Akeroyd recorded his thoughts, actions, and reflections in a personal diary. Most entries documented his thoughts on challenges he faced and ways he intended to resolve the issues. These issues arose

---

[20]   Or IG as many of his documents refer to his role.

[21]   Lynn and Armstrong, 1996.

from his experience as inspector of schools in the Gippsland and Bendigo regions of Victoria (Australia) and included those stories of students and teachers he felt were important for him to gain a deeper understanding of varying circumstances. These stories may support gaining a deeper insight into causative factors regarding students' disadvantage or disengagement from attending school. In addition, some stories helped to record the efforts of teaching staff to help address student and community concerns within the local community. Through the practice of journaling, Akeroyd adopted the reflective perspective of an educator to assist in making sense of each intellectual and strategic challenge he needed to address. This practice was particularly helpful to help gain insights into the ways Akeroyd tried to make sense of his role and consolidate his plans for the vision he was forming for Victoria's penal system. Through these writings, he left a trail of breadcrumbs for someone to pick up and gain some insight into the extraordinary and previously unheralded period of penal reform in Victoria's, Australia's, and indeed the world's penal management history which occurred in the turbulent times between two world wars, through a major universal economic depression, and leading into the cold war period!

Through his dedication to rigorously review, develop, and establish systems and processes to address criminal behaviours, Akeroyd provided insights into his approach to provide a rationale and context to reform policy and practice within Victoria's prison system. However, Akeroyd's notes also showed there were others with differential perspectives to his. Some of these differences were expressed by politicians and community leaders of the time, some by academics and some by those working in the prison system. These differences highlighted the diversity of opinion about the function of prisons and brought to light the diversity of oft-hidden assumptions about the link between understanding the nature of crime and criminality and the emerging policies guiding the ways to deal with those in custody. Identifying and analysing the underpinning ideological thinking behind the various policy positions and public statements of the time provides insights to the formation of policy, the implementation of reforms, and the public debate taking place in this turbulent historical time. Further, it also provided insights into the legacy of Akeroyd's reforms which are still apparent in contemporary prison policy and practice.

This book then analyses Akeroyd's experiences in three phases of his time: his early years, middle years, and later years before drawing together the nature and themes of his achievements and his failures. Interspersed between Akeroyd's stories are the reflections on contemporary prison education experiences and an attempt to contextualise these experiences with some of those challenges faced by Akeroyd.

Finally, the book responds to Eliot's challenge to extract meanings arising from these experiences for prison educators, policymakers, prison management, and those involved in creating experiences supporting prisoners' transition from prison to post-prison life.

The examination of Akeroyd's influence in shaping prison and prisoner management reform in Victoria and the processes he used unearthed three broad key discoveries. These are as follows:

- There was significant education-based reform activity in the Victorian prison system which was unique compared to the rest of the Western world at the time and is still unique today.
- Through Akeroyd and his contemporaries, there was robust extensive public debate about revolutionary ways to manage

crime and criminality within the Victorian community as well as within prisons.

- There was an emergence of critical criminological thinking predating those trends emerging in the USA and the UK many years later.

These discoveries contradicted previous claims there was little or no prison and prisoner management reform in this period. As his story unfolds, it becomes clear Joseph Akeroyd played a central role in laying the foundation for long-term prison and prisoner management legacies through his education-led reform. His battles were not easy, and an examination of the system Akeroyd inherited lays bare the challenges bestowed upon his role through the evolution of prison management principle practices embedded in history.

CHAPTER 4

Prison and Prisoner Management History and Theory Context – 1920s and Before

Crime and criminality have been a focal point of community interest and debate for centuries. Many societies embedded different approaches to dealing with those exhibiting behaviours contrary to those expected of citizens of communities of the time. Even before the Middle Ages, there were many records of ways communities identified aberrant behaviours and meted out punishment accordingly. Foucault wrote about four basic forms of punitive tactics ranging from exiling or banishment (in ancient Greek society); enforcing redemption practices (Germanic societies); marking or mutilating bodies (such as the public Western societies); and, in latter days of the eighteenth century, confining people.[22] Underpinning these tactics was the refinement of justice system approaches to address criminal behaviours. These refinements were mapped in the transition from feudal accusatory methods to a more state management inquisitory approach (such as the infamous church-led Spanish Inquisition) and the emergence of a judicial-based examination systems which form the base for contemporary approaches.

It was not until the late eighteenth century that imprisonment became the main source of confining offenders in Western societies. Even at these early times, the role of prisons and the processes in criminal justice systems leading to the management of offenders was

---

[22]   Foucault in Rabinow (1997).

subject to extensive public debate. This debate continues in current times with as much fervour and passion as it did in earlier times.

An examination of Akeroyd's reflections and musings in Melbourne throughout the 1920s through to the 1950s witnesses an increased focus in community debate about the role and function of prisons in the Victorian community. These debates led to the emergence of significant and enduring criminological reforms in the post-Akeroyd periods.

At the risk of oversimplifying the attributes and differences between the theories, it is important to state the position there are differing viewpoints in Western society explaining the reason behind crime, criminality, and ways to deal with those deemed criminal. It is worth examining these theories in some detail as the interplay of these theories becomes important to unravel in the Akeroyd and post-Akeroyd periods.

In the lead-up to Joseph Akeroyd's appointment, there were three major theories explaining the nature of crime and criminality as well as the approaches to dealing with criminals holding influence in public and political debates of the time. In contemporary discourse, these theories are known under the broad titles of classicism, conservatism, and positivism.[23] Identifying the broad attributes of each of these major theories provides a context to examine the ebb and flow of debates at the time and also analyse Akeroyd's approaches to prison and prisoner management from the commencement through to the end of his career. In current days, there are many other theories which Young referred to as minor theories. This is not to say that minor theories were not represented in some form in Akeroyd's times, but rather they were not formally recognised or named in Akeroyd's days. However, throughout this book, there is evidence

---

[23]   Young, 1981; Taylor, Walton, and Young, 1979.

on the emergence of alternative or critical criminological thinking that was not thought to have emerged until many years later.

4.1   Classicist Theory

The classicist school of thought developed in the late eighteenth century responded to the 'arbitrary systems of justice . . . and the barbarous codes of punishment by which the law was upheld in the period of feudalism and absolutist monarchies.' [24] This approach recognised the rule of law and the adherence to contract as sacrosanct. It was based on the premise that reason was embedded within the individual and that society was constructed of many classes of people meeting their respective needs by applying reason. Hence, society was seen to be managed by a structure of reason as evident in the systemic advent of government, legislation, and law.[25]

Within the classicist framework, a crime or a criminal act was seen to be an infringement of a legal code with that behaviour deemed detrimental to the personal safety and property of people who had agreed to live in 'contract' with the state. According to classicist theory, rational people avoided engaging in any behaviours which contravene the law. Hence, according to the theory, people committing crimes were considered to have made irrational decisions.[26]

As Young stated,

> *In the classicist paradigm, the whole concept of the causes of crime relates to the question of rational motivation. Within a consensual majority, where reason and self-interest are in*

---

[24]   Young in Fitzgerald, 1981, p. 253.

[25]   Fitzgerald, 1981; Cohen, 1985.

[26]   Young, in Fitzgerald, 1981.

a proper balance and the costs of crime clearly outweigh the
benefits, no one would be tempted to commit crime hence, by
definition, this would be an irrational calculation.[27]

Thomas Hobbes, sometimes referred to as the father of classicism, posited the view that the state would exert control irrespective of what eventuated. Hobbes drew a link between civil obedience and peaceful societal coherence.[28] Under their premise, it was logical to assert that every person within society was subject to the sovereign power of the state and needed to be accordingly taught such was the case. According to Taylor, Walton, and Young, the Hobbesian perspective went further to argue that once an individual became aware of the link between subjectivity to sovereign power and peaceful coexistence, then he would logically agree to adhere to the laws of the state unless he was irrational.[29] The fundamental premise underpinning the classicist viewpoint is that citizens are considered to be 'naturally independent' but are bound together within society through social contract that is overseen by the monarch or the state in return for protection of rights, property, and safety.[30]

Classicist theory provided a focus on the legal framework to identify, address, and redress individuals contravening the law. It means 'rational' people must judge the nature and extent of any criminal act and treat suspects in a just and rational manner. The judiciary, court systems, and the establishment of juries represent the

---

[27] Fitzgerald, 1981, p. 260.

[28] According to Lloyd and Sreedhar (2014), Hobbes held different versions of his of his political philosophy. On one hand he held the view that, under social contract theory, subjects were bound to follow the rules of the sovereign authority. However, Hobbes also argued that subjects had the right to disobey or resist a sovereign power if they felt their lives were in danger.

[29] Taylor, Walton, and Young, 1973.

[30] Young in Fitzgerald, 1981.

rational person. The core assumption underpinning the theory is that people committing criminal acts must be considered irrational in their decision–making. In this instance, the law is the agent responsible for punishing offenders before educating them to become law-abiding citizens. Convicted criminals require an education system and legal system geared towards rehabilitation to ensure a criminal is restored to a law–abiding citizen once their punishment has been served.[31] However, the critical feature of the classicist approach to punishment, as noted in Bentham's position, rested with the codification of the laws and punishments commensurate with the degree of harm inflicted by the criminal act.[32]

In essence, classicist theory emphasises the responsibility of each individual within society to maintain social order and that the framework of the legal system provides the basis for 'social contracts'.[33] Through the lens of the theory, the individual is seen to be responsible for their own actions, and any engagement in criminal acts is subject to a punishment commensurate with the harm generated by the criminal act.

4.2   Conservatist Theory

The conservatist school of thought had its roots in the adherence to traditional organisational structures and societal organisation. Young argued that 'conservative theory arose as a reaction against the ideas of the French Revolution . . . it has always stressed the organic nature of society, defending the traditional order against the

---

[31]   Young, 1981.

[32]   Ignatieff, 1981.

[33]   O'Toole, 2002, p. 178.

individualism and rationalism of the emerging bourgeoisie'.[34] The nature of the conservatist approach is summed up by Nisbet who stated,

> *From conservatism's defence of social tradition sprang its emphasis on the values of community, kinship, hierarchy, authority and religion, and also its premonitions of social chaos surmounted by absolute power once individuals had become wrenched from the context of those values by the forces of liberalism and radicalism.*[35]

In relation to crime and criminality, conservativist thinking considered acts which threatened societal order had to be criminalised. It included acts that not only threatened authority and community values but also offended morality or undermined authority. According to Young, the conservativist considers the root of criminal behaviour lies in the pursuit of personal gratification, the undermining of traditional loyalties, and the consequent unwillingness of the individual to accept discipline.[36] Maintaining social and authoritative order becomes the central tenet which dictates a punitive regime is required as a symbolic deterrent both for the individual and for the broader community. The concept of punishment as a deterrence arises from such an approach. Hence, it may be argued that the conservativist outlook reinforces the concept of communal values within the wider community at the expense of treating the individual.

---

[34] In Fitzgerald, 1981, p. 275.

[35] Nisbet, 1970, p. 11.

[36] In Fitzgerald, 1981.

4.3   Positivist Theory

The positivism school of thought emerged during the nineteenth century and, as Young argued, was based around the 'the unity of scientific method'.[37] There are many varieties of positivism within the fields of criminology and social sciences, but the most popular interpretation identified that biological, physiological, psychological, and social influences all contribute to the creation of the criminal.[38] The positivist theories claimed that the predisposition to the formation of a criminal resided within the individual. As Young stated, positivism contended that 'social order is consensual and that crime is a product of under socialisation'.[39] Within this theoretical position, some schools of thought adhered to an individual determinist perspective. Eysenck held the view that people were substantially different both in their abilities and in their degree of socialisation capabilities and experiences.[40] Young provided such explanations to the cause of crime and criminal behaviour in terms of the following: innate genetic and/or physiological determinants of the individual, family background which resulted in under socialisation, and the social milieu which lacked coherent and consistent consensual values.[41] In social policy terms, the positivist school of thought required education and training programs to be structured around diagnosing an individual's needs with the intent to rehabilitate them to re-enter society.

---

[37]   1981, p. 267.

[38]   See Young, 1981; O'Toole, 2002; Cohen, 1985; and Walton, Taylor, and Young, 1973.

[39]   1981, p. 267.

[40]   Eysenck, 1969, 1977.

[41]   Young, 1981.

Whilst the positivist thinking was essentially based on applying scientific methodology, Bessant and others argued 'lots of different versions' drew their respective positioning within the broader positivist school based on applying a scientific method based 'partly on induction, and empiricism and partly on deduction and the use of mathematics or statistics'.[42] Taylor, Walton, and Young sought to distinguish between positivism as it applied to social and psychological theory and that which was used in the area of criminology.[43] Whilst all aspects of positivism were based in the committed application of scientific theory to individual behaviour and dispositions within a social context, criminological positivism often adopted an alternate perspective to the prevailing classical criminological practice. The emergence of positivism within a criminological context arose as an alternative perspective to the previously dominant classicist perspectives.

Positivism comprised three major characteristics, all of which were critical for a scientifically methodical approach to treating offenders.[44] The characteristics included the quantification of behaviour, the determinism of behaviour, and scientific neutrality. Regarding positivist methodology, Taylor, Walton, and Young wrote,

> *The premises and instruments which are alleged to be successful in the study of the physical world are seen to be of equal validity and promise in the study of society and man. Insisting on this premise, positivists have proceeded to propound the methods for the quantification of behavior, have acclaimed the objectivity of the scientist, and have asserted the determinate, law governed nature of human action.*[45]

---

[42]   Bessant et al., 2006, p. xvi.

[43]   Taylor, Walton, and Young, 1973.

[44]   See Taylor, Walton, and Young (1973).

[45]   Taylor, Walton, and Young, 1973, p. 11.

In summary, positivism in its many forms holds the position that criminal behaviours are determined through the individual's interactions with their environment and that such criminality can be treated. A critical component of positivist perspective is that scientific methodologies play a central role in understanding and identifying criminality as well as in treating criminality.

These major theories were solidly embedded in broader community thought and practice at the time Akeroyd commenced his role albeit many aspects of positivist thought were still emerging. Many of the prison and prisoner management practices in place at the time emanated from the views of dominant political positioning at times as well as the custom and practice entrenched up over many years of Australia's convict transportation history.

As Akeroyd's experiences are examined throughout this book, the major arguments the language used by protagonists give clues to the assumptions made about ways to address crime and criminality according to prevailing or major criminological theories of the time. However, as Akeroyd's experiences unfold over the longevity of his appointment, we witness his questioning of current approaches and practices as he attempts to make sense of effective ways to run the penal system in Victoria. Accordingly, we will examine the emergence of other ways or, as Young wrote, the emergence of the minor theories within criminological discourse which help to make sense of dealing with crime, criminality, and criminals through our prison system (with particular focus on the role of prisoner education).

CHAPTER 5

My Story: Practice and Rhetoric

T he first four years of my experience teaching in the prison system were particularly challenging. The challenges did not come from the prisoner students per se, nor did they necessarily come from the prison management. These challenges were mainly personal and kept gravitating around clarifying an understanding of my role as a prison educator.

5.1 The Early Years

My colleagues of the time (around 1977–78) also struggled to come to a common understanding of focus of the role of a prison educator within a security-conscious environment. In 1978, the *Education Magazine* reported on teachers' perceptions of their roles often in what was perceived to be, at that time, an antagonistic (if not outright hostile) environment.

> *Education is not highly regarded . . . if you are not even reading, writing, or even doing arithmetic, then you are not doing anything.*[46]

Another stated that from the traditional administrative viewpoint, 'education should be strict and not enjoyable. Prison officers, on the whole, see their role as purely custodial and would regard . . . helping

---

[46]   *Education Magazine*, 1978, p. 7.

him (a prisoner) as signs of weakness'.[47] Others, however, reported tremendous officer–teacher relationships and cited examples where teachers sat on a range of prison operation committees to provide advice and insights into prisoners' behaviours or attributes to assist decisions of classification and/or welfare planning. However, when asked about what prison education can achieve, the teacher responses varied from person to person and location to location.

> *Perhaps we help to prevent reinforcement of criminal values. It would be pretentious to suggest prison schools are decriminalizing men but maybe we are sending out people a little more in touch with the community, a little less hostile . . . Prisoners are very isolated; take little interest in the outside community; lose sympathy and sensitivity. Even short-term people are often recidivists and prison becomes a way of life . . . We must never preach.*[48]

In the same magazine, David Biles, a prison teacher at Pentridge and later renowned criminologist, reflected on his days teaching in the prison system. He particularly focused on the challenge of working as a teacher in an environment where punishment appeared dominant. Of great interest was a story that Biles related where a prisoner stole some glue from a class he was conducting. By regulation and statute, Biles was compelled to report this theft to the prison governor, but he chose to manage to retrieve the glue by eliciting the support of willing prison officers and dealing with the prisoner face to face, ultimately engaging this prisoner to undertake more and more education programs.[49] Whilst this article considered the effectiveness of a non-punitive approach to issue resolution, it also identified

---

[47] *Education Magazine*, 1978, p. 7.

[48] *Education Magazine*, 1978, p. 8.

[49] *Education Magazine*, 1978, p. 15.

the risk and challenge of a teacher utilizing traditional teaching or educative approaches within a prison setting which saw itself surviving through rigorous adherence to strict rules of operation.

It was reassuring to me reading these stories about my colleagues teaching in Victorian prisons. These stories served to illustrate the challenges faced by teachers within a prison setting, particularly the challenges of understanding and playing a role when, in so many instances, there is great inconsistency in the understanding of the role and/or of the function of the prison environment. Many teachers saw their roles to humanize an environment whilst prison officers often saw their role to isolate individuals with a humane containment environment. Some prison officers saw their role to maintain the emphasis on punishment of offenders whilst they were in prison.

5.2   The Later Years

In January 1989, prison education in Victoria underwent a major reform when the responsibility for managing the provision of education and training services moved from Schools Division or the Victorian Education Department to the state's Technical and Further Education (TAFE) sector. This is the most significant piece of prison education reform since Schools Division assumed the responsibility for provision of education services in Victoria in 1954.

This period of reform brought forward significant challenges to those involved in prison education to justify and validate the reason for their existence and the rationale of how the programs offered supported prisoners and prison management. The key change was to directly align prison education programs with improving employment outcomes for prisoners. The experiences of working in a context of significant change challenged co-workers, administrators, new host organisations, prison management, and prisoners alike. The continuous discussion centred on the rationalisation of the role of prison education. One example of the changing perceptions occurred two years before the 1989 Victorian prison education reform but occurred in the period of political and government departmental debates in the lead-up to that reform. This experience provided an example of conflicting perspectives on the purpose and role of education can erupt in public debate.

In August 1987, I was requested to provide support for Julian Knight who had been recently imprisoned following a highly publicized crime. Julian was a rarity in Victoria, in Australia, and across the world at that time – the first mass murderer to be captured alive.[50] The authorities believed it was critical to allow criminologists, psychiatrists, and similar professionals to interview this person who committed the crime to try to understand the motivations and actions of a person committing such a crime. This drive to understand the thinking behind such crimes became even more critical following a second mass killing in the Melbourne Central Business District (CBD) where the perpetrator took his own life prior to capture.[51] The key directions provided to me were to ensure Julian was actively engaged in some form of education pursuit to engage his mind thereby reducing any risk to harm himself. Accordingly, Julian was enrolled in a range of courses and activities with the intent to engage

---

[50] As mentioned earlier in this book, apart from the NSW Myall Creek massacres (1838) where the four assailants were hanged for their action (presumably after a trial), I am being mindful that many mass killings of indigenous people across Australia occurred prior to the 1987 Hoddle Street massacre but were considered sanctioned actions at the time and did not result in criminal convictions for non-indigenous persons.

[51] Frank Vitokovic shot and killed nine people in the Melbourne CBD four months after Knight's Hoddle Street shootings.

him in study and allow him to fill in the time he was spending in the prison hospital. These courses included units in a higher education course as well as hobby leisure programs. The higher education course included elements of study in a unit titled strategic studies. The Department of Corrective Services (as it was called at that time) was pleased with the response to quickly engage this prisoner in a variety of studies to assist maintain his interest and engagement with studies whilst allowing other professional the time to study him. Hence, the role of prison education in this instance provided a critical service supporting prison management, and the greater corrections-related services to engage prisoners in worthwhile activity whilst in custody.

However, several years after this time, prison education came under significant criticism for what was thought to be inconsiderate provision of studies particularly for Julian. This criticism came from within the Office of Corrections bureaucracy and from the popular press. It was argued that this prisoner should not have been enrolled in a unit of strategic studies because of the claimed links between this student's life in the defence forces and the possible links between this background and his offending behaviours. These claims resulted in an investigation as to why this student was enrolled in these studies. For me, this was a significant indication of a change in the Corrective Services' consideration of planning programs from the focus on supporting good order, management, and security of prison management to a more treatment-focused approach intended to address perceived criminogenic factors within prisoners. It also highlighted the challenge of the Corrections bureaucracy policy positioning to labile public perspectives (and consequently changing political perspectives) regarding the function of prisons and the nature of imprisonment. In particular this event also landmarked a change in assessing the value of education and training programs to their direct impact on addressing criminogenic behaviours.

The consideration of prisoner programs being implemented to directly address specific criminogenic behaviours became formally entrenched in the early 2000s in Victoria upon the advice of the Bearing Point Review which became a critical driver for advising program delivery policy and the resultant allocation of resources for prisoner education.

I was intrigued by the seeming double messages being continually implemented through the education and prison management authorities. In simple terms, there were the utilitarian actions of needing to maintain the practice of good order, management, and security (the overarching focus of the Corrections Act 1986) whilst striving to marshal resources to address the offending behaviours of prisoners through the basic psychological/criminological models underpinning the 2003 Bearing Point Review.[52] These two perspectives (somewhat simplified in my mind as a practitioner at the time) conflicted in that one was an unspoken assumed driver, yet the other was the public rationale for what needed to be done. I felt that once practice and rhetoric became disassociated then, there was fertile ground for an 'anything goes' practice to be implemented if the underpinning principles became diffused. This provided fertile motivation to examine the nature of reforms in prison and prisoner management, particularly in Victoria.

---

[52] Bearing Point Review, 2003.

CHAPTER 6

The Nature of Reforms in Prisons

The word 'reform' appears more and more frequently in contemporary newspapers and political speeches. As the old joke goes, change is the only constant in contemporary society. The word 'reform' is consistent with change, but the term 'reform' carries a connotation of change for improvement. Within the prison context, the term 'reform' has a dual edge to it: reform in the way prison management processes and related systems (such as legal systems) are changed and the ways incarcerated individuals are changed. Implicit in this concept of reform is change for the better. To examine the significance of Akeroyd's influence on prison reform in Victoria, it is important to reflect on the nature of prison reform prior to and after Akeroyd's time. By looking at prison reform trends, achievements, and failures in Australia as well as across the Western world, gaining an appreciation of the challenges facing Akeroyd and the steps he took to address these challenges enabled a clearer insight into the complex world of prison and prisoner management. Further, given Akeroyd's and his successors' educational backgrounds, a focus on the relationship between prisoner education reform and penology adds an important dimension to identify, analyse, and record Akeroyd's achievements and failures.

6.1 Prison Reforms

The first step in examining the extent and nature of Akeroyd's reforms is to understand the history and nature of prison reforms. The advent of the prison is a comparatively modern phenomenon following the establishment of the first prisons emerging from the American and British workhouses in the late 1700s.[53] Since that time, there has been continuous community, political, and academic debate regarding the function of prisons with most of the debate focusing on the effectiveness of prison and prisoner management practices. Young believed the debates centred on two broad themes with the first relating to varying perceptions about the nature of crime and criminality at a specific time and the second examining how to deal with people convicted of committing crimes.[54] The two core streams provided the platforms for reform in prison and prisoner management practices from the inception of prisons through to contemporary times.

The relationship between reforms in the ways prisons have been managed and the different approaches on the ways prisoners are managed is intertwined. At various times over the history of penology (as the study of the punishment of crime and of prison management is often referred), there have been differing emphases on forming and reshaping policy. These manifested in a variety of underpinning policies and practices between the various jurisdictions in Australia and overseas. Differing approaches in punishment, sentencing, treatment, education, and classification can often be linked to specific criminological theories holding prominence at particular times. Examining the interplay between the various theories and related policy, practice, and language used to explain these theories in the times before and after the Akeroyd period gives insights into the significance of reforms in the Akeroyd period.

---

[53]   Gehring and Eggleston (2007), Ignatieff (1981; 1983), and Lynn and Armstrong (1996)

[54]   Young, 1981.

Foucault wrote the emergence of the early concept of the prison as we know it today emerged in the early seventeenth century. This was a time when there was a shift from the spectacle of the public punishment of criminals to a consolidated approach to detain and manage groups of offenders. This is the period Foucault explained the function and functionality of prison architecture evolved with the emergence of discipline practices to render the individual docile and therefore easier to manage within the place of incarceration.

To achieve this outcome, architectural models emerged enabling custodians to observe without being observed and to control the inhabitants. This architectural and design approach, Foucault noted, was replicated in organisations required to house and manage groups of people; and this included workhouses, schools, hospitals, and army camps. Foucault noted similar themes in architectural design in each of these facilities based around the requirement of observation, supervision, and discipline to ensure obedience of the incarcerated. It was at this point Foucault connected the concurrent structural development of the prison with that of schools. He did so by reflecting on commonalities such as isolated accommodation areas (i.e. cells and classrooms) aligned along lineal corridors thereby allowing observational supervision; focus on discipline practices; and use of discipline terminology (such as the interchangeability of the term 'discipline' with managing behavioural limits with defining topics of content such as subject areas – mathematics, science, etc.). Whilst Foucault's observations examined the linkage between education and prisons which occurred well over four centuries ago, they also established a continuing interconnection between the evolution of prisons, prison design, and programs (including the role of education) within prisons related to the prison reforms.

Whilst Foucault viewed prison reforms in a critical sense, there were significant reformers in the emergence of prisons as we know today. Jeremy Bentham and John Howard were two key people identified with the emergence of prisons from the workhouses during the early eighteenth century who took the designs of prison to the next stage. British economist and philosopher Bentham was lauded for developing an architectural model which informed the physical layout planning for prisons through to modern days, while Howard, the sheriff of Bedford, was responsible for shaping prison and prisoner management practices in the formative stages of the early prisons. Both men had long-lasting impacts around the world in terms of prison building structure and prison management practices. Bentham's impact shone through the architectural design of prison buildings, especially through the establishment of the panopticon structure where prisoners in cells could be observed continually from a central location.[55] Howard, on the other hand, established himself early on as an authority on managing prisoners' 'salvation' through self-reflection in isolation.[56] Both Bentham's and Howard's models were adopted around the world following continual growth of incarcerated people and the subsequent transport of prisoners to Australia and America. Further development of their models occurred in America where the penitentiary model evolved. The American penitentiary structure was then replicated in both the UK and Australia in the early 1800s, and prisoner management reform moved toward the Quaker-influenced Auburn model of prisoner management within a building comprising single cells.[57] Otherwise

---

[55] Lynn and Armstrong, 1996.

[56] Ignatieff, 1983.

[57] See Lyn and Armstrong, 1996; and http://www.quakersintheworld.org/quakers-in-action/50/Influence-on-Prison-Design.

known as the 'silent system', the Auburn model involved prisoners being subjected to a regime of rigidly imposed silence with severe penalties for any caught breaching the silence.[58]

Whilst Bentham and Howard were widely recognised as founding fathers of prison reform in terms of prison architecture related to form and function, Ignatieff pointed out that prison reform from the late eighteenth and early nineteenth centuries shifted the prison operations focus from its role and place within society to a more mystical enclosed prison-centric focus.[59]

The developments in penology in this period were largely confined to the world within the walls of prisons. It was not until the mid-to-late twentieth century that historiographical studies reflected on the actual reform of the prisons by analysing reform in a much broader social context. Analysing these retrospective investigations, Ignatieff (1981) concluded penal reform in the late eighteenth and nineteenth centuries could be analysed through three separate areas: the movement away from punishments inflicting physical pain, the emergence of the prison (and imprisonment) as the major penalty for major offences, and the expectation that punishment and reform would be interlinked through the penitentiary.[60]

6.2   Reforms in Prisoner Education

Whilst Foucault and others mapped the periods of prison reform up to the period of Akeroyd's appointment, Gehring, Semmens, and Braithwaite examined prisoner education reform. According to Gehring (1993), there were five general periods of correctional

---

[58]   Lyn and Armstrong, 1996.

[59]   Ignatieff, 1981.

[60]   Ignatieff, 1981; Foucault, 1977; and Rothman, 1971.

education history covering reform, prison reform, citizenship, cold war, and the current cultural period. Gehring's term 'correctional education' is synonymous with 'prisoner education'. However, Gehring along with many contemporary prisoner education practitioners use the term 'correctional education' to describe providing educational programs and services to correct a prisoner's behaviour. It should be noted that throughout this book, the terms 'correction education' and 'prisoner education' are interchangeable and relate to providing education, training programs, and services to prisoners during their incarceration.

Gehring used Kuhn's paradigm change model to define his views on changes within corrections education. According to Gehring, the inability to resolve a problems or issues using, in Kuhn's terms, 'normal science' leads to a paradigm shift[61]. The failure by 'normal science' to resolve the issue sparks a crisis situation which leads to the introduction of an 'extraordinary science' process to rationalise or adjust the anomalies within the scope of the existing paradigm. If the anomaly remains unresolved, then the crisis period leads to revolution and, consequently, the formation of a new paradigm.

Gehring's identification of five periods of correctional education history appeared to relate to the progression of prison reform explored earlier in this section. It should be acknowledged that the periods of citizenship and cultural aspects take different perspectives in the United States compared to the British and Australian contexts. While Gehring commenced his analysis of prisoner education history from the period of enlightenment until the mid- to late-1800s, he did recognise disparate approaches to providing education services dating back to the late 1700s with references to the establishment of the Sunday school movement at England's Bridewell Gaol by Robert

---

[61]   Gehring, 1993, p. 8

Raikes and William Rogers (among others) at Philadelphia's Walnut Street Jail in 1789.

In the main body of his analysis, Gehring's 'period of reform' correlated with the same period of Ignatieff's and Cohen's 'period of enlightenment'. It also coincided with Bentham's and Howard's and others' beliefs that improving a prisoner's literacy would enhance their capacity to read and comprehend the Bible. Gehring (1993), as did Eggleston (1998) and Semmens (1999), strongly argued that the period of prison reform along with introducing prisoner education as a complementary arm commenced during Maconochie's stewardship of Norfolk Island in 1840–1844.

Maconochie was recognised for introducing a more humane approach to dealing with prisoners at Norfolk Island. Maconochie wanted to move the punishment-focused regime to an environment where the prisoners saw some hope for a life beyond the prison.[62] To this end, Maconochie introduced his famous 'marks' system which rewarded prisoners for positive behaviour as they progressed through the stages of his sentences. Maconochie supplemented this program with access to meaningful tasks, increasing degrees of autonomy, and increasing access to entertainment (particularly music). It was Maconochie's marks system which was revolutionary at the time, and this system saw a prisoner work through various stages. The prisoner progress was not only dependent on the individual prisoner's development, but it was also based around group responsibility to support one another. As Hughes outlined,

> *They would work together and mess together. Each man in the group would be responsible for the marks of others as well as his own. If one backslid and lose marks, all would.*

---

[62]   Hughes, 1986.

In this way they would learn mutual dependence and social responsibility.[63]

This approach to monitoring, recording, and evaluating each individual's progress in demonstrating improvement in his capacity of mutual dependence and social responsibility became a rudimentary form of prisoner classification. This was recognised by a significant point of differentiation between Maconochie's time and those who both preceded and followed him.[64]

Maconochie's time at Norfolk Island also finished abruptly when the prevailing government required a more punitive response to prisoner management, and his services were terminated. However, his legacies influenced practice beyond the Norfolk Island shores. The impact of Maconochie's work in establishing the reformatory prison concept was first picked up and expanded upon in Ireland during the early 1860s by Sir Walter Crofton before later being adopted from the late 1870s until the early 1900s at the first US reformatory prison at Elmira. The Elmira model was subsequently implemented by many US states. The superintendent at Elmira, Zebulon Brockway, commented that 'the unique characteristic of this period was the educational idea of it all'.[65] Gehring identified the significance of this period in the evolution of correctional education by concluding that 'this was an international correctional education period marked by shared purpose – to improve the world by implementing effective programs'.[66] From this point, Gehring's interest in further evolution focused on developments largely within

---

[63]   Hughes, 1986, p. 501.

[64]   Semmens,1999.

[65]   Brockway, 1969, p. 242.

[66]   Gehring, 1993, p. 17.

the United States. He observed the next American milestone to be the emergence of what he described as the citizenship period. Gehring quoted William George, whom he credited in 1911 with 'ushering in the citizenship aspiration' by laying down the key premise for correctional education under the question 'Do you wish to produce good prisoners or to prepare good citizens?'[67] To Gehring, it was an extension of the groundwork laid down by Maconochie and later by Crofton and Brockway rather than a new direction or arguably, in Gehring's terms, a new paradigm. Gehring also stated that little reform occurred in correctional education development in the Western world during the early part of the twentieth century through to the Second World War / cold war era. Regarding this period, he noted,

> *Instead of being on the cutting edge of teaching and learning . . . the definition of correctional education[68] was reduced to mere education in an institutional setting.[69]*

Gehring's observations appeared to focus primarily on the stasis in prisoner/corrections education reform within the American and European jurisdictions which was at odds with progressive attitudes evident in Australia, particularly Victoria, during that same unique historical period.

---

[67] Gehring, 1993, p. 18. The citizenship focus also gained traction in prisoner education directions in the UK, but this occurred in the 2000s – a much later time than the US (Faulkner, 2003).

[68] Every aspect of correctional education was impacted (over this period). In the US, correctional educators adopted a definition of learning that linked them to the behavioural-oriented medical model.

[69] Gehring, 1993, p. 19.

6.3   Reforms in Prisoner Education in Australia

The role and practice of delivering education and training programs in Australia, and particularly Victoria, battled with the prevailing struggle of understanding the role and function of the prison ever since they were first established. Both Braithwaite (1999) and Semmens (1992), albeit independently, sought to classify the dominant themes describing the perceived prevailing function of the justice system in Australia, including the role of prisons, over time. They both adopted a similar framework to emphasise the roles expected of prison at given times throughout history with both mapping the evolution of the prison function (and hence the transition) through reform from one era to another.

The first era both Braithwaite and Semmens referred to was regarded as the era of retribution. During this period in mid–1800s, the function of the prison was primarily seen as a symbolic and actual tool of punishment for criminal behaviour. According to both, the era was characterised by regular hangings and flogging which contrasted markedly with the subsequent era of reformation where prisoners were put to work as form of punishment. The intent was to expose criminals to people of good example to facilitate change in the individual. The rehabilitation era emerged next under the guise to enable prisoners to leave prison with more skills than when they entered. The final era, reintegration, considered prisoners as part of society and actively engaged prisoners in activities linking them to the broader community[70].

Along with Braithwaite, Semmens noted a lack of clear delineation at any one point in time showing a definitive transition from one

---

[70]   Semmens, 1992

stage or one era into another.[71] In fact, an analysis revealed that distinctive themes emerged then faded before re-emerging over time. Each analyst (Blake for the education perspective, Gehring for the worldwide corrections education perspective, and Semmens and Braithwaite for the prison-focused perspectives) held slightly different views on the emergence and receding of themes with questions remaining whether any one specific theme ever disappeared.

Having already implemented prison reform at Norfolk Island in the 1840s, Maconochie's influence was also evident in the 1860s–1890s in Tasmania in response to a common outcry at a rise of juvenile delinquency. Petrow (1995) explored the phenomenon of the rise of juvenile industrial schools and reformatories in Tasmania from 1860 until 1896. The different initiatives sponsored by moral reformers and philanthropists in industrial schools catered for neglected and destitute young people whilst training schools accepted convicted young people who would otherwise have been imprisoned. Petrow reported the phenomenon of addressing juvenile delinquency occurred simultaneously throughout the colonies but varied in relation to government leadership on reformatory initiatives. In Tasmania, the government played a subordinate role to the clergy who adopted a leading role in engaging moral reformers to implement initiatives. A 'homeliness' atmosphere developed amid an expectation to nurture inmates, but Petrow found the new approach came under critical focus during the late 1890s as schools and reformatories increasingly favoured disciplinary practices over reformative practices. Like Maconochie's experiences many years earlier, the trend of oscillating between reformative practices through rehabilitative approaches and the more austere punitive approaches is evident once again.

---

[71]   Semmens, 1992.

The experiences in Victoria, however, were different to those in Tasmania. In his book *Vision and Realisation*, Blake (1970) identified three phases of prison education development in the Victorian prison system from 1858 until the late 1940s. The first phase, American Pentonvillians, greatly influenced the early Melbourne penal programs (1844–1853) as indicated by the emergence of the penitence and reformative approach. Prisoners were physically separated from peers and exposed to 'good influence and regular worship'.[72] From 1857 until 1924, prison education delivered by chaplains failed to elicit any recorded debate within education, prisons, or public arenas. In fact, funding was completely withdrawn for teachers after 1890 due to the Depression.[73] It appeared that the emphasis on prisoner education in Victoria, Australia, reflected the international trends identified by Gehring regarding prisoner education entering a hiatus in terms of activity, funding, and debate.

However, unlike the trends in the United States and the United Kingdom, the second phase commenced in 1924 when the significance of prisoner education enjoyed a resurgence following Joseph Akeroyd's appointment as inspector general in Victoria. Lynn and Armstrong identified the second phase under Akeroyd's administration that witnessed a new focus on prisoner education and training. Lynn and Armstrong found that 'if prisoners could be reformed, it would be through reformatory treatment of which education was the cornerstone'.[74] It was important to note the commitment to prisoner education or training was enacted in legislation in Victoria during this period. In 1928, the Victorian State Government reinforced the

---

[72] Armstrong, 1980, np.

[73] Blake, 1970. Subsequently acknowledged by the Victorian Education Department. It recorded that allowances were made in the prison budgets for books and some secular instruction provided by the chaplains.

[74] Lynn and Armstrong, 1996, p. 231.

commitment to prisoner education and training in the Goals Act of 1928 which authorised the inspector general to provide trade or vocational training for prisoners. Prisoner training was implemented during this period amid an expectation prisoner would conform by establishing good work habits that would see them returned to the community as a reformed character.

6.4   Prison and Prison Education Reforms in Victoria

Limited resources existed apart from the inspector general annual reports presented to parliament to offer any insights into the evolution of the Victorian prison system as well as allied prison management and prisoner management practices. Armstrong (1980), Lynn and Armstrong (1996), and O'Toole (2006) independently recorded reforms in Victoria's penal system to assist drawing some connections between the inspectors general of the time and the prevailing practices prior to and after Akeroyd's time.

From Armstrong's research, we find Victoria only had a few small and insecure prisons from its early failed penal settlement in 1803 at Sorrento until the gold rush years. Until 1843, any serious offences were dealt with by the courts of New South Wales. Plans for Victoria's first large gaol only got under way in 1845 when the Supreme Court started sitting in Melbourne.[75]

Armstrong recorded that life in Victoria in the early days was 'not so charming . . . battles between colonists, blood sports and convict tension often disturbed the peace', and a dualistic approach to punishment was applied by the courts depending on whether the offender was a free citizen or a convict.[76] To illustrate the disparity,

---

[75]   Armstrong, 1980.

[76]   Armstrong, 1980, p. 5.

Armstrong recorded that 'a convict was sentenced to 50 lashes for drunkenness whilst the next accused, (a free settler with whom the convict was drinking) was fined five shillings'.[77]

The period from 1840 until the 1870s was a turbulent time in which the success of any prison operations rested on the capability of the presiding inspector general.[78] Prison operations appeared to be brutal, as evident in the 1857 Select Committee of Inquiry into (Inspector General) John Price's[79] administration that 'an important milestone in the development of a more humane system with improved facilities'.[80] Lynn and Armstrong described the Price era as one of 'unnecessarily' severe punishment which 'crushed out . . . the last spark of humanity'.[81] They also concluded that 'a major feature of Price's administration was his total domination of the system' which supports their earlier assertion that the power wrested in the inspector general's position set the tone for prison and prisoner management.

Price was appointed inspector-general of penal establishments in Victoria in January 1854. The newly established colony was confronted with grave problems arising from the explosive influx of gold seekers, who included many former convicts. The inadequate gaols were supplemented by hulks, moored in Hobson's Bay, on which conditions were appalling. Public disquiet forced investigations, and in 1856 the Legislative Council and the Legislative Assembly each appointed a select committee. The Legislative Council committee sat intermittently from 27 November 1856 to 29 July 1857, and

---

[77] Armstrong, 1980, p 4.

[78] See Lynn and Armstrong . . .

[79] This refers to the infamous inspector general John Price, not to the prisoner John Price mentioned earlier.

[80] Lynn and Armstrong, 1996, p. xvii.

[81] Lynn and Armstrong, 1996, p. 39.

*the Legislative Assembly committee from 8 January 1857 to
September 1857. Price gave evidence before both committees,
but he was dead before returned a report. On 26 March 1857
he visited Williamstown to investigate complaints about
rations by convicts from the hulks employed there on public
works. While he was listening to some grievances a party
of convicts gathered around him. Missiles were thrown and
one struck him heavily; as he turned away he was knocked
down and severely battered about the head and body. On
the next afternoon he died from his injuries. At the inquest
fifteen convicts were committed for trial. They were tried in
four groups, and seven were convicted and sentenced to death.
Three were hanged on 28, three on 29, and one on 30 April
1857. Accounts of the trials leave the impression that some of
the executed men may have been wrongly convicted.*[82]

The period following Price witnessed the development of the panopticon building which housed solitary confinement as well as ensured constant prisoner surveillance observation by warders. Prisoners wore masks anytime they were outside their cells and were forbidden from conversing with warders unless necessary.[83] William Champ, the inspector general from 1857 until 1868, was renowned as a strict disciplinarian who severely punished any prisoners caught breaching regulations. However, he introduced some areas of reform such as new work options for prisoners. Whilst Champ was heavily criticised for failing to classify Pentridge prisoners,[84] he was recognised for attempting to broaden the scope of prison work options.[85]

---

[82] Barry, 1969.

[83] Lynn and Armstrong, 1996.

[84] Lynn and Armstrong, 1996.

[85] Lynn and Armstrong, 1996.

When John Price was murdered at Williamstown in March 1857 Champ was recommended to the government of Victoria by Denison to succeed Price as inspector-general of penal establishments in Victoria, a position he held until his resignation on 31 December 1868. He was largely responsible for the building of Pentridge gaol, and his administration was strikingly successful; according to a penal officer who served under him for eleven years, 'no board of enquiry was ever appointed to investigate charges against any of the officials, the management of the department was never questioned, nor did any comment appear in the public press unless in praise of his public career.[86]

There was a growth in the number of regional prisons both during Champ's time and under his successor George Duncan's reign as inspector general until 1880. Many were classified as industrial and reformatory schools, which meant Duncan and his successor H. F. Neal were appointed into the dual roles of inspectors general and inspectors of industrial schools. Duncan was a deeply religious man who raised the profile on moral reformation of prisoners by introducing prison chaplains and teachers.[87] Further, he introduced incentives to reward prisoners for employment and good behaviour.[88] However, such initiatives appeared to be countered by his extremely strict prisoner management regime as borne out by the fact both he and subsequently Neal were dismissed for improper practices – including the use of severe corporal punishment.[89]

John Castieu was a prison governor and later became inspector general in a career spanning 1880 until 1884. Unusually at this time,

---

[86]   H. A. White, *Crime and Criminals*; Ballarat, 1890, p. 130; Barry, 1969.

[87]   Lynn and Armstrong.

[88]   Lynn and Armstrong, 1996, p. 104.

[89]   Lynn and Armstrong, 1996, p. 102.

Castieu not only left detailed diaries reflecting on his experiences living in Melbourne but also recoded his reflections on the application of criminal law and criminal justice practice at the time. This was seen to be unusual because, until Joseph Akeroyd, it seemed rare for prison administrators to record such personal reflections.[90] Not only did he leave his diaries as a legacy, he also was recognised as an artist of note with his sketches of Melbourne life exhibited at various galleries at the time. As governor of the Old Melbourne Gaol, Castieu was the official state government witness to the execution of the infamous bushranger Edward 'Ned' Kelly on 11 November 1880.

William Brett (1884–1890) followed Duncan, Neal, and Castieu in the role after Castieu had been similarly dismissed due to his lack of administrative capability when staff problems compounded and weakened prisoner discipline under his watch.[91] Brett was lauded over his 16-year reign for his strong leadership particularly introducing a prisoner classification system. It appeared Brett segregated prisoners based on their sentence length and the nature of the criminal behaviour. In his 1885 annual report, Brett recorded his concern that:

> *the moral atmosphere in prison is replete with so much injury to character that, independent of the corruption arising from the companionship of the hardened and depraved, acquaintance with the interior of the prison produces impressions most unfavourable to reformation. . .. It is therefore of great importance that first offenders be able to work out their own deliverance from such fate through their own exertions whilst exposed to the temptations and vicissitudes of everyday life.[92]*

---

[90]   Finnane, 2004.

[91]   Lynn and Armstrong, 1996, p. 106.

[92]   Annual Report, 1885, p. 6.

Accordingly, he divided the classifications of prisoner in accordance with the management regime. First offenders were treated with a lenient approach and kept separately from others, juvenile offenders were met with corporal punishment, and hardened criminals were met with solitary confinement.[93] Interestingly, Brett defined the difference between the application of solitary confinement and separate confinement in accordance with the British Habitual Offender Act. By doing this, Brett, unsurprisingly reflective of the times, acknowledged and deferred to the British imperial influence in the formation and application of criminal justice methodologies of the time.

However, Brett specified the importance of selecting staff able to discern when to apply punitive approaches and when to provide lenient support to prisoners. Brett's appreciation of the importance of recruiting staff with capabilities to discern situational awareness appeared to reflect Alexander Maconochie's revolutionary Norfolk Island approach to prisoner management.

Despite his initiatives, Brett was also transferred from his role following a 'daring escape' which attracted public attention.[94] Captain John Evans assumed the role until 1903 during which time he followed his predecessor's model in segregating prisoners according to specific classifications. These classifications included the following: prisoners in solitary confinement (for punishment, or where specified by the courts), 'specials' who were deemed hopeful cases that were separated from other prisoners, 'restraints' for the younger offenders, and selected ordinary prisoners who worked in areas of responsibility within the units.[95]

---

93   Annual Report, 1885.

94   Lynn and Armstrong, 1996, p. 108.

95   Annual Reports, 1891, 1894, and 1899.

The 1933 annual report included a retrospective record on earlier reforms in Victoria's penal system.[96] In this report, the Evans period was characterised as a shift away from solitary confinement as a punishment. While he failed to introduce any specific education programs, Evans was acknowledged for supporting skill development in the prison industries.[97]

In the periods leading up to the Akeroyd appointment, there were four further inspector general appointments including Edward Connor (1903–1910), William Callaway (1910–1914), John Freeman (1914–1921), and R McIver (1921–1923). Of these, Callaway proved a most interesting appointment in that he was never in fact officially appointed to the position but instead retained the position as deputy inspector general.[98] He was also undersecretary for the State of Victoria, and he held several other government posts after relinquishing the deputy inspector general role. In the government roles, Callaway continued to maintain an interest in, and contributed toward, commentary on prison and prisoner management beyond the term of his appointment to deputy inspector general.

The introduction of the Indeterminate Sentencing Act of 1907 in the lead-up to Akeroyd's appointment proved to hold great significance during this period.[99] Under the new statute, the courts had the power to place a prisoner on an indeterminate sentence with their release date to be determined by the Indeterminate Sentences Board. The board decided whether prisoners subject to the laws would be housed in reformatory prisons to access education, work, and post-release

---

[96]   Written by Inspector General Joseph Akeroyd as part of his retrospective on the history of Victorian prisons.

[97]   Annual Report, 1933.

[98]   Lynn and Armstrong, 1996, p. 122.

[99]   Freiberg and Ross, 1999.

employment support. Callaway favoured the indeterminate sentence as an effective means to shift from punishment to education. He recorded his commitment in his 1910 annual report:

> As criminals are human beings and not inanimate machines, their disposal is a matter of education and the treadmill and other brutalising modes of punishment have given way to the rational scientific method.[100]

Lynn and Armstrong argued that Callaway failed to implement the strategies he preached by concluding that 'the emphasis on education was not in evidence during his administration, nor for another decade after his departure from the prison scene.'.[101] Further, Lynn and Armstrong argued that Callaway favoured using 'coercion for deviants' and that the application of the indeterminate sentence was appropriate as punishment for the individual.[102] Callaway wrote:

> The fundamental principle is not that the punishment should fit the crime but that it should fit the criminal. He was imprisoned not for what he did but for what he was. The indeterminate sentence says to him 'you are imprisoned because your violation of the law has shown that you are unfit to be free'.[103]

In broad terms, Lynn and Armstrong found that the period leading to Akeroyd's appointment contributed little toward prison operation reform, and they argued:

---

[100] Annual Report, 1910, p. 5.

[101] Lynn and Armstrong, 1996, p. 122.

[102] Lynn and Armstrong, 1996, p. 123.

[103] Annual Report, 1910, p. 5.

*The first half of the twentieth century was a static period
for prisons which were not the subject of political passions.
There were no major scandals or inquiries of note, nor were
there signs of the arbitrary or capricious use of power by
administrators. The prison system was dormant and there
were few demands for changes to the system.*[104]

Despite this and Gehring's observation, prison reform activity in the first half of the twentieth century in Victoria was far from dormant.

Prior to and after Akeroyd's time, there were numerous recognised reforms dealing with trying to perfect the best way to establish a rationale to describe the reason people offend and working out the best ways to deal with those in custody. For Akeroyd, the intersection between the perceived functions of prison and prisoner management and the role of education in personal reformation is significant to gain a greater understanding of the nature of crime and criminality. Gaining insight into this intersection was critical for Akeroyd to develop effective social policies designed to address the nature of crime and the impacts of crime on offenders, victims, and society in general.

During that time, Joseph Akeroyd was inspector general of Victoria's penal system. This is the most senior bureaucratic position within the Victorian public service focused on managing the state's prisons and prisoners. Appointed to this senior position directly from his role as an inspector in Victoria's school sector, Akeroyd held this position between 1924 and 1947, becoming the longest-serving inspector general in Victoria's history. Throughout this time, Akeroyd kept formal and informal records of his daily operational and strategic challenges. Access to these private papers provided insights into his

---

[104]   Lynn and Armstrong, 1996, p. xviii.

experiences and strategies to reform practices and mindsets in many areas of prison and prisoner management but particularly around education, sentencing, classification, and punishment for which Whatmore was later recognised. Through access to these papers and records, insights into significant but previously unheralded prison and prisoner management reform activity become apparent.

6.5   Appointment of Joseph Akeroyd to the Role of Inspector General

Akeroyd applied for the position of inspector general, and his application was considered and subsequently approved by the cabinet on 12 October 1923.[105] It remains unclear whether Akeroyd was asked to apply for the position, or he applied of his own volition. His successful appointment was recognised by the then director of education, Mr Tate, who expressed pleasure at Akeroyd's appointment and advised,

> *A large number of officers trained in the Education Department had been appointed to responsible positions, and though . . . their transfer somewhat weakened the education department, it gave a great fillip to the ambitions of younger officers.*

Mr Tate went on to explain that such appointments resulted from a defined strategy:

> *Of giving ambitious young officers facilities for obtaining higher qualifications . . . [and] . . . this policy was producing results which were beneficial to the public service generally.[106]*

---

[105]   Chief Secretary's Correspondence 1923, PROV, VPRS 8291, P000.

[106]   *Argus*, 30 November 1923, p. 11

This statement refers to Tate's apparent strategy encouraging officers from the Education Department to work in senior positions within the public service and that it may be reasonably inferred that Akeroyd was one beneficiary.

Akeroyd's diary entries also indicated he had a strong civic-minded focus that appeared to motivate him in his role both as a teacher and later as an inspector of schools. His civic responsibility was evident in his capacity for workforce management and his commitment to keeping disengaged young people connected to education. His diary entries also demonstrated his empathetic understanding that multiple strategies were paramount to keeping young people engaged in education. He especially referred to the application of trade training skills for students disengaged from the academic curriculum. While his diaries remained silent from the immediate period leading to his application to the position as inspector general through to his appointment and subsequent official transfer on 21 November 1923[107], it appeared his education-based values provided the basis for his planning once he assumed the role the following year. Akeroyd's educational principles and values to implement significant change in prison deployment and prisoner management are evident in both his diaries and the public debates recorded in the daily press. His alignment of the principles of teaching with the principles of penology provided a powerful insight into his approach to the challenges or prison and prisoner management before him.[108]

Along with his other diary entries, Akeroyd valued the role education played in providing people with the skills to become effective contributors to society. While no evidence exists linking Akeroyd's thoughts and approaches to any influential educationalist

---

[107] Chief Secretary's Correspondence, 1923, PROV, VPRS 8291

[108] 28 January 1928, PROV, VPRS 6604

philosophy, his papers and practices demonstrate a strong belief in the links between education and psychology. There may be some people who found alignment between Akeroyd's approaches to education policy and practice to the then pre-eminent influential American educationalist John Dewey. It may be possible that in linking psychology and educational practice, Akeroyd had been influenced by Dewey's approach to connecting learning experiences with student development. However, no direct evidence exists proving that Akeroyd recognised any such link. Regardless, to Akeroyd, 'the method of the psychologist'[109] remained extremely important to him, and the link between education and psychology played a major role in the approaches he brought to prisoner education and prisoner management practice.

Whilst his diary and personal papers provided insights into his personal commitment to civic principles, his military experiences also helped shape his determined and disciplined approach to shaping and implementing prisoner management reforms.

Whether this strategy extended beyond Akeroyd's period is unclear, but it is of interest to note that the two next heads of prison services (Alex Whatmore and Eric Shade) were also educationalists. Regardless, this means that Victoria's prison system was managed by those with education backgrounds, and this spanned a period almost 50 years, from 1924 to 1972. This remarkable achievement in longevity of educationally qualified leadership in the most senior prison management bureaucracy compared to other jurisdictions in Australia and across the Western world.

Whilst these three men shared an educationalist background in common, it cannot be assumed that they operated under similar principles. One notable difference between Akeroyd and

---

109

his immediate successor, Whatmore, is evident in their recorded approaches to the corporal punishment of prisoners, particularly regarding the role of flogging or whipping offenders. In the context of public debate about the role of corporal punishment of offenders in South Australia, Western Australia, and Victoria in March 1950, The *Western Australian* newspaper reported the difference between Akeroyd's pro-corporal punishment position and Whatmore's anti-flogging position. Whilst Whatmore was 'an ardent anti flogger . . . Akeroyd advocates the lash for those who deserve it'.[110]

As Akeroyd's positioning on prison management reform and prisoner reform is unravelled through his story, it is poignant that reflections of his achievements focus on his oft pro punishment position.[111] It is Akeroyd's stance on using flogging as a form of punishment that he was, and still is, remembered;[112] and arguably this perception underpinned views that the period leading up to Whatmore's time was considered punitive and, by inference, lacking prisoner management reform.[113] However, examination of Akeroyd's private papers and his personal diaries led to gaining further insights into the extent of Akeroyd's activity and insights rendering this period of 1924–1947 as one of unheralded reform in which many enduring prison and prisoner management practices were formed. By mapping prison reforms before and after Akeroyd's period, insights into the power of Akeroyd's influence can be realised.

---

[110] *The Western Australian*, 17 March 1950, p. 2.

[111] Report of the Statute Law Revision Committee (1948) VPARL 1947-48 NoD1 pdf.

[112] It is also noted that even today, senior Department of Justice Corrective Services officials reflect on Akeroyd's contribution in relation to his advocacy for corporal punishment.

[113] See both Semmens (1999) and Gehring (1993).

CHAPTER 7
My Story: Classifying People

I was always fascinated by the symbolism within the operations of prisons. There are so many practices embedded in what I assumed were historical, but which were not questioned. Apart from the language and practices ensconced from the naval heritage (e.g. the use of the word 'billets' to describe cleaners, the ringing of the bells at naval times [i.e. 'at six bells'], and many more), the symbolism surrounding the classification process was always intriguing.

Classification is a prominent process within the prison management practices. In the classification process, prisoners are assigned a security status, have their sentence (case) plan goals and targets reviewed, and are the critical repository of the information guiding further location or parole decisions. The classification process effectively stamps the identity of the prisoner for his or her life in the prison system.

I specifically remember John Price. He ironically shared the same name of one of the notorious prison governors in Victoria's early years who was murdered in Williamstown by disgruntled prisoners. Like a few of his contemporaries, John spent his youth as a serving member of Australia's defence force. John was convicted of the double murder of his girlfriend and his friend. John was also involved in a profoundly serious event in Victoria's prison history. There was an assault of a young Salvation Army volunteer visitor resulting in her suffering long-lasting physical injuries. This event was a horrific experience for this young woman, for the volunteer association, and for the prison.

John's involvement in this event saw him classified as a high-security risk and labelled as 'an ultimate psychopath'. This classification and assessment of him was registered in his case file; and this was brought up at every sentence review, security review, and case plan review throughout his prison life. Accordingly, his prison classification was maintained as high security.

John did not help matters when he, along with two other prisoners, escaped from the notorious H Division and held a protest on the portico roof of A Division. (I will tell a story of this event a little later!)

From another perspective, I found John to have an incredibly active and enquiring mind and was constantly seeking to be intellectually challenged. He became one of the first prisoners to undertake and complete an undergraduate degree whilst in prison. Throughout this time, John was keen to explore his own understanding of himself and a role that he could play in this world.

This capacity to want to extend his own understanding, the drive to find what contribution he could make given his circumstances, led me to question whether we were dealing with an 'ultimate psychopath'. This young man tragically ended his own life in the early 1980s. For what reasons he did this I am not sure, but I do sense that the realization that the challenge to him to disprove the view others held of him became insurmountable for him. I can only hypothesise.

Another student, Ray, was serving his second life sentence for murder. Ray had a temper that landed him in trouble several times when in the community. Labelled for life as a double murderer, Ray undertook remote undergraduate studies through Deakin University. Driven by his own experiences growing up in a severely disrupted family life, Ray's passion for study arose from his desire to recreate a safe family structure within prison settings. Through this study, he managed to create surrogate family structures to help bring, in Ray's thoughts, stable family influences within an extraordinarily chaotic living environment. His 'out of left field' thinking elicited extreme responses from within the prison. These responses ranged from great respect by staff and inmates for helping to reduce disruptive influence on young prisoners through developing and implementing compensatory parenting roles. Ray became another death statistic in prison. After his passing (and I will write a little more about this later), it was fascinating to witness the number of older prisoners clamouring to take on Ray's role and leadership, continuing this innovative approach to support young (and older) prisoners gain some semblance of family. Ray challenged the stereotyping of ascribing the tough, brutal double-murderer behaviours with a criminal typology whereas others also witnessed compassionate behaviours to care for his 'family'.

However, my views of prisoners as individual students were balanced with insights into crimes committed. Norm (not his real name) was one of the most affable, easy-going characters I met in my time as a teacher in prisons. Norm was the model student – diligent, articulate, and passionate about his studies. I was involved in planning workshops organised by the department of justice, and there were invitees from all the stakeholder agencies connected with managing prisons and prisoners. I was honoured to be selected to represent the education aspect of prisoner and prison management. Throughout the course of the workshops, I was placed in discussion groups with representatives from the victims of crime organisation. As it turned out, one of the representatives, Noel, was the father of the young women killed by Norm in a domestic violence event. I did not discuss specific student matters with Noel, but I was moved (if not shaken) by the depth of unresolved hurt Noel carried with him. In saying this, Noel was not vindictive in any overt way toward Norm (if he felt vindictive, I certainly did not see or hear any evidence through his manner, speech, or actions), but his grief was palpable. I always think of Noel and other people who have suffered loss or physical and emotional damage resulting from the behaviours of my students. I did not allow these feelings to intervene in my approach to teaching nor in my desire to help create a learning environment in which prisoner students can create a broader range of decision options available to them. However, my meetings with Noel (and later others pin similar positions to Noel) fostered my insights into the impacts offending behaviours have on offenders, victims, and our society in this complex world in which we live. Sometimes the simplicity of classification defies the complexity of people and events.

CHAPTER 8

Learning the Ropes – Akeroyd's Early Years

Akeroyd used various methods to record his thoughts and observations either to consolidate his emerging insights or to communicate and test with others throughout his tenure. There appeared a three-phase progression in Akeroyd's insights into prison and prisoner management landmarked by the emergence of different ways of recording and communicating his thoughts and actions.

During the initial phase dating from 1924 until 1930, Akeroyd turned to his personal diary to record his thoughts and reflections which he later translated into annual reports to communicate key messages to the government of the day. The second phase, spanning 1931 until 1940, heralded a shift in the documentary evidence base amid a marked reduction in diary entries in favour of a growing number of public presentations and public debates in the daily press. The third phase signified an increase in Akeroyd's reflections on prison and prisoner management policy and practice via formal proceedings such as government-led enquiries and reports from 1941 until 1947.

Akeroyd refined his approach to individual prisoner reform amid divided community opinion towards moves to change the existing prison system. He encountered challenges to reforms he strove to implement in respect to the dimensions of punishment, sentencing, prisoner classification, and educating both prisoners and prison officers. This chapter maps his privately and publicly recorded experiences and reflections to analyse challenges faced and support received during the three phases of Akeroyd's engagement as inspector general.

Akeroyd's first week as inspector general proved eventful. Not only was he trying to understand his new role, but he was also thrust into dealing with the unexpected challenges arising from working in a prison. His early diary reflections not only appeared to revolve around whether prison life assisted the offender in developing requisite skills to make a positive contribution to the community upon release, but also reflected on the number of critical incidents needing attention.

On 3 January 1924, his first day in the role, Akeroyd's reflections forecasted his vision to establish education–based reform:

> *They received no definite training and evidently leave prison with as little marketable skill as they entered. There seems room here for some definite schooling probably in trade work.*[114]

Later the same day, he recorded a further observation:

> *The whole of the industries – woodwork, boot making, woollen, blacksmithing, plumbing etc [sic] are under the care of Uren who is a builder by trade. Experts are in charge of tailoring, boot making and woollen manufacturing departments. Otherwise everything is run by prison labour. The difficulty of obtaining good work is obvious. There seems room for other teaching experts.*[115]

Akeroyd continued to visit all prison sites during his first weeks where he recorded his observations about the lack of structure and

---

[114] VPRS 6604, diary entry 3 January 1924.

[115] VPRS 6604, 3 January 1924.

discipline. He specifically documented concerns about lax discipline at Castlemaine Reformatory, C Division at Pentridge, and French Island.[116] He observed a distinct need for education and training programs as well as for teaching staff, which he subsequently acted upon as he noted on 11 January 1924:

> *Delivered to Chief Secretary report on Castlemaine Reformatory escapees. He was satisfied. He agreed to the creation of position of school master at Castlemaine after consultation with the Premier.*[117]

Whilst the education perspectives appeared to occupy his initial reflections, Akeroyd noted the escapes from Castlemaine and fires in Pentridge Prison in his early diary entry. These entries provided some initial insights into the daily challenges faced in managing the state's prison system. However, his early days were to be tested with a significant escape attempt from Pentridge. Akeroyd's diary recorded the uncovering of a plot designed by the well-known gangster Squizzy Taylor to aid the escape of the 'notorious criminal' Angus Murray from Melbourne Gaol. Akeroyd in concert with the chief secretary, Dr Argyle, and the police, prepared an undercover investigation to capture prison officers and prisoners involved in the escape plot.

According to Akeroyd's diary, this plot, apparently hatched in 1923, was unearthed on 10 January 1924:

> *At 5pm. Was informed that a plot was afoot to release Angus Murray next Saturday . . . (the plan) was to put him on a boat with Buckley, the captain of the ship already*

---

[116] VPRS 6604, 9 January 1924; VPRS 6604, 9 January 1924; and VPRS 6604, 15 January 1924.

[117] VPRS 6604, 11 January 1924.

bribed. Gleeson and Costello are temporary warders at the Melbourne gaol. Some days ago Costello asked Gleeson to come into a hotel with him for a drink. There they met Squizzy Taylor, Ida Pender and two other men. A plan was laid to get Murray out of gaol next sat night. Two men would come over the wall near Costello, tie him up, get the key, tie up Gleeson, let Murray out (his cell would be known) and haul all back again over the wall. Gleeson is to receive 250 pounds) down and 100 (pounds) after the job. Gleeson has seen Costello receive notes from Taylor when on duty. Taylor has written in the earth alongside Gleeson 'a pound for a . . . (unclear)' and then rubbed all out with his foot. Gleeson has reported this. Supt Potter has the matter in hand. . . . McCormack of the Melbourne gaol reports that he can hold the gaol. To ensure both men being on duty on Sat. night Costello has arranged an exchange with a permanent warder. McCormack agreed at first but demurred later as he did not want two temporary men on duty at the one time. (it was) agreed to make all preparations as if the plan was allowed to develop, the Premier to give his decision tomorrow as to whether to hold our hands or to go on and attempt the scoop.[118]

On 13 January 1924, Akeroyd further wrote,

The political situation developed seriously for the Government last night and the Premier went off today without giving a decision. The Chief Secretary after consultation with Nicholas and myself decided to go on with the scheme and endeavour to catch the lot.

In the meantime the scheme has been changed to 7.45am today. Gleeson goes on duty at the tower at 7.15 am. The

---

[118] VPRS 6604.

prisoners will come into the remand yard about 7.20am. Murray was then to go into the bathroom alone, come back with silk pant and singlet, come out get away over the wall into McCormacks [sic] yard, thence will go to Victoria Street where a car would be waiting facing East, the driver reading a paper. Gleeson was to receive a signal from Murray before he made his dash, right hand over his head. Gleeson was then to take out his handkerchief as a signal to the driver of the car. Murray was to be provided with a hook& a dozen or so towels for the ladder. He probably would have a gun also. While he was preparing three desperate criminals were to engage Warder Leslie in the remand yard in an argument & if necessary gag him. Three armed men were to be outside the wall to cover the escape. Costello was to meet Taylor at the Railway Crossing at Park St at 10 am to receive his money and Gleeson was to receive his whack at home at 2 pm.

The position was discussed by Potter, Hawkins, Bourke, McCormack & myself in Potter's office last night. In the gaol the night warders would be kept back, Murray would be seized in the bathroom & the place and prisoners searched. Gleeson to take no notice but to give the signal at 7.45am.

The police part: The detectives would be kept back and at 7.45 would rush the various points. Two P.C. men would be stationed in McCormack's yard at 5 am in case Murray got away.

At 7am today I reached the detectives office and found everything complete – cars tuned up ready, men told off. By phone I found the gaol similarly prepared.

At 7.45am the detectives moved and picked up Taylor's car with faked number and reading newspaper as given to us. . . . The driver was arrested and charged with loitering with intent. A car went out and immediately searched Taylor's place and brought him in. I advised getting Costello at once but (was) ruled against. Unwise. At appointed time he could not be found. Taylor gave nothing away. Said his car had been stolen in the night.

Went over to the gaol at 8 am. Murray had been seized a little too soon and nothing found on him. The whole place was searched and hook, towels cut ready and a flask of whisky just finished, yesterday's Smiths Weekly and several other papers and a bunch of envelopes & writing paper, letter written by Murray, one pound note, & a letter apparently written by Costello to Taylor and other items. Nothing on Murray. Advised Gleeson asked for protection and at 11 am left for home.

14/1/23 [sic] After a conference with Chief Secretary, Mr McPherson, Mr Nicholson & myself the attached (press release) was drafted and given to the press. Nothing fresh occurred. Costelloe gave away nothing. Gleeson has now been suspended pending developments.

It is not evident from Akeroyd's notes that he anticipated his first two weeks in the job would entail intensive involvement thwarting an escape of the condemned prisoner Angus Murray planned by the notorious Squizzy Taylor. Not only did this planned escape occupy his focus, but there were also several other incidents occurring in the prisons. A series of fires were lit in Pentridge Prison, and a plug of dynamite was also found at Pentridge at the same time the Taylor-inspired escape was unfolding at Melbourne Gaol. It was within his first two weeks dealing with a series of major and minor security issues that Akeroyd questioned the cause and effect surrounding these events and started to form the opinion there was a laxity of discipline within warders' approach to their role. Akeroyd noted from that time forward, he committed his focus to 'the necessity for tightening of the discipline within staffing ranks (be) made manifest'.[119] This will be a consistent theme throughout Akeroyd's twenty-three reign as inspector general.

Staff discipline and staff professionalism were not the only focus in his first year. His educationalist heritage was never far from the forefront of his thinking as he recorded his observations throughout his visits to Victoria's metropolitan and regional prisons. In the first month, he recorded his major statement espousing the principles underpinning his approach to the role of inspector general. Akeroyd's diary entry on 28 January 1924 revealed his commitment to rapidly implement education reform to drive further reform within the prison system:

> On Wednesday night visited Castlemaine with the (Indeterminate Sentences) Board. Received by the Mayor. Enunciated the three principles of (1) classification (2) work of an interesting nature and (3) right ideals with living conditions conducive to self-respect. These are the principles underlying teaching and they also appear to underlie penology.[120] Next day spent some time at the Board meeting. The plan for Hand is to allow him to teach from 8.30 – 12 noon and from 7 to 9 at night. He will plan entertainment, debates etc and generally take charge of the recreational work of inmates.[121]

This diary entry provided the strongest clue to Akeroyd's emerging philosophy on prison management by drawing parallels to key principles

---

[119] VPRS 6604, 13 January 1924.

[120] My underlining.

[121] VPRS 6604, 28 January 1924.

underpinning teaching. A later diary entry revealed Akeroyd's plans to implement change swiftly were not necessarily shared by the board at this point in time. On 4 February 1924, Akeroyd recorded,

> *Afraid the Board is ruled by Morris — too lenient. Takes the view of expediency not that of true reform.*[122]

Hence, Akeroyd's reflections on his early days in the new role not only demonstrated his drive to implement 'true reform' based upon educational principles but also hinted at his frustration towards resistance that was hindering the reform process. Recognising this was just over a month since he started his new role, his diary comments provided clues about his ambitions to implement educational principles to drive prison reform and reveal his great interest in understanding the relationship between the causalities of crime and criminality. Akeroyd anticipated that understanding the link would help create effective systems and processes to make the prison system work. Above all, his words pointed to a personal drive to implement reforms in a way that others had not envisioned in the years before him and that would endure in the years that followed him.

His drive for understanding the nature of crime and criminality saw Akeroyd turn to the world of science to help set a framework. Akeroyd started to document the life histories of prisoners to find clues that explained the behaviours of male and female prisoners.

One of the first case studies he compiled was that of Angus Murray, the prisoner at the centre of the Squizzy Taylor–inspired escape from the old Melbourne Gaol in early 1924. Murray was to be the first prisoner executed in Akeroyd's time as inspector general. The lead-up to the execution witnessed large crowds attending protest rallies in Melbourne with Anglican clergy, Trades Hall Council, and

---

[122]   VPRS 6604, 4 February 1924.

Labour politicians presenting vocal entreaties to the then premier, Harry Lawson, to overturn the death penalty.[123] Despite this pressure, Lawson refused to overturn the court's decision, and Murray was executed on 14 April 1924.

Akeroyd collected letters sent to Murray and letters sent by Murray to others over those last few days of Murray's life. Many of these letters sought to comfort Murray facing impending mortality whilst Murray reflected on his last few days of life.

Making sense of the causal factors leading to criminal behaviour meant Akeroyd could adopt appropriate remedies relevant to the specific individual. He documented his assessment of one prisoner named Eric Gordon in his diary as follows:

> *Bulumnaal murder . . . Intelligence 95 IQ MA 15 3/12 normal. Quite good reasoning ability in concrete situations. Abstractions not so good. Visualising power very good . . . Morally*[124] *is dead. There is no make up for higher virtues.*[125]

Unlike his predecessors, Akeroyd undertook extensive assessment of prisoners entering the system and introduced the application of the Stanford Binet IQ test to ascertain the individual's intellectual status on arrival[126]. He continued to record individual prisoner details in his diary until 1928 without offering any rationale regarding the reason for choosing these prisoners other than an apparent strong interest in offenders convicted of capital crimes. Using the results from these tests helped Akeroyd formulate some understanding of the individual's capability for personal reform as well as highlight areas

---

[123] Duff, 2014.

[124] Akeroyd's underlining.

[125] VPRS 6604, 20 July 1924.

[126] VPRS 6604, 20 July 1924

where a case plan may assist the individual's return to the community as an effective citizen.

He demonstrated his commitment to education principles on his September 1924 diary entry following his visit to Janefield. It was evident that Akeroyd started to formulate his recommended approach to the role and function of Janefield as a 'proposed site for defective home' during this visit. In his diary entry, Akeroyd listed four principles to be followed with the fourth principle being 'Hand the whole show over to the Education Department'.[127] This diary entry not only demonstrated his recognition that education played a major role in reforming juvenile offenders but also landmarked his concern for them once the youngsters left the prison system. It is at this early juncture in Akeroyd's appointment that raised the twin issues of reconciling his educative approach to prison management against the need for punishment.

It is clear in his personal reflections that Akeroyd believed punishment should played only a minor or incidental role in prison:

> *You will begin to realize how I view a prison or a reformatory —*
> *as a place of education not of punishment — education away*
> *from evil habits and thoughts to thoughts and habits habitual*
> *to good citizens.*

> *This does not mean prisons are not places of punishment,*
> *but punishment is only incidental — it is an accompaniment*
> *not the main aim.*

> *Of course there is punishment in the long hours of isolation*
> *at night time, in the discipline, the shutting off from friends*
> *and relatives, the penalties for breaches of discipline etc.* [128]

---

[127]   VPRS 6604, 5 September 1924.

[128]   VPRS 6603, undated paper)

In October 1925, Akeroyd was invited to speak to student teachers at the Victorian Education Department's Teachers' College at the university grounds in Carlton. In his speech notes, Akeroyd claimed that criminals fell into two main classes which, in his own words, Akeroyd identified as follows:

> (1) *Those who show some definite taint [sic] in mind or body, either from birth or acquired, that makes it impossible or almost impossible for them to conform to laws.*

> (2) *Those who are victims of bad environment or training who could quite possibly conform to laws.*[129]

Drawing on his experience as an educator and gathering prisoner case information, Akeroyd believed it was critical to link the characteristics of the two distinctly separate criminal classes to an appropriate method of treatment. He elaborated about class 1 criminals as follows:

> *Except among imbeciles, and of these I have only found two in 20 months work I cannot find that mental deficiency as such is a main cause of criminality. It is the psychopathic or aberrational mental traits (as you please) that lead to criminality, not mental deficiency in itself.*

> *These psychopaths are few in number. They require long and careful training and much testing before release.*

> *It is a moot point, too, whether psychopaths should be segregated wholly from normal criminals. Certainly they are destructive to discipline, but a gaol wholly composed of psychopaths would be an awful place, and the influence and*

---

[129] VPRS 6603, 7 October 1925.

example of normal human beings must do much to steady
up these unfortunates.[130]

During the same speech, Akeroyd also defined the criminals he believed had been affected by environmental factors (class 2).

In these cases it is notable that very many have lost one or
both parents. Very often a stepfather or stepmother appears
in the picture.

Again one often stumbles on scenes of poverty, hunger, dirt,
immorality, thrifthlessness [sic], poor discipline or other lack
of discipline etc.

From good homes in the material sense one can sometimes
trace as a contributory cause lack of harmony between parents.

Very seldom is the school or the church mentioned and one
fails to find any very definite impression left by teachers or
ministers of religion.[131]

In the latter scenario, Akeroyd advocated a multilevel approach for treating the specific class of criminal. Further, Akeroyd was conscious that as the second class of criminal spent little time within the prison system, it was critical to adopt a coordinated approach to capitalise on the limited time available to reform the individual. The first step, Akeroyd believed, was removing the prisoner's 'distinct antisocial grudge' to enable progress to be made.

Very often when first received into prison, he has <u>*distinct*</u>
<u>*antisocial grudge*</u>[132]*_looking upon warders as his enemies.*

---

[130]   VPRS 6603, 7 October 1925.

[131]   VPRS 6603, 7 October 1925.

[132]   Akeroyd's underlining.

Before any progress can be made this must be removed, and in fact, it soon disappears under kindly treatment. The prisoner is trained to think that punishment comes from the law officials (the court), that the prison officials are under orders of the court to hold him for a certain length of time, and, that, during that time, these officials will help to place him in such a position, that, when he leaves prison, he will be more fitted than before for the battle of life.

Akeroyd went on to detail what reforms can be achieved once the prisoner lost their grudge:

(1) Ideals. First let us put ideals – ideals of conduct and of living. Good and beautiful thoughts. Training in tolerance for one's fellows and his possessions.

First we must have a fine tone in our institution, and this can only come from a fine type of officer in daily associations with the prisoners – wise, kindly, upright, firm, and well educated with some knowledge of the mental types to be found . . .

The second is in the provision of a school where a trained teacher of good personality is daily in contact with these lads for several hours a day.

Next these lads must be trained in discipline. Discipline from above first, leading later to self-discipline. I find nothing so good as the physical exercises and games taught in the schools . . .

Practically none of these prisoners remain in prison longer than twelve months. Consequently a trade cannot be taught . . . all can be trained to handle tools.

> *It is anticipated that (the workshop) will be placed under the care of a trained technical teacher who will instruct these youths in practical geometry, sheetmetal work and woodwork – the basis of all trades.*

Akeroyd outlined the final step involved instilling 'a sense of responsibility to the community'.

> *Consider the people we are dealing with. Reared without sense of responsibility to the community in which they live. Accustomed to spend as much time as possible in pleasure with no thought of self-improvement – living only for the moment. How in twelve short months can one cause the door to open of service to the community.*[133] *It is a difficult matter. The mind must first be prepared by discipline and training.*
>
> *Again the whole atmosphere of the place must help. The daily talks of the superintendent should be vitalizing and only a broad visioned educated man can do such work. The school helps, but I am afraid that we fall far short of the ideal.*[134]

Akeroyd's thoughts registered both in his early diary entries and in other documents clearly set the platform for his approach to prison management system reform, in particular individual prisoners. As Akeroyd strongly believed that education principles aligned consistently with those of penology, he also introduced science-based thinking in his bid to understand reasons behind criminal behaviour to effectively reform offenders.

While Akeroyd's policies had many advocates within Victoria, he invited Dr Morris Miller, Director of the State Psychological Clinic

---

[133] Note that Akeroyd did not include the question mark in his notes.

[134] VPRS 6603, 7 October 1925.

of Tasmania, to comment on the Victorian prison system during his visit, and this was reported in the *Herald*.[135] The article outlined the call for treating the mental defectives separately from other prisoners as well as reviewing the term 'indeterminate' to include prisoners serving indeterminate sentences within the scope of reform. Such remarks prompted extended debate in the newspapers and official reports over the nature of indeterminate sentencing which peaked during Akeroyd's middle years.

While the indeterminate sentence debate surfaced in 1925, a public debate on the underlying causes of crime and criminality emerged in the following year. In an article published in the *Herald*, Dr C. R. McRae, one of Browne's contemporaries on the executive Board of the Australian Council for Educational Research (ACER), questioned earlier positions on the causes of crime and criminality as well as the appropriateness of programs to redress such causes.[136] According to McRae, the arguments purporting 'defective moral sense' were illogical because he argued 'morality is entirely the outcome of experience'. He also found any direct relationship between mental defect and delinquency to be equally spurious by quoting Dr Fernald: 'Every feeble-minded person is a potential criminal, needing only the proper environment and opportunity for the development of the criminal tendencies'.[137] McRae further argued that:

> ...*since the mythical 'defective moral sense' or 'inherited criminal trait' is never among the causes of juvenile delinquency, and mental defect is a comparatively rare cause, I may proceed to indicate . . . the real causes. (These*

---

[135]   *Herald*, 8 January 1925.

[136]   *Herald*, 29 May 1926.

[137]   *Herald*, 29 May 1926.

> *are) . . . defective discipline at home which may be either*
> *too lax or too strict . . . some unrealised wish rankling in*
> *the unconscious . . . a family history of vice or crime . . .*
> *(and) . . . poverty.*[138]

Such arguments appeared to have preoccupied Akeroyd in his middle and later years as he weighed the issue of pre-disposition to criminality against criminality arising from under-socialisation or environmental influences.

The early stages of Akeroyd's appointment witnessed interesting public and private debate from Akeroyd and his colleagues from the education world as well as others boasting prison management interest. The ensuing dialogue not only attracted people with a positive interest from education and allied fields but also sparked contributions coming from the broader political arena. While prompted early in Akeroyd's career, the nature of the issues continued to pique Akeroyd's interest as his career progressed.

The controversy surrounding effective prison management and reform programs continued throughout 1924 with debate extended to present prisoners' views that the state of the Victorian prison system was 'a vicious one, tending to increase rather than lessen crime . . . little effort is made in our gaols to teach trades to convicts; that the Indeterminate Sentences board is given powers that are too arbitrary and that prisoners are herded together indiscriminately, resulting in contamination of first offenders by hardened criminals'.[139] The *Age* and the *Argus* newspapers independently reported on Chief Secretary Mr Tunnecliffe's presentation on the government's approach to prison reform following a recent prisoner strike protesting against continuing indeterminate sentence. Tunnecliffe was reported

---

[138]   *Herald*, 29 May 1926.

[139]   *Herald*, 19 April 1924.

as saying that 'the policy of the Labour Ministry was that prison treatment should be reformatory and not punitive'.[140] The *Argus* reported that Tunnecliffe had interviewed Akeroyd and had 'every confidence in Mr Akeroyd's ability, but he realised that Mr Akeroyd was seriously handicapped through the lack of proper classification of prisoners'.[141] Mr Tunnecliffe suggested recalcitrant prisoners be looked after at the Beechworth prison where 'facilities for education, development and reform of prisoners would be made'.[142]

Both newspapers also reported the importance the chief secretary placed on dealing with youthful criminals by noting the level of youthful offenders had remained unchanged despite the general prison population decreasing during the past 50 years. However, only the *Argus* reported on the challenge the government faced regarding the court–imposed sanction of whipping.

> *Mr. Tunnecliffe said that the Labour party was opposed to corporal punishment, but as the sentence had been awarded by the court he, as Chief Secretary, would have to see that it was carried out . . . Personally, he was convinced that a man could not be reformed by flogging, which only had a brutalising effect.*[143]

In the early phase of his career as inspector general, Akeroyd commenced to articulate his thoughts and prepare his positioning for future developments in prison and prisoner management through annual reports in his concerted effort to engage the government and broader community. The inspector general was required to submit

---

[140]   Argus, 18 August 1924.

[141]   *Argus*, 18 August 1924.

[142]   *Argus*, 18 August 1924.

[143]   *Argus*, 18 August 1924.

annual reports to the government of the day – more specifically both houses of parliament – entitled 'Penal Establishments, Gaols, and Reformatory Prisons' for the previous year.

The year prior to Akeroyd's 1924 appointment, Mr C. S. McPherson prepared the review for 1921 and 1922. In 1924, when Akeroyd presented his first report, he was reporting on events that had occurred during 1923 for which he was not, at the time, responsible. It was notable that the reports prior to Akeroyd's appointment merely provided a summary of the statistical information without commentary. The reporting style changed under Akeroyd with his inaugural report presenting statistical information as prescribed in previous report formats but also included a chapter which appeared to invite a challenge for parliamentary debate. In his 1924 report, Akeroyd presented chapters on education, industries, indeterminate sentences, probation, discipline, and tone. He also presented several graphs detailing the following: intelligence testing including cumulative and distribution graphs of prisoner IQ, school attainment, and prisoner mental age. Therefore, 1924 marked the year education featured in Akeroyd's plans to present the state government with baseline data on prisoner education and intelligence attributes.

Akeroyd maintained a similar approach with the annual reports until 1932 with only minor additions here and there. Whilst Akeroyd used the annual reports to articulate his views, his critics used alternative forms of media such as newspapers to publicly address their concerns about his directions.

8.1 Other Voices at the Time

While Akeroyd's thoughts reflected his personal position, it was evident that many of his contemporaries from education, research, politics, and the church shared his outlook at the time. However, it was equally evident that many in the Victorian community also challenged his views. To reflect on divided public debates occurring concurrently with Akeroyd's evolving position, consideration is given to both the supporting and contrary positions.

The Honourable Samuel Maugher, chairman of the Indeterminate Sentences Board, addressed the Methodist Church on approaches to managing crime and criminals as recorded in the *Warrnambool Chronicle* by reflecting on the international focus toward prison reform. Maugher was reported as saying,

> *Prison reform and the treatment of prisoners never received more attention than at present time. In Canada the old prisons are being discarded for forest settlement and development. The indeterminate sentence is being universally adopted. In America long overdue reforms are in progress and the establishment of prison industries is being undertaken. In the homeland one of the effects of the Great War has been to give a fillip to prison reform in a remarkable manner.*[144]

As Maugher's address was presented to the Methodist Church, he couched many observations and comments within a religious context by reminding the church that 'many of the world's best men have been prisoners – criminals as we loosely call them'.[145] Maugher presented his perspectives on the prison system and treatment of prisoners in the context of 'Jesus and John and Peter, James and Paul were each under arrest or in prison many times. . .. Germany arrested and imprisoned Martin Luther . . . one of the greatest Scotchmen, John Knox, was for years a galley slave'.

---

[144]   14 March 1924.

[145]   14 March 1924.

Using religious analogies, Maugher attempted to persuade the church that prisons needed to reform individuals before they returned to the community. However, Maugher cautioned that prisons must embrace the framework of 'humane scientific treatment of the unfortunate' by stating,

> *The only justification for any prison system is that to help the prisoner and protect society and prepare the prisoner for restoration to society . . . This is what the new penal science in contrast with the old penal law, attempts to do. To correct or cure the conditions in the person has caused the commission of the crime by placing him in a prescribed environment under medical industrial education, and other scientific care and discipline and to reform the person so he is likely to take care of himself and his family after his discharge.*[146]

Interestingly, the same newspaper article reported comments from a Miss Dorgan who reflected on the value of education to women prisoners:

> *Education has done a great deal of good, no doubt, but it has also given us a well-educated and smooth spoken lot of crooks . . . Miss Dorgan approves of the new system of teaching trades to male prisoners, and occupations such as sewing, raffia and laundry work to women . . . but she doesn't believe in coddling criminals or in the abolition of capital punishment.*[147]

In 1924, many newspaper articles reported on the importance of introducing a 'human touch' into prisons to support the prisoners'

---

[146] *Warrnambool Chronicle*, 14 March 1924.

[147] *Warrnambool Chronicle*, 14 March 1924.

intellectual growth. Mr Maugher was reported in the *Herald* as follows:

> *If the idea of making imprisonment reformative instead of purely punitive is ever to be more than the pious aspiration of good and kindly folk, a radical change must be made to the penal system . . . The first great need is to the introduction into the prison itself, as tutors and exemplars, of bright, strong, resolute young men, skilled in letters and not unskilled in handicrafts. The average warder is an efficient gaoler; his office bars him from being guide, philosopher and friend. The personal touch on the reformative side is as yet unexploited . . . where . . . it could be most valuable as a national asset.*[148]

In July 1924, George Browne, Vice Principal of the Teachers Training College at Melbourne University, in evaluating the effectiveness of American programs, pleaded for a 'vigorous scientific campaign against crime' to be introduced.[149] Browne reflected on previous regimes of handling prisoners and their offending behaviours.

> *The method of meeting criminal offences with severe punishments has never been successful in seriously diminishing crime, for the reason that many offenders are constitutionally unable to exercise the same control over their actions as their more normal fellow beings.*
>
> *It is not very long since the accepted treatment for insane persons was to flog them until their particular devils left them. This we regard now as hideous cruelty, but future centuries may consider our methods of dealing with criminals equally as cruel and ineffective. We punish them and let them*

---

[148]   *Herald*, 29 November 1924.

[149]   *Herald*, July 1924.

go, and soon they are back for their next dose of punishment.
Is there not a more scientific procedure than this?[150]

Using case studies from the Detroit (USA) program as a template for dealing with offenders, Browne advocated for prisoner classification along similar lines to that of Akeroyd:

(1) The victim of a bad environment, who can often be cured by being given a fresh start under better circumstances.

(2) The criminal of definite feeble mindedness, who can only be easily be detected and segregated before much harm is done.

(3) The high grade criminal, intelligent and crafty, with an hereditary taint in his mental and moral make up.[151]

Like Akeroyd, Browne placed significant importance on developing case studies that sought to understand offenders' backgrounds by identifying factors contributing to offending behaviours but also called for the use of intelligence tests to indicate the mental age of the offender.

Browne strongly believed combining the case history with the intelligence test would benefit the first two classes. However, he admitted the existing indeterminate sentence strategy served the needs of the third class of offenders.

How to deal with the third class is still a problem. The Indeterminate sentence seems the best solution so far; but the

---

150   *Herald,* July 1924.

151   *Herald,* July 1924.

> *first and second classes, if allowed to continue in a criminal career, remain a permanent reproach to the State.*[152]

The Detroit program, according to Browne, established therapeutic communities based on a village concept and an industrial colony 'where similar cases receive firm but sympathetic treatment . . . where the gaol was merely a place of retribution, the village community becomes a hospital for the morally sick'.[153]

There was evidence that not everyone embraced Akeroyd's initiatives during the early years of his tenure. Various elements of the community, including prison staff, some prisoners, and some members of the public, recorded their dissatisfaction towards Akeroyd's philosophical approach to prison and prisoner management. In the early days of his appointment, Akeroyd spelled out his directions and philosophical position on his expectations of prison staff in an undated document. Akeroyd made the following comments about staff selection and training:

> *The first necessity is good staff. The members of the staff must be men of good personality, interested in their work, upright men who rule more by force of character than by force of might – if I may put it so.*

> *To this end they are carefully chosen. They must conform to a certain physical and mental standard – in the mental standard being judged by mental tests . . . After being placed on duty they are kept in temporary positions under supervision until they prove themselves and are then placed on probation.*

---

152   *Herald*, 1924.

153   *Herald*, 1924.

During the period of probation they are required to pass
examinations . . . before being made permanent officers.
Then before receiving promotion they must pass examinations
in the principles and practices of prison Management and in
the Laws & Regulations relating to penal establishments
and goals.

Many of them will be able to compile histories of criminals,
note the salient points of those histories and give the best
methods of dealing with any particular person.[154]

Prison staff questioned his approach through both prison officer associations and the press to publicly voice their dissent in his early years. W. C. Callaway, former chief secretary, wrote a letter to the editor of the *Argus* in July 1924 purporting to speak on behalf of warders at Pentridge Prison in response to Akeroyd's proposal to initiate promotion of warders though an examination process. Callaway's position tended to reinforce the previous regime of promotion on seniority and experience. However, his letter also showcased Callaway's concern that the underpinning principles of education were unsuitable in prison operational management:

A boy fresh from school could, with six month's preparation,
pass a better examination in penology than a warder with
a quarter of a century's good service, unhabituated to the
acquisition of book knowledge, which in practice has often
proved so futile. . . . Practical experience should be the sole
standard of advancement.[155]

The debate continued through 1925 and 1926 with prison warders lobbying a delegation of politicians to the chief secretary of

---

[154] VPRS 6603, undated paper.

[155] *Argus*, 16 July 1924.

the time, Mr Argyle, which both the *Argus* and the *Age* reported on one such delegation on 17 June 1925:

> *For the seventh time in the past four years representatives of the penal warders waited upon the Chief Secretary with requests for . . . removal of various sources of grievance at Pentridge and other prisons. . . . The deputation was supported by three members of Parliament – Messrs Keane, Cain and Jewell. . . . And advanced a claim . . . to review the decisions of the Inspector general in cases of warders who appealed against the withholding of increments . . . and asked for promotion by seniority.*[156]

On the same issue reported in the press the following day, Mr Callaway stated,

> *The Pentridge warders do not hail with joy the apparent ambition of the inspector general to fill the higher posts with school men. School fills a very useful place in the social organism, but to carry its traditions through life surely indicates a narrow horizon.*[157]

In another letter to the editor, Mr Callaway also publicly questioned Akeroyd's philosophical approach to managing prisoners by casting doubt on his scientific and sympathetic outlook:

> *All prison systems should be progressive in order to be effective, as penology it [sic] not like mathematics, an exact science. Mr Akeroyd is an officer of high ideals, but his practical knowledge is limited, and the treatment of criminals cannot be mastered in six months.*[158]

---

[156]   *Age*, 17 June 1926.

[157]   *Age*, 18 August 1924.

[158]   *Age*, 18 August 1924.

In the same article, Callaway stipulated his preferred approach to treating prisoners.

> *When London suffered from the epidemic of garrotting, the lash put an end to the terror, and it may check the robbery under arms so prevalent in our midst at present. It is puerile to talk of brutalising the tiger, and the best remedy for violence and cruelty is homeopathic. Sympathy is well, but sentimental treatment of crime is utter folly.*[159]

In these responses to Akeroyd's initiatives, Callaway provided the voice to those prison officers in a couple of matters. Firstly, Callaway expressed disapproval to Akeroyd's 'scientific' or 'mathematical' approach to penology, and secondly, Callaway voiced concerns about the concept of a therapeutic approach to dealing with prisoners. Whether these concerns are based on theoretical differences against Akeroyd's positivist approach or whether these concerns were based on simply doing the work differently is not clear from the evidence available, but it is clear there was a strongly presented case against Akeroyd's reform vision.

In terms of work practices and work conditions, prison warders repeatedly challenged the state government's commitment to their working conditions in four presentations reported in four years. Both the *Age* and the *Argus* on 17 July 1925 reported on the warders' claims for improved pay and removing various sources of grievance. Their claim, presented to the chief secretary by three members of Parliament, included a specific request to establish an appeal board which bypassed the inspector general in response to Akeroyd's plan to base promotion on merit rather than seniority.

---

[159]   *Age*, 18 August 1924.

Akeroyd's early years were marked by his firm agenda to reform prisons and prisoner management underpinned by his dual commitments to prisoner education and using scientific methodology to identify causes of crime to develop programs to address identified causes. His approach led to a stronger focus on prisoner education and training for both younger boys and men in reformatory prisons. He extended his agenda to improve prison officers' education in his move to instil a more disciplined approach to prisoner management which brought him into marked conflict with prison warders. While the prison warder dispute remained a consistent element throughout Akeroyd's middle and later years, it was in his early years that the strong agenda for introducing what he called scientific methodology into prisoner management practice was established. Akeroyd's diary entries recorded strong evidence of his desired approach to prison reform through his various references to scientific methodologies to gain evidence for reforming actions, as well as the subsequent movement towards treatment and encouraging robust community debate.

CHAPTER 9

My Story: Expect the Unexpected

General reflection about the role of a teacher and the process of teaching conjures an environment which is largely controlled, safe, and managed through a broad shared agreement of expected behaviours and professionally managed experiences to facilitate the learning experiences for students. I know this is a 'safe' picture of what happens in schools, and I also know that things can go awry. Working in a prison environment can be all these things as well except when the students escape from a secure classroom to stage a bloodied, self-mutilating protest on the roof of H Division or the day when the bomb exploded in A Division or the day that one of your students has an out-of-body experience from a severe heart attack.

These events are generally not expected in any normal classroom environment but, in a blasé way, are not a surprising aspect of life in a maximum-security prison. The A Division bomb incident was one of those events that was bizarre to the observer participant.

In every way this was a normal day in the prison classroom. The students had been escorted back to the division for lunch when there was a low but ominously powerful thud which rattled windows and shook the thick bluestone walls of the division. I went out the classroom (sited just adjacent to the front entrance of A Division) to witness the glass skylight above the A Division circle shatter, sending shards of glass in 360 degrees. This was then followed by billowing black smoke pouring out the now-broken window frames three stories above the area I was standing. Next, the blast of billowing black smoke gushed out the front door of A Division.

What happened next is indelibly etched in my mind. Following the stream of smoke was a mass of men pouring out the front door – prisoners and prison officers alike. These men ran to a point about 15 meters from the entrance, then they stopped in their tracks. They turned around as one to look back into the open front door as the smoke still made its way out, then after a hiatus of maybe 10 or 15 seconds, then they ran back into the building again en masse. Not a word was spoken (or that I heard).

Here was a group of prisoners and prison officers drawn together in this single yet remarkable event – the community of the prison assembled not based on their roles but as a collection of individuals brought together by a common threat or common event. Their collective reactions were so in tune with one another – here was a community that did not separate prisoners from prison officers for that instant.

There were times when the harmony was non-existent. There have been stories about prison officers being taken hostage at different times over history, but in August 1987, it was the first time a group of prison educators was taken hostage by John Dixon Jenkins. Dixon Jenkins was imprisoned for making bomb threats to schools in an attempt to voice his concerns over his perceptions on the threat of nuclear war. Dixon Jenkins held seven people hostage (four teachers and three prisoner students) with the threat to blow up Bendigo prison with an incendiary device unless his demands for a nuclear-free world were met.[160] Whilst the hostage situation was diffused peacefully after five days, the impact on those held captive was devastating with some of the captives unable to resume their teaching career as a result of the trauma experienced. This event impacted all prison educators at the time. Even though many

---

[160] *Age*, August 1987.

educators believed their role was respected and valued by inmates, it manifested an underlying concern and awareness that events can change in an instant.

Whilst this event showed a different perspective of prison life following a common traumatic event, the time that prisoner 'Ray' suffered a heart attack also provided a different perspective. This was around the same time as the A Division bomb incident.

Ray was a full-time education student and was involved in an arts undergraduate course. He had an interesting theory on building surrogate family structures within the prison environment with the intent to support the growth and development of the young prisoners in the division. His ethnographic study was seen with some suspicion but also with some interest by the prison authorities and the prisoner group. I will not go into his study but say that Ray, undertaking his second life sentence, suffered a major heart attack whilst in his cell. Ray recalled the experience vividly and explicitly. He was able to do this, he explained, as he was able to observe everything that went on from his out-of-body experience. He related to me that he went from feeling extreme pain to feeling no pain, but he was able to observe everything that went on from a point above his body. He described how one prison officer, someone with whom he had many battles with over the years, fought so purposefully to resuscitate him even though it looked to all intents that Ray was certainly dead. The prison officer persisted with his CPR, organised other officers to get the ambulance, and was continually speaking to Ray, encouraging him to live. At the same time, Ray was able to observe another prisoner sneak in behind the officer, unplug Ray's clock radio, and take it out of Ray's cell. Ray described how he followed this prisoner to his own cell and saw where he secreted the clock radio. The next thing Ray described was the severe pain returning.

Ray was taken to the hospital only to release himself from the hospital three days later. He told me that on his return to A Division, he went straight to the other prisoner's cell and removed the clock radio to return it to his own cell. The learning for Ray, however, was the respect he gained for the prison officer who worked so hard to resuscitate him. This challenged Ray who did have a clear them and us perspective to realise that this prison officer went well over what Ray felt was the call of duty to bring him back from the brink. Nothing is what you expect, and you need to expect the unexpected. Ray died from a massive heart attack two days later after telling me his story.

CHAPTER 10

Akeroyd's Perspectives – Middle Years (1931–1940)

During the middle years, Akeroyd maintained his focus on using a scientific approach to understand the nature of crime and criminality through developing his case study methodology. He also continuously lobbied government and judicial agencies to rethink the role of prisons within the community.

Evidenced in the marked decline in diary entries in the late 1920s and 1930s, Akeroyd noticeably shifted from recording his thoughts in his diary to increasingly expressing his views in the public media. Akeroyd's aspirations for a science-based prison and prisoner management regime played out in his speeches, public presentations, and annual reports. During this period, Akeroyd strengthened his resolve to better use psychology to underpin his policy approach to program development particularly in his moves to help young offenders by improving reformatory schools in Janefield and Bayswater. While his focus remained fixed on prison classification and improved treatment of offenders, particularly younger people, Akeroyd likewise presented his strong views on the role of punishment within criminal justice management.

In the early 1930s, the issue of punishment of offenders was playing a larger role in the public debate. On June 20, 1931, Chief Secretary Tunnecliffe publicly expressed his personal opposition to capital and corporal punishment in accordance with the prevailing Labour Party position that was 'to eliminate the more brutal forms of punishment, and to help men by giving them adequate employment and a better form of prison treatment'. Tunnecliffe felt that punishment for criminal behaviour was being 'invariably reserved for the poorer classes'.[161] However, at the same time, the judiciary and Parliament appeared at odds in regard to punishment with the former having established the standard of corporal (and capital) punishment as a legal response to the crime committed while the political position (as reflected by Akeroyd's key employer at the time) condemned corporal and capital punishment. Akeroyd was left to implement punishments determined by the courts which meant his middle years presented the added challenge of reconciling differing perspectives alongside his own personal views.

In an article written for the Honorary Justices' Association of Victoria, Akeroyd plainly stated his perspective on the key principles underpinning the 'modern penal system'. Akeroyd wrote, 'There are two attitudes, and two only, that may be adopted towards the criminal.[162] The first and oldest is conveyed in the very word penal . . . it means "of or pertaining to punishment".' The second attitude, according to Akeroyd, was 'the attitude of understanding and sympathy'.[163] As Akeroyd stated, 'It is the method of the psychologist. It recognises that crime is not a single isolated fact in a man's life; but that it is a mental symptom of mental origin.'[164]

To explore the differences between the two principles, Akeroyd outlined his understanding of key theoretical perspectives underpinning the function and role of a prison by clearly recognising the changing perspectives. In his words, Akeroyd provided a framework for the punitive approach identifying key points of rationale: he firstly established that the regime that he inherited was

---

[161] *Herald*, 20 June 1931.

[162] Justice of the Peace, 1932.

[163] Justice of the Peace, 1932.

[164] Justice of the Peace, 1932.

based on the conservatist principles of punishment of individuals for greater public safety and to adjust criminals' behaviours through punishment. Of the regime he inherited, Akeroyd wrote,

> *Penal institutions, gaols, prisons, houses of correction, etc., were simply places of punishment, designed to punish those convicted of crime. . . This hostile attitude was justified in terms of social utility . . . for the greatest good not only to the individual but to the community was assured.*[165]

Akeroyd argued that the punitive approach had been instituted for four reasons, namely retribution, reformation, deterrence, and social solidarity. In debating the reasons, Akeroyd argued the concept of retribution

> *…considered that the criminal should pay back in suffering for the harm he has inflicted on the community as a sort of moral compensation. I find this reason . . . very difficult to understand. It seems to me the counterpart from the point of view of the community revenge, and I fail to see any social utility whatever in it.*[166]

Akeroyd started then to state his position on punishment by criticizing the approach of the previous regimes of using punishment to reform criminals. In terms of the concept of reformation, he wrote,

> *It is held that by punishing criminals you reform them. This end is achieved in either of three ways: - by creating a fear of the repetition of the punishment, by creating the conviction that crime does not pay, or by breaking the criminal habits*

---

[165]   VPRS 6603 undated.

[166]   VPRS 6603 undated.

formed . . . but punishment as a means of reformation is greatly over − rated. Reformation follows punishment only when the prisoner desires a change in his mode of life, possess [sic] sufficient insight into his inner life to find the reason for his criminal acts, wisdom to plan wisely, and sufficient strength of character to carry out his plans.[167]

Akeroyd spelled out his position on the deterrent impact of punishment as follows:

It is argued that the infliction of suffering upon those convicted of crime has very great value in preventing others from criminal acts, and may even defer the criminal himself from committing another crime . . . But those of us who work among criminals know that for them punishment has very little real value considered as a deterrent, as it makes no real change in the man's character.[168]

Finally, Akeroyd reflected on the role of punishment as a public deterrent as follows:

It is asserted that punishment of criminals is an instrument for the development amongst the general public of ideals and attitudes hostile to crime, and that respect for laws grows from the ideals and attitudes thus created . . . But would it not be truer to assert that respect for laws is felt when those laws are representative of the morality of the nation.[169]

Akeroyd supported his argument by citing American prohibition laws and illegal betting in Victoria by arguing that 'severe punishments are inflicted (for both prohibition and illegal betting), but there is no

---

[167]   VPRS 6603 undated.

[168]   VPRS 6603 undated.

[169]   VPRS 6603 undated.

sign that respect is growing for those laws, but rather the reverse'.[170] After outlining his concerns about the structure and philosophy of the punitive approach, Akeroyd went on to espouse the values of another approach that advocated an 'attitude of understanding and sympathy' which he claimed had been emerging worldwide.[171] He called it 'the method of the psychologist' and compared its underlying principles of sympathetic understanding akin to a medical approach.[172]

> *It is closely akin to the methods of the medical man in the realm of physical illness. Confronted with a problem, he looks to the symptoms, traces them to a cause, and treats the cause.*[173]

In applying such principles to prison and prisoner management, Akeroyd argued it would lead to the following:

1. *The abolition of definite sentence.*
2. *The complete investigation of each prisoner's personality and history, i.e., the preparation of a case history.*
3. *Treatment based on the knowledge obtained.*
4. *Reformation of the reformable.*
5. *Adequate supervision and help after release until the prisoner is in a stable occupation.*
6. *Elimination from the community either by segregation or otherwise of the unreformable.*[174]

---

[170] VPRS 6603 undated.

[171] VPRS 6603 undated.

[172] VPRS 6603 undated.

[173] VPRS 6603 undated.

[174] VPRS 6603 undated. Akeroyd used the numbering presented in this quote.

Throughout the middle years, Akeroyd continued to explore and further refine his understanding of prisoner typologies. In the initial years of this phase, Akeroyd had established two broad categories in planning appropriate reform programs which he continually challenged by applying his own research gleaned from case studies. In a 1935 paper, he designated the two categories to be indeterminate sentence prisoners and 'others' with the latter consisting of 'specials' or 'restraint' subcategories. The 'specials' consisted of young prisoners Akeroyd described as 'accidental' prisoners that were provided employment either in a store or in an office environment with those 'who are backward in education are required to attend school'.[175] On the other hand, the 'restraint' group is kept separate because of their 'intractable' nature (as Akeroyd considered them in need of correctional treatment.[176]

Akeroyd started to focus a further classification relating to sexual offenders as he started to explore in-depth the nature of mental deficiency and its relationship to criminality.

In 1936, Akeroyd introduced a new chapter into his annual reports that focused on sexual offenders that he classified as follows:

(a) *The first division consists of those who are certifiably insane under the Lunacy act.*

(b) *The second division consists of mentally abnormal persons – psychopaths – who are not certifiably insane.*

This division again falls into two sub classes –

Those who commit sex offences; and

---

[175]   VPRS 6603, 1935, p. 9.

[176]   VPRS 6603, 1935, p. 9.

Those whose offences, whether larceny, housebreaking, shoplifting are the result of mental conflict due to abnormal personality . . . may be convicted of incest rape, carnal knowledge or . . . other perversions. But his offences are not the result of any abnormal personality, but his lack of morality.[177]

This text indicated that Akeroyd acknowledged and accommodated conservatist perspectives in explaining crime and criminality within his private or public debates. It was from this basis that Akeroyd commenced his public appeal for greater acceptance to the positivist approach of using psychology to gain an understanding of a person's motives to act immorally. Interestingly, the conservatist approach towards anti-social behaviour involves a regime of punishment designed to correct the offender actions. However, Akeroyd discounted the consequential action in favour of his preference for a therapeutic response by teaching the criminal:

to wipe away old habits and form new ones in accordance with ethical behaviours. . . . <u>Will punishment prevail?</u>[178] By itself No. Punishment is merely a negative remedy. In itself and by itself it gets nowhere because it does not teach ethical standards and train the recipient in the practice of those standards.[179]

In promoting his vision, Akeroyd stated,

Prisons will become on the one hand education institutes (education being used in the widest possible sense) in which

---

[177] Annual Report, Penal Establishment, Gaols, and Reformatory Prisons, 1936, pp. 9–10.

[178] Akeroyd's underlining.

[179] VPRS 6603, 1935.

those who have offended will be trained to take an appropriate place in the world of decent citizenship, and, on the other hand, those deemed irreformable (and these are a goodly number) will be isolated from the chance of injuring their fellow men and trained to work for the good of the state.[180]

In 1935, Akeroyd presented his thoughts to a broader audience through a radio broadcast 'Can Criminals Be Cured?'[181] In the notes prepared for his broadcast, Akeroyd reflected on directions he envisaged for prison operations and prisoner management. He reasserted his basic premise that inadequate moral training in the criminal's background remained the major contributing factor leading to criminal behaviour. Hence, Akeroyd presented his approach to curing the criminal in terms of education 'in the principles and practices of right living'.[182] He went on to specify that education in prison involves:

(a) *highly trained staff.*

(b) *small prisons preferably of an open nature such as forest or farm camps where the officers can be a living vital force in the spiritual welfare of each prisoner.*

(c) *ample work of a productive nature in which the man can be interested and where he can see something for his labour.*

(d) *ample provision of an uplifting nature for the right use of lecture hours . . . make ample provision for the prisoners' leisure hours in the way of books, facilities for higher*

---

180   VPRS 6603, 1935.

181   VPRS 6603, 20 June 1935.

182   VPRS 6603, 20 June 1935.

education in theoretical and practical subjects, sports,
educational talks, concerts, wireless programs, etc.[183]

In 1936, Akeroyd expanded his support for young offenders by suggesting Janefield ought to be used as a place to house and treat young offenders exhibiting mental deficiencies. Janefield, originally established in 1912 as a health sanatorium for tuberculosis sufferers, was re-opened in 1937 as residential treatment centre for young intellectually disabled offenders.[184] Janefield also established a reformatory school within its operations, and it was noted that Akeroyd signed his letters regarding reformatory schools to the chief secretary from 1936 through to 1939 as inspector of reformatory schools. Indeed, as Akeroyd first suggested in 1924, at least a part of Janefield was handed over to the Education Department.

Akeroyd extended his quest to make sense of understanding the causal factors leading to criminality in his formal reports to the government by exploring links between mental deficiency and criminality. Again, Akeroyd's views were played out in the public arena through the press as he advocated a shift away from the formerly punitive approach into the scientific, positivist approach to prisoner and prison system management. In addition to Akeroyd's use of annual reports and public presentations to fuel debate, he appeared to focus on, and foster the recognition for, the discipline of criminology as a means of understanding the driving forces behind criminal behaviour. The increasing frequency and intensity of debate revealed Akeroyd's push for public policy reforms towards reducing crime and the frequency of citizens exhibiting criminal behaviour

---

[183]   VPRS 6603, 20 June 1935.

[184]   Following Akeroyd's considerations and recommendations formulated in his 1924 diary entry.

as well as using scientific rationale to develop a clear and rigorous approach towards prisoner management regimes.

Tracking the interplay between the main perspectives was evident not only in the language of the debates but also through the means in which these perspectives were communicated to the public arena, namely the public forum (including the newspapers and political and academic spheres) as well as the private world of Akeroyd.

In 1939, Akeroyd consolidated his vision of a prison as an education institute by outlining the aims of a reformatory school as well as specifying qualifications and attributes required by staff running the school. In a circular, Akeroyd spelled out the aims of a reformatory school as providing moral as well as vocational training.[185] In the same circular, Akeroyd specified the importance of educational qualifications of staff involved in the elementary school. For example, the superintendent was to be a man of 'good education . . . take charge of daily assemblies . . . and direct the attention of both staff and pupils to some worthwhile thought'.[186] Similarly, the elementary schoolteacher and overseers are required to be trained teachers and officers are to be selected from 'young men of outstanding personality, fine ideals and good education and have trained in such institutions as (a) teachers training college, (b) such schools as Dookie or Longernong Agricultural colleges'.[187]

This circular was also important because it highlighted a key area of Akeroyd's responsibility but not one which was readily addressed in his own papers. Whilst Akeroyd clearly held a focus on the education and training component of prison management, he also focused on ensuring the skills of the industry supervisors were

---

[185]   F 0234, VPRS 6603, 1 June 1939.

[186]   VPRS 6603, 1 June 1939.

[187]   VPRS 6603, 1 June 1939.

consistent with current industry practice. He also focused on the viability of the prison industries. Despite the very stringent financial times resulting in cuts to prison maintenance, non-replacement of staff, and escalating prisoner numbers (from 756 in 1920 to 1301 in 1930 and back to 1181 in 1940), Akeroyd held prison industries to be accountable for financial viability.[188] Despite the financial and resource challenges, Akeroyd maintained his focus on prisoner and prison staff training throughout the middle years of his tenure.

As in the early years, Akeroyd faced conflict from differing quarters throughout this period amid challenges from prison staff opposed to his management strategies, particularly in his drive to promote suitably qualified staff members on merit within the system. Politicians also challenged his views, particularly government ministers, opposed to implementing the practice of early release. Finally concern about inadequate financial and capital resources supporting the new strategies he proposed also became an issue for public airing. While disputes with prison wardens over his steadfast approach to promotion remained a consistent element through Akeroyd's years, fresh debates about early prisoner release and concerns about limited resources gained increasing traction in the public arena. Not only was Akeroyd in public conflict with his employees, but he also now found himself at odds with the attorney general. In 1931, the *Argus* reported the attorney general Mr Slater was in dispute with Akeroyd over the release of prisoners. According to the *Argus*, the attorney general authorised the release of six prisoners 'who served only portion of their sentences' on two separate occasions in 1931.[189]

---

[188]   Lynn and Armstrong, 1996.

[189]   *Argus*, 6 June 1931.

In January 1931, the attorney general, who had recommended the early release of several prisoners, acknowledged in two instances he disregarded Akeroyd's advice. Of significance is the *Argus* reporting of the apparent distance between Slater's and Akeroyd's approaches to early release.

> *It is not the function of the responsible Minister to revise decisions of the courts I order to carry out such experiments on penal practice as may appeal to him. Provision is made for the release of prisoners after the processes of law have operated, because, in very exceptional cases, circumstances may arise which render a departure from the course which the Courts have laid down . . . When the processes of justice about which no secrecy is permitted are frustrated by executive acts only casually revealed speculation on their cause is not unnatural. Mr Slater's explanation of his principles in the administration of his department is no more consoling than the conjectures, which, lacking his assurance might seem to afford the explanation of the Ministry's decisions.*[190]

Also, in June of that year, according to the *Argus*, Akeroyd presented a report to the attorney general recommending that each of the nominated prisoners should serve their complete sentence as he believed the time served within custody would better serve the reformation of the character rather than releasing the prisoners to their own devices in the community. On one prisoner, he reported, 'He is very irritable. When released, if he does break out and lose control of himself, he will certainly use the knife.'[191] On another prisoner, Akeroyd stated, 'Prison has had a deterrent effect on him, but I think that the greater effect will be by making him serve his

---

[190] *Argus*, 5 January 1931.

[191] *Argus*, 6 June 1931.

whole sentence.'[192] On a third, he recorded, 'I do not recommend this release on bond. . . . I am sure that prison will not be harmful for him but will give him an opportunity to recover some serenity of mind, and, with guidance, work out a course of action that will ensure no further crimes of this kind.'[193]

Within one week of the publication of Akeroyd's views, there were further newspaper articles reporting views on the need to maintain corporal punishment both to reform prisoners and to deter criminal behaviour.

In the *Herald* on 17 June 1931 an unnamed 'ex-official' provided graphic detail to the newspaper about floggings using the cane, birching, and the 'cat': 'Speaking from an intimate knowledge . . . I have no hesitation in saying that the administration of a flogging for certain offences is not only wise, but necessary'.[194] In denouncing Akeroyd's approach to prisoner management, the unnamed 'ex-official' argued in the same article that 'the public will have cause to regret it if, through a false sentimentality for the criminal, flogging is done away with'.[195] Such examples highlighted the polarized positions that Akeroyd's approach to prison reform using education and psychological principles often conflicted with those from within the prison system and the public alike who held differing theoretical positions.

The judicial approach to corporal punishment reflected the theory that perceived punishment served the established government's needs by deterring individuals from re-offending. The public debate on punishment in prisons gained some momentum in the newspapers in

---

[192]   *Argus*, 6 June 1931.

[193]   *Argus*, 6 June 1931.

[194]   *Herald*, 17 June 1931.

[195]   *Herald*, 17 June 1931.

1931 following an article outlining an initiative to introduce wireless into the Geelong prison.[196] Its publication sparked a series of articles debating the merit of using whipping as an effective punishment against prisoners. One article quoted a prison authority arguing that 'a whipping seldom has an evil effect or even a degrading one . . . The objections to corporal punishment are based on unsound, sentimental reasons that do great harm through mere ignorance'.[197] Further reports in the *Herald* in subsequent days quoted ex-prison officials denying flogging was a brutal act and instead resulted in 'well under 7 per cent ever com(ing) back to the gaol'.[198] Further articles discussed the deterrent aspect of flogging all prisoners except ones convicted of sexual offences.

> *Flogging fails in one set of crimes – sexual offences which, according to this authority who knows criminals backwards, are generally committed by mentally defective men who are unable to control themselves. Mental homes, failing a lethal chamber are the only means of dealing with these.[199]*

Unlike the conflicting views expressed in the early Akeroyd years, the focus on the role and application of punishment became more explicit in his middle years. The arguments presented publicly came from those with experience of working in the prison system. There did not appear to be any critical views presented in the press or by other means by members of the public. It is unclear whether the criticism presented came from an informed knowledge base or from comfort of maintaining a practice to which prison staff are

---

[196] *Herald*, 10 June 1931.

[197] *Herald*, 16 June 1931.

[198] *Herald*, 17 June 1931.

[199] *Herald*, 17 June 1931.

accustomed. Whilst the extent of the debate represented in the press is limited in the number of articles recorded, the nature of the debate presents a critical juncture in the Akeroyd reform process. For the first time, the criticism of his approach to treatment is challenged publicly by those supporting the maintenance of the punitive regime. However, Akeroyd's engagement with the press elicited support from media to broaden their approach to reporting matters of prison and prisoner management. In response to criticism in the press on Akeroyd's position on punishment, Ray Curtoys, editor of the *Argus*, wrote to Akeroyd,

> *I confess what you had to tell me threw a new light upon what is a tremendous social problem. It may be that what I conceive to be a sense of my public duty to the public may impel me to return to the subject again someday and even to call into question the acts of the Attorney General but you may rely on me to deal with the matters with a sympathetic understanding and a real appreciation of your efforts to make broken men whole.*[200]

Perhaps unwittingly, Curtoys appears to succinctly specify Akeroyd's driving but perhaps unstated mission to 'make broken men whole again'!

Concurrent newspaper reporting indicated a time of concentrated public debate over a range of issues compared to Akeroyd's earlier years in the role. The press coverage included a range of issues including, at one stage, the use of the wireless for prisoners. The *Herald* on 10 June 1931 challenged Akeroyd not only about the use of wireless radios at Geelong Prison but also regarding his intention to extend access to wireless radios to those serving at Pentridge.

---

[200] 4 December 1931.

Akeroyd's response to the wireless issue demonstrated his renewed focus on educative processes to support prisoner development when he stated, 'As to wireless . . . Why not? It is educative and instructive, as selected programmes are always good.'[201] Whilst he was addressing the criticism of some aspects of his approach to keep prisoners appraised of what is happening in the world outside the prison, albeit through the means of radio, he was also coming under criticism about the ways he managed staff.

In the later years of his middle phase, the Victorian government's chief secretary's office criticized Akeroyd's approach to staff management as evident in an unsigned, undated document in 1935. The document alleged the number of escapes[202] had increased markedly under Akeroyd's stewardship while warders 'totally unfitted for the duties that they have to perform' filled the system. The anonymous writer stated, 'It is quite plain that in 12 years of administration the I.G.[203] has destroyed the discipline, the high standard of which it is taken nearly a century to attain.'[204] The document also alleged many instances of what the writer described as improper handling of prisoner incidents and staff issues:

> *The new IG encouraged espionage among staff, and he has*
> *been heard to boast that he knows more about the private lives*

---

[201] Also printed in the *Herald*, 10 June 1931.

[202] Records noted there were three major escapes from Pentridge in the Akeroyd period. These were J. K. Monson who escaped in1926 and was recaptured in Perth, Western Australia; George Howard (1939) who was recaptured inn two days; and K. R. Jones (1940). The previous recorded escapes from a secure setting were in 1901, but there were five further escapes in the ten years following Akeroyd's retirement. The annual reports and Akeroyd's notes indicated there were escapes from low-security settings, but there were no consolidated quantifications of these.

[203] *IG* refers to inspector general as abbreviated by the writer of the letter.

[204] VPRS 6603, undated.

of his subordinates than they do themselves. . . . Prisoners
were encouraged to tell tales on one another. So much of this
sort of thing was carried on that the ignorant sort the idea that
the I.G. must have obtained honours for the subject when he
gained his Arts degree.[205]

Akeroyd disputed the claims raised in the unsigned document and questioned the identity of the anonymous authors. Regardless, the document revealed the disharmony among some staff resistant to Akeroyd's approaches as evident in the apparent cynicism towards Akeroyd's scientific approach to understanding crime and criminality. The author(s) wrote, 'He immediately set himself up as a criminologist, psychologist, reformer etc. . . . as a psychologist the I.G. is supreme.'[206]

The conflict with staff continued through the middle year's phase which culminated in 1939 with Akeroyd calling a meeting to address all Pentridge warders following the anonymous publication of an article in a newspaper that discredited his actions in dealing with warders convicted of trafficking. At this meeting, Akeroyd implored the prison warders, 'Then why send someone to blackguard me? Why send a man to slander me?'[207]

Not all the resistance faced by Akeroyd came from the rank and file, however, with the final area of resistance arising from inadequate funding hindering Akeroyd's attempt to implement his reforms to the extent he planned. In his 1935 annual report to the government, Akeroyd argued comprehensively that establishing a philosophical basis to identify the factors contributing to 'criminals in the making' linked to the importance of prison functioning as a

---

[205] VPRS 6603, undated.

[206] VPRS 6603, undated.

[207] VPRS 6603, notes from meeting at Pentridge, 13 June 1939.

treatment centre for young prisoners.[208] Akeroyd further used the platform to condemn existing physical facilities as unsuitable for 'modern methods of prison administration'.[209] In putting his case for greater consideration for facility works, Akeroyd wrote,

> *Owing to the need for rigid economy little money has been available for repairs and renovations to gaol buildings and yards several years past, while improvements have been out of the question. The result is that considerable expenditure has become necessary. Apropos to this matter I would draw attention to the inadequacy of existing buildings to conform to modern methods of prison administration.*[210]

Sourcing adequate funds to support his initiatives remained a major concern for Akeroyd. Given the unique time in history amid the onset of the 1929 Great Depression and the period falling between two major world wars, it could be well conceived that Victoria was experiencing financial difficulties. Insufficient access to extensive evidence makes it difficult to hypothesise whether it was the prevailing economic situation or other contributing factors centred in the differing perspectives of the key players that played a more dominant role in the limited funding for prisons.

Akeroyd adopted various means to connect with different groups and individuals to communicate his directions, share his learning, and address his critics and landmark his achievements. He often used specific communication vehicles to connect with the groups or

---

[208] Annual Report, Penal Establishments, Gaols, and Reformatory Prisons, 1935, p. 9, Parliamentary Papers, Victoria.

[209] Annual Report, Penal Establishments, Gaols, and Reformatory Prisons, 1935, p. 9, Parliamentary Papers, Victoria.

[210] Annual Report, Penal Establishments, Gaols, and Reformatory Prisons, 1935, Parliamentary Papers, Victoria, p. 9.

individuals he wanted to influence. He used annual reports to present opinions on prison and prisoner management issues; he implemented change of practices through speaking directly with staff members; and he used public media, such as the radio, to inform the broader community. He also engaged with academia for the purposes of researching changes in practice as well bringing outside expertise into prison operations.

Akeroyd's use of annual reports became an important means for Akeroyd to engage with the government throughout his middle year's period. The 1932 annual report provided an example of communicating his approach to expand the practice of writing extensive prisoner case studies to ensure there was an evidence base to implement programs to facilitate personal change. This was the first time that such an approach was brought to the government's attention, and by writing this, Akeroyd appeared to inform the government that he was taking an approach to focus on individual prisoner needs. In this 1932 annual report, Akeroyd made it clear that

> *special emphasis, however, must be placed in getting in touch with individual prisoners, learning their histories, gaining their confidence, and encouraging them to amendment of life. It is just this personal touch which helps to bring about a change in attitude of mind, and to strengthen a resolve to follow a different course of living.*[211]

Whilst this report landmarked his approach to implement programs based on changing attitudes, he also recorded his initiative to broaden prisoners' minds through lectures on the 'Science of Everyday

---

[211] Annual Report, Penal Establishments, Gaols, and Reformatory Prisons, 1932, p. 15, Parliamentary Papers, Victoria.

Living' and 'Psychology'.[212] This annual report was significant by forecasting Akeroyd's commitment to scientific approach to gather evidence about individual needs and engage prisoners in science-based programs to address these needs. In doing this, Akeroyd was preparing the government for this change in approach and, arguably, building a science-based rationale which would be difficult to refute without an evidence base.

Whilst the 1932 annual report prepared the way for introducing the science-based approaches, Akeroyd used later reports to strengthen his viewpoints and influence government thinking about crime issues. In the 1933 report, Akeroyd deviated from previous reports by introducing additional chapters apparently designed to elicit debate within the government. In one chapter entitled 'Does Crime Pay?' Akeroyd recorded his ponderings on what factors influenced criminals to offend, including making the following observations based on information he had collected on a prisoner's individual wealth:

> *It would appear from the foregoing that crime is not a very profitable pursuit, or else the criminals squander the proceeds of their crime. Probably those that benefit most from the commission of crime are the receivers who manage to retain their freedom whilst those who plunder for them that go to prison.*[213]

This statement could be interpreted in several ways, but the key message was that Akeroyd appeared to be using his information to bring a greater awareness to the government about the nature of

---

[212] Annual Report, Penal Establishments, Gaols, and Reformatory Prisons, 1932, p. 16, Parliamentary Papers, Victoria.

[213] Annual Report, Penal Establishments, Gaols, and Reformatory Prisons, 1934, p. 8, Parliamentary Papers, Victoria.

crime and criminality. Presumably, he did this to establish a more fertile space for a deeper policy discussion within the government, or possibly opening the opportunity for him to become more influential in assisting government thinking about crime matters.

In another chapter in the same report, Akeroyd provided a retrospection of the previous 100 years of the Victorian penal operations. Akeroyd summarised positivist directions emerging under his guidance to demonstrate to the government how his reform had resulted in significant achievements compared to previous years. It was also telling that in the same report, Akeroyd reflected on pressures managing limited staff numbers with many 'fulfilling duties of higher ranks in an acting capacity . . . and the engagement of temporary staff from the railways'.[214]

Akeroyd continued his commitment to improving educational opportunities within the penal environment during his middle years. Akeroyd clearly established his philosophical position on punishment and treatment during his talk to the Melbourne Teachers' College students and staff, as quoted earlier, when he questioned whether punishment would prevail. He responded in the negative to his rhetorical question by emphasising that prisoners' ethical standards could be improved through teaching and practice.

> *Teaching and practice are required. The more one works amongst criminals the more one becomes convinced that two outstanding factors in the curing of the criminal – education in the broadest sense; and supervision and guidance after release.*[215]

---

[214] Annual Report, Penal Establishments, Gaols, and Reformatory Prisons,1934, p. 16, Parliamentary Papers, Victoria.

[215] Annual Report, Penal Establishments, Gaols, and Reformatory Prisons, 1935, p. 9, Parliamentary Papers, Victoria.

In the 1938 report, Akeroyd asserted that the approach he had taken to initiate education programs into the prison system became the 'only'[216] way for prisoners to achieve the reform required by themselves and the community. Akeroyd stated,

> *It is now generally recognised that by training and teaching only, can that ambition and capacity to stand alone in the struggle of life be attained in the men who have drifted into crime largely through the environment in which they lived.*[217]

As Akeroyd used his reports to elicit debate, a parallel phenomenon was simultaneously developing amid the science of criminology emerging as a defined discipline for public debate and informing public policy. Through Justice Barry, Anita Muhl, an internationally recognised criminologist of the time, was invited to lecture at Melbourne University where she connected with many others including Joseph Akeroyd who subsequently wrote a foreword for her book *The ABC of Criminology*:

> *The science of criminology is a fascinating subject of great importance to the community, for it deals with the physical, mental and moral makeup of the individuals who offend against the law and who are commonly known as criminals.*[218]

Through his writings, broadcasting, coverage in the daily press, and everyday meetings, Akeroyd used the scientific authority of criminology to further support his arguments of prison and prisoner reform. Other than the odd minor addition, Akeroyd maintained a

---

[216] Akeroyd's words.

[217] Annual Report, Penal Establishments, Goals, and Reformatory Prisons, 1938, p. 14, Parliamentary Papers, Victoria.

[218] Muhl, 1941, p. 9.

consistent structure in writing his annual reports up to 1932 with his persistent focus on using both science and his case study methodology to promote discussion about the nature of crime and criminality. From 1932 until retiring in 1947, he witnessed significant developments in the positivist approach including the establishment of the Centre for Criminology at Melbourne University. It is also in this period that evidence emerged of significant challenges to Akeroyd who remained frustrated at the inability of prison operations to implement changes. Akeroyd recorded his reflections on Victorian prison and reformatory operations as follows:

> *Castlemaine Reformatory Prison to me constitutes a paradox. Here we have modern methods of medical and psychological examination, vocational training etc., being applied in an environment typical in every respect, and to an extent not found anywhere else in Australia, of the old prison system, with its rigid insistence on the old penal principles. The boys are continually reminded by the administrative authority that they are there for help and training so they can be readjusted to the community to which they return as self-supporting, self-respecting and valuable members, and they are not held in any punitive sense. . . . BUT they are surrounded by every evidence of the old prison life and discipline of the most rigid type.*[219]

Arguably, during this period of Akeroyd's appointment, he developed a clear strategy to provide an elegant explanation of a treatment-focused model of prison and prisoner management based on an evidence raised through scientific methodology. Using this approach, Akeroyd also aligned himself to key allies who espoused similar sentiments by reinforcing key message to the community

---

[219] VPRS 6603, p. 17.

through respective avenues. Akeroyd used his formal reports to the government, media coverage, and the newfound Centre for Criminology at Melbourne University and other key education-based research organisations (such as Australian Council for Education Research and Melbourne Teachers' College) to assert a definite legitimacy (verified through scientific methodology) underpinning his opinion and practice.

CHAPTER 11

My Story: Time Stands Still

The sally port is that security space where vehicles, and sometimes individuals, transition between the street entrance and the prison buildings and yards. At Pentridge, all staff reporting to duty proceed through a security pass checking area, sign in, then enter through a locked gate into the sally port to walk to another locked gate before entering the prison proper. There were many other locked gates to be negotiated before the teachers would access their teaching space. However, in the first stages of this process, I, like all my colleagues, would walk past several prison officers standing in the sally port and manning each gate.

I was not alone always feeling that the prison education staff were viewed with suspicion by the prison officers. We were dressed in civilian clothes, seen as 'do-gooders', and generally viewed as security risks for either bringing in contraband or taking out messages. I do have to admit that there were instances over time of teaching staff breaching security rules; and there were times in my later years of having to manage situations where staff inadvertently, or in some cases deliberately, contravened security protocols. These instances only heightened the sense of distrust by uniformed staff toward 'civilian' staff. This distrust manifested itself in various means, but the one aspect that really rankled with me occurred when the prison officers in the sally port would observe me entering the port but then turn their back on me as I walked toward the gate to the prison. Sometimes I felt some prison guards would ignore me at the gate to keep me waiting simply for the sake of it.

I set myself a challenge to address this behaviour and win respect for me and my colleagues. So I started to acknowledge each prison officer in the sally port with a direct, cheerful, and personal 'good morning'. I set a long-term goal to have each prison officer say good morning to me before I said good morning to him or her, and I knew that if I had every officer say good morning first, then I built a platform for extending this mutual respect to other aspects of a positive education staff–prison staff relationship.

This strategy worked well early with many of the prison staff readily engaging in the good morning and actively good morning me before I could good morning them. All but one who was very reluctant to engage. He would constantly turn his back on me and not visually engage let alone verbally engage.

I love to take on a challenge, so I would make a point to get in his line of vision and wish him a specific good morning. It became a game that raised the interest and humour within the other prison staff to see when he would acknowledge me. In reflection, it was almost a humiliation exercise, but it also became a powerful motivation exercise as I felt all the other prison officers were creating the environment to compel him to acknowledge me.

Then one day it happened! He acknowledged me first with a good morning before I said good morning to him. That was a great moment for me, but the ultimate moment came almost six years after this landmark event.

I left teaching at Pentridge to return to teaching in mainstream schools and in the youth justice sector only to return to Pentridge in January 1986. On my first day back as I travelled through the same entry regime as I had years before, there was my old 'adversary' in the sally port, welcoming me with a good morning and asking how I enjoyed my Christmas break! He had not realised I had been elsewhere for almost six years! It goes so show that in prison, time means so many things to many people, but also for many others, time stands still!

On that very same day, a second event occurred that blew my mind.

In December 1985, I was a senior teacher in the security section of Baltara Special School. Baltara was a facility for young boys aged between the ages of 9 and 15 who were held in care due to the nature of offences or extreme risk to their health and well-being resulting from their behaviours. Working in the high-security locked section with two other teaching staff, we were supporting up to 15 young boys with education programs.

Over the Christmas break period whilst the education programs were closed, many of these boys my team and I were teaching escaped the facility. They were taken to the youth detention facility (named Turana) where they were then involved in a major riot only then to be taken to Pentridge to be managed.

It was so disheartening to find my students of my last education program as boys in Baltara were my first students on my first day back at Pentridge, the maximum-security prison in Melbourne. This was a frightening episode of the speed that some young men travelled through our juvenile justice system into the adult corrections system.

But that was only half the story. Young 'Morry',[220] as we called him, was one of those Baltara students fast rolling to Pentridge and told me that 'Macca Moo Cow' was in the yards! This Macca was David McColloch, one of the childcare officers I worked closely with in Baltara's high-security section. With his broad Scottish accent, Macca was an amazing motivator and, I thought, an amazing role

---

[220] So many of these students had not yet reached the age of 15, yet here they were in a maximum-security prison!

model for many of these young men. The newspapers revealed Macca had an alternate life and was heavily involved in drug sales and stand-over tactics in the community. This was so alien to the Macca I knew, and this was a great shock. It wasn't long before I caught up with Macca as he enrolled in education programs. Macca still maintained this role as a mentor to many of these young men, and I mean mentor in the most positive sense. He not only mentored these young men, but also became a strong advocate for prisoners negotiating with prison management and arranging for legal advice for those bewildered by the legal system or struggling to find their way. As he had not taken Australian citizenship (or so I assume), Macca was recently deported to Scotland.[221]

---

[221] Jailhouse lawyer to fight deportation by Peter Dutton (theage.com.au).

CHAPTER 12
Akeroyd's Later Years (1941–1947)

As in his middle years, many of Akeroyd's recorded comments about, and his positions on, issues were captured through third-party reports such as newspapers and government reports initiated by others during the final phase of his tenure. Akeroyd no longer appeared to record observations in his diary, and any documented reflections in terms of letters and reports had also drastically diminished in the later years. Whilst his personal and private reflections were not as evident in his later years as they were in the previous years, his achievements and challenges were readily recorded in the daily press and other public media. Through evidence provided by these media, Akeroyd's s final years provided a mixture of his position on a range of important areas. Four significant areas characterised Akeroyd's final years as inspector general, including the reported impact of the poor condition of prison stock, the inconsistency in the processes of promoting staff, the inquiry into punishment within prisons, and a strong public position postulated on dealing with sex offenders. The poor prison stock exemplified Akeroyd's battle to fully implement all his program ambitions amid scarce financial resources following the Great Depression and world wars. His perceived inconsistency in managing staff promotions compared to the rigour he applied in earlier years revealed the possibility the job was wearing him down. The corporal punishment inquiry highlighted Akeroyd's challenge in reconciling earlier conflicting perspectives between punishment and reform. The strong position adopted in classifying and managing sexual offenders had consolidated Akeroyd's view that the psychologist/criminologist played a distinctly more effective role than the medical scientist (in this instance psychiatry) in dealing with sex offenders. To clarify each of these points further, each of these issues is considered in turn.

The later years' period provided a range of challenges to Akeroyd's management of prison stock. These challenges ranged from the handing over of Pentridge Prison and Geelong Prison for use as military prisons and the increase in prison industry production to support the war effort.[222] Apart from small referencing in the annual reports, newspapers articles prompted major discussion about ageing and inadequate prison stock during Akeroyd's time. In 1944, the newspapers reported Victoria still languished behind other countries despite many inroads being achieved under Akeroyd's leadership. Articles published from 1944 until 1947 reported his achievements against the apparent lack of support for his initiatives from the government(s) of the day. The *Truth*'s 28 October 1944 headline 'Prison Reform No Mere Ideal, Report Shows Much Already Done' outlined the reforms introduced by Akeroyd over the years.

> *The changed system of punishment at Pentridge . . . has worked wonders. In 1923, discipline was at a low ebb . . . the treatment of prisoners was far from ideal . . . the system of studying the prisoners' problems sympathetically and training instead of merely punishing them is paying good dividends for Pentridge.*[223]

The article went on to explore the main handicaps to achieving Akeroyd's goals:

---

[222]   Lynn and Armstrong, 1996.

[223]   *Truth*, 28 October 1944.

Progress in the education of prisoners has stopped somewhat short of the desired objective because of obsolete and unsuitable buildings and equipment and because the true functions of prison is not adequately appreciated yet.[224]

The position remained consistent with an earlier article written by Edith Onians:

There has been a marked improvement in our prisons during Mr J. Akeroyd's humane administration. Still, we are sadly behind other countries in the treatment of prisoners and their aftercare.[225]

Ms Onians likened the Victorian prison program status to prisons in England, America, and Sweden in particular, commenting on the depressing appearance of the Victorian prison uniforms and the 'dark and forbidding' structures like Pentridge Prison.

R. K. Gerrand reported on the state of the Victorian prison stock as follows:

Hundreds of prisoners at Pentridge live in buildings only one step ahead of the hell hulks and stockades they replaced nearly 100 years ago. Some of the gaol's oldest and worst buildings are still in use, very little changed, and more crowded than ever.

Gerrand observed little had been done to improve building stock since 1926 and criticised chief secretaries (up until the chief secretary of the day) for failing to commit funds to improve the prison. Gerrand described the impact of the poor-quality facilities on education and reform programs:

---

[224] *Truth*, 28 October 1944.

[225] *Age*, 14 October 1944.

Modern re-education work is out of the question with the present buildings. Complete redesigning of the whole place is needed.[226]

Geraldine Turner followed up on Gerrand's article with the following commentary:

That the modern gaol is not a place for punishment, but a place where offenders are sent by the courts as a punishment, and from which they should emerge as better citizens, prepared to take a responsible place in the community is a firm belief of Pentridge governing authorities. But with the facilities with which they have been struggling at Pentridge since 1924 it is almost impossible to achieve this purpose.[227]

The newspaper articles appeared to support Akeroyd's intended and actual reforms with Gerrand writing in a follow-up article:

The Government must already be aware of the needs from the reports of the Inspector General (Mr Akeroyd) in whose term of 21 years a great chance [sic][228] has been made the whole outlook and organisation of the prison. His recommendations on many vital issues appear to have been ignored. . . . Pentridge school, doing excellent work with miserable equipment for its task, needs to be made a technical school . . . one of the most serious deficiencies of the present system is the lack of special institutions, buildings, equipment and staff for the rehabilitation treatment.[229]

---

[226] *Herald*, 31 May 1945.

[227] *Herald*, 3 June 1945.

[228] This typo was, I believe, to be 'change' rather than chance.

[229] *Herald*, 6 June 1945.

On 22 July 1947, Undersecretary L. Chapman criticised Akeroyd's proposal that positions of responsibility be filled from within existing staff ranks. In his letter to the chairman of the Public Service Board, Mr Chapman (undersecretary to the chief secretary) disagreed with Akeroyd that an internal prison officer be appointed to a senior position within the penal system. Mr Chapman argued that despite him and Mr Akeroyd long agreeing to fill senior posts externally, Akeroyd had reversed his decision and appointed an inside applicant for a senior position. According to Chapman, the about-face went against advice offered by both the undersecretary and Akeroyd's own deputy. Chapman expressed his concerns to the chief secretary about Akeroyd's decision:

> *I cannot help feeling that he is retiring from the department he has allowed his regard for one or more officers within his department to outweigh his judgement as to what he previously urged was necessary in the interests of the community and the inmates of the gaol . . . I feel is a surrender to sentiment at the expense of departmental needs.*[230]

The letter raised concerns that Akeroyd's change of heart demonstrated an uncharacteristic divergence from his early disciplined approach to staff training and recruitment against defined qualifications. It may suggest he was becoming tired and/or worn down after significant years in a demanding job heralding radical reform in prison and prisoner management. Conversely, it may also reveal his changing viewpoint in response to constant challenges to his stated positions. Regardless, Akeroyd's attitude shift towards staff management, recruitment, and promotion practices in his later years appeared to align with the apparent change in his view on the role

---

[230] VPRS 6603, 22 July 1947.

and function of prisoner punishment, and this indicated his deeper foray into examining the emerging impact of criminological theories or prisoner management practices.

Akeroyd confirmed his alignment with the emergence of the criminological revolution in Melbourne where he connected with Anita Muhl in the early part of the final phase of his career as stated in her book:

> *It is the object of the science of Criminology to ascertain its own department, as do the Physical Sciences in theirs, the relation of Cause and Effect.[231] It strives to find causes and to control effects. If criminals are treated in bulk, so to speak, or if on rule only, the rule of punishment, be applied to them, it cannot do this. Seldom does rigorous punishment alone fan this spark of flame.[232] Far more often, understanding and sympathy, following on from some soul- stirring experience, light the way that leads to this new outlook.[233]*

The quote reflected Akeroyd's position on punishment that coincided with his views held in his early career phases. However, in the final stage of his career, Akeroyd questioned the role punishment played in reforming individuals to such an extent that by the end of his tenure, his position had changed. In 1947, Akeroyd was called before the state government inquiry into corporal punishment in order, according to inquiry chair, the Honourable A. M. Fraser, for the committee 'to obtain your [i.e. Akeroyd's and government medical officer Dr Allan's] views concerning corporal punishment

---

[231] Akeroyd used the capital letters in this quote.

[232] Akeroyd refers to the spark divine which at times enables even the worst of men to rise superior to his surroundings and say, 'I have finished with my former life. From this day on I shall live the life of the ordinary, average, decent citizen' (Muhl, 1941, p. 2).

[233] VPRS 6603, 1941, p. 2.

under the terms of the Crimes Act'.[234] The panel questioned both Akeroyd's and Dr Allan's experiences and observations in respect to the role corporal punishment played as part of prisoners' sentences. Akeroyd referred to specific case studies (including his first-hand conversations) to describe the impact whipping and birching had had on several inmates. His responses indicated that Akeroyd now saw some merit in corporal punishment based on conversations he had with the punished prisoners.

Akeroyd related the following observations to the inquiry regarding two prisoners he called Dick and G. Regarding Dick, Akeroyd asked,

> 'Now Dick, what made you the man you are?' He started to say something, but I interrupted him and said, 'Now, Dick, do not try to pull the wool over my eyes; we know each other too well for you to attempt that. Was it the whipping that made you what you are?'[235]

Akeroyd outlined the prisoner's story to the panel before adding commentary about his own learning from Dick's experience: 'It is my firm belief that in every case to which I referred the whippings did good in that they enabled the afterwork on the person to fall upon fruitful ground.'[236] However, in the case of G Akeroyd admitted punishment had had no impact on the individual:

> I spoke with him after he had received his punishment with the 'cat' . . . I said, 'How did you feel about it?' He replied, 'I have had worse hidings than that in a pub roughup.' The

---

[234]   VPRS 6603, Report of the Inquiry, 1947, p. 5.

[235]   VPRS 6603, Report of the Inquiry, 1947, pp. 6–7.

[236]   VPRS 6603, Report of the Inquiry, 1947, p. 7.

*punishment did not affect him either way. You could not have
done anything with that man; he was beyond the pale.*[237]

Akeroyd also spoke of a young prisoner who after his release
had returned to gaol charged with murder: 'Whipping might have
stopped him but certainly talking to him would not.'[238] Akeroyd's
position on corporal punishment was recorded as follows:

> *I endeavoured to ascertain what effect the whipping had
> upon the prisoner. For the purpose I would have a long
> interview with him prior to the infliction of the whipping
> and make a report to the secretary of the Law department
> for the information of the Attorney general. Some days after
> the whipping, when the prisoner had somewhat recovered
> from its effects, I would have another talk with him and
> report in writing the effect the whipping had on him. I came
> to the conclusion that, generally speaking, whippings did
> good [sic].*[239]

Akeroyd further refined his position by stating that whipping
should be reserved for men convicted of brutal crimes rather than
psychopaths or criminals convicted of sex crimes.[240] In those cases,
Akeroyd recommended sending the offenders to a mental health
institution as the most effective remedy.[241] The debate extended to
ascertain Akeroyd's position on capital punishment. In his personal
notes, Akeroyd recorded that he witnessed and oversaw four hangings.
Akeroyd advised the inquiry he remained unconvinced capital

---

[237]   VPRS 6603, Report of the Inquiry, 1947, p. 7.

[238]   VPRS 6603, Report of the Inquiry, 1947, p. 9.

[239]   VPRS 6603, Report of the Inquiry, 1947, p. 6.

[240]   VPRS 6603, Report of the Inquiry, 1947, p. 7.

[241]   VPRS 6603, Report of the Inquiry, 1947, p. 9.

punishment had any long-lasting deterrent impact on prisoners but conceded, in some instances, prisoners refused to carry guns for fear of taking 'the drop'.[242]

Akeroyd's wavering position on corporal punishment, and to punishment in general, contradicted the position he adopted in earlier stages of his incumbency. The transcript from the inquiry suggested Akeroyd no longer opposed punishment as was his earlier position by providing clues that Akeroyd saw corporal punishment as 'doing good' for particular types of criminals. It is also apparent that Akeroyd used what he perceived to be scientific methodology to judge the benefits of whipping by discussing the experience with the affected prisoner after the punishment had been meted out. In other words, Akeroyd used his own education background to gain insights from the experience for both himself and the affected prisoner.

While his marked turnaround in attitude towards punishment was noticeable, so too was Akeroyd's drive, even in his later years, to further classify and understand certain types of criminal behaviours, particularly in the case of sexual offenders.

Akeroyd's final annual report provided a vehicle to share his parting thoughts on dealing with sex offenders. He dedicated a significant chapter of his report (one and a half pages out of the eight-page report) on questioning plans to segregate sex offenders from other prisoners to offer them therapeutic treatment. Akeroyd rejected claims that separating sex offenders would prove either a productive or effective remedy amid his doubts the 'realm of medicine' being capable of providing 'worthwhile results'.[243] It appeared Akeroyd's comments arose in response to an emerging

---

[242] VPRS 6603, Report of the Inquiry, 1947, p. 8.

[243] Annual Report, Penal Establishments, Goals, and Reformatory Prisons, 1947, p. 6, Parliamentary Papers, Victoria.

sympathetic feeling between psychiatry and the judiciary for more therapeutic support for sex offenders.[244] Akeroyd's position was predicated on his observations that segregating sex offenders from others would 'heighten the tendency to sex criminality' and 'so far as can be found no evidence has yet been produced that psychiatric treatment or treatment by purely medical means has yet produced worthwhile results'.[245] Akeroyd further argued that assimilating sex offenders into the broader prison population allowed for greater supervision and observation by prison officers best placed to judge the likelihood a prisoner would reoffend.[246] Underpinning this position, Akeroyd argued that applying an indefinite sentence principle to sex offenders was a necessary step to give prison officers the confidence to pronounce a sex offender ready to return to the community without reoffending.[247] Akeroyd's position drew criticism from the *Melbourne Truth* which reported, 'This report was written in 1947, not 1847!'[248]

Another significant event for Akeroyd also occurred in these later years. His son John was a medical practitioner and served as a doctor supporting Australian troops in Rabaul and New Britain in World War II. John was captured by the Japanese forces and was held prisoner of war in a prison in Rabaul before being shipped to Japan. Despite the beatings and poor health, John was highly regarded for the support he continually provided to the incarcerated Australian

---

[244] *Melbourne Truth*, 2 January 1948.

[245] Annual Report, Penal Establishments, Goals, and Reformatory Prisons, 1947, p. 6, Parliamentary Papers, Victoria.

[246] Annual Report, Penal Establishments, Goals, and Reformatory Prisons, 1947, p. 7, Parliamentary Papers, Victoria.

[247] Annual Report, Penal Establishments, Goals, and Reformatory Prisons, 1947, p. 7, Parliamentary Papers, Victoria.

[248] VPRS 6603, unnumbered.

and allied troops. In so many ways, John reflected similar attributes as his father.

In his papers, Joseph kept copies of correspondence from John as well as a recorded timeline of events John faced throughout his ordeal. Whilst Joseph did not leave any written evidence of his thoughts at this time, the sad irony cannot be ignored of Joseph managing the incarceration of prison inmates in Victoria whilst his son suffered extreme violence through beatings and witnessing executions of his mates whilst incarcerated in Rabaul and Japan.[249] One wonders how much impact this had on Joseph reflecting on his role in his latter days leading to his decision to retire or conversely adding extreme pressure on trying to articulate his position on punishments whilst his son was the recent recipient of brutal beatings in Japan at the same time.[250]

---

[249] Major Robert V. Glasgow, citation for MBE, in service record of Captain John Finch Akeroyd VX18194, National Archives of Australia, Canberra. This officer was 'repeatedly beaten and knocked about because of the strong stand he took regarding sick and ailing men, he never weakened, and a great deal of credit goes to him for the few deaths recorded in this particular camp'.

[250] People - Akeroyd, John Finch - Lost Lives - The Second World War and the islands of New Guinea (jje.info).

CHAPTER 13

My Story: Mouse

T he name Mouse was often applied to a prisoner who was adept at being able to fossick resources from anywhere in the prison. Mouse was often a fellow of slight stature but effervescent nature who buzzed in and out of the various groups within the prison. Just about every prison at every time had a Mouse. One such Mouse provided me with an important lesson about the different perspectives people held on what a prison was and what it did.

On this day, I was in the circle of A Division in Pentridge Prison. The circle is the hub of the division where the wings of the prison intersected. In the panopticon model of prison structure devised so many years before, the circle provided the station for prison officers to maintain vigilance on the happenings in the wings of the prison. I had been waiting for a group of prisoner students to be called in from the exercise yard when one of the senior prison officers escorted a group of women from a hospital auxiliary into the circle. The prison often played host to various philanthropic groups, and this group of approximately ten women was being shown into the division and to view the cell of Bill O'Meally, one of Victoria's longest-serving and notorious prisoners. Quite often, when groups were brought into the prison, they were taken to Bill's cell whether the prisoner agreed or not to entertain visitors. Bill would say to me in his inimitable way, 'Ron, Ron [he always used double speech!], Pentridge, Pentridge. Used to be a farm — a farm. Has pigs! Pigs! Still does!'

Whilst I was watching the prison officer open the cell door, the group of women formed a circle around the open door, peeking in, but not venturing in through the open door. Mouse walked past me after coming straight out of the showers, his modesty covered only by a single white towel which was held together at the front by only his right hand. In his left hand, Mouse carried the soap he had used in the shower. To this day, I have no idea how Mouse manufactured this situation, but the next thing I saw him in the middle of the circle of auxiliary ladies, apologising profusely at his lack of decent clothing and of interrupting the visit to the cell when suddenly the soap, still slippery from the shower, shot upwards from his grip. To trap the soap on the smooth slate floor, Mouse was scurrying around in the circle of women scrambling to pick this bar of soap whilst desperately hanging on to his towel when suddenly his false teeth came flying out of his mouth on to the floor. To capture both his teeth and the soap, Mouse let go of his towel and was scrambling, head down, chasing the two escaping items around the legs of the now shrieking and terrified women trying to avert their eyes from the naked (albeit a mumbling apologetic) man scrambling around before and between them. As the prison officer (with a smile on his face as I recall) gathered the women together and shepherded them out of the A Division Circle, Mouse looked up at me and winked.

I doubt whether this scenario would have made sense outside a prison setting. The elements of this scene are quite diverse: a group of women undertaking, I suppose, a voluntary philanthropic role visiting a prison (for some reason unknown to me); being escorted by a prison officer into Bill O'Meally's cell (without obtaining his permission); and being exposed to a naked male prisoner whilst in the hub of a major prison division in full view of prisoners and prison staff. The only element that made sense to me at the time was that Mouse made his message quite clear in his unique way. Mouse's performance sent the message that whilst these people are in prison, it did not mean that these people were not entitled to some degree of respect.

CHAPTER 14

Analysis of Reform in the Akeroyd Era

J oseph Akeroyd's diary signalled his clear intent to change approaches to those prison and prisoner management practices he witnessed in Victorian prisons in those first days of his appointment. His intent was recorded on 24 January 1924 after his meeting with the Indeterminate Sentences Board. He wrote, 'Afraid the "Board" is ruled by Morris – too lenient. Takes the view of expediency, not of true reform.'[251] Whilst Akeroyd did not spell out what he meant by true reform, his note implied that prison management practice or policy at the time did not reflect his expectation of reform. Akeroyd did provide some insights into his approach to reforming the approach to prison and prisoner management in Victorian prisons when he wrote in his diary of his meeting with the Reformatory Prisons Board and the mayor of Castlemaine regarding his approach to the management of prisons and of prisoners.[252] It was this diary entry in which Akeroyd enunciated his three principles of teaching which underpinned his approach to penology. With these words, Akeroyd outlined the intention to align education principles to change prison management approaches and practice.

As Akeroyd was to find out, prison reforms are and were not easy or swift to achieve. According to Gehring and Semmens, little of the prison and prisoner management activity in the lead–up to Akeroyd's appointment was considered reformatory. Akeroyd

---

251   Akeroyd diary, VPRS 6300.

252   VPRS 6604, 28 January 1924.

inherited a system teetering 'near collapse' with little, if any, useful information recorded by his predecessors to guide him in his role.[253] This was interpreted to mean that there was very little change in prison management practice from the post-Maconochie punitive approach to prisoner management from the early days of prison establishment of the 1850s through to Akeroyd's appointment.[254] Further, it was interpreted to mean that there was very little focus on reforming individuals apart from the imposition of strict punitive regimes (of which work was often used as a means of punishment).[255] In short, Akeroyd inherited a prison system which operated under a punitive approach for nearly seventy years and was in a poor financial state coupled with deteriorating prison building stock.

On his appointment, Akeroyd immediately focused his reforms in two key areas. The first area concentrated on his drive to transform the individual prisoner into a model citizen.[256] The second area focused on a broader approach to reforming prisoner management processes to enable prisoner reform to occur.[257] As expressed in his undated papers, Akeroyd clearly believed that the key to prisoner reform lay in understanding the specific circumstances leading to the prisoner's behaviour and using that knowledge as a platform to reform the prisoner.[258] It is the focus on the reform of the individual through the application of 'treatment' programs and his approach to address these two areas which stands Akeroyd apart from his predecessors.

---

[253]   Paterson, 1989, p. 144; O'Toole, 1998.

[254]   Semmens, 1999.

[255]   Semmens, 1999.

[256]   Akeroyd's papers, VPRS 6604; Muhl, 1941.

[257]   Annual Reports, 1924–1947.

[258]   VPRS, 6604.

Evidence placing Akeroyd's approach within the positivist framework arose from the methodology he employed to gain an understanding of the criminal and subsequent treatment regimens. This positivist approach was further evidenced through the strategies he put in place and the language he used. His methodology for analyses was based on the concept of individuals' psychological and sociological attributes and deficits as well as policy and program determination based on remediation principles.[259] Akeroyd insisted on using his understanding of scientific methodology to provide evidence for decision-making. More specifically, he focused on the biological, physiological, psychological, and social attributes of each individual prisoner amid his firm belief that each factor contributed to the offending behaviours of the individual to varying degrees. Above all, Akeroyd remained convinced that the predisposition toward criminality was embedded in the under-socialised individual with his writings identifying three main characteristics that contributed to such under-socialisation. He reflected on the genetic and physiological attributes of the individual that led to an inability to be socialised such as an ineffective family background and child-raising practices as well as a surrounding social environment lacking moral values that Akeroyd and others ascribed to their understanding of an effective community. Akeroyd drew on his education background and experience to develop programs designed to address behaviour shortfalls he believed arose from individual prisoners experiencing inadequate socialisation. Above all, Akeroyd planned and implemented such programs with a spirit of sympathy and empathy towards individual prisoners based on the evidence he gathered from detailed assessment and case planning. Whilst the 1910 annual report referred to the importance of introducing a scientific

---

[259]   Undated papers, VPRS 6604,

approach to prisoner management, Akeroyd was the first inspector general in Victoria on record to introduce coherent and consolidated approach to adopt a rigorous and, in his eyes, scientific approach to prisoner management within the Victorian prison system.

While Akeroyd appeared to stamp his commitment to the positivist approach from his very first day, he also engaged a series of strategies to consolidate and reinforce his support for positivist reform. Whether such strategies were premeditated actions by Akeroyd or rather they occurred as a confluence of like-thinking allies at a particular point in time remains unclear. However, it is evident that Akeroyd's strategies established the positivist perspective as a consolidated alternative to the prevailing punitive perspectives. A significant strategy involved creating a circle of influential and supportive allies charged with reinforcing and reaffirming the positivist position in support of Akeroyd in aspiring to his goals as well as driving reform within their respective spheres of influence. Akeroyd drew his allies from the education sphere as well as experts working in the field of psychology. Akeroyd enjoyed considerable support in his early days from former educational colleagues including Dr C. R. McRae and Ken Cunningham from the Australian Council for Educational Research and Dr G. S. Browne, principal of the Melbourne Teachers' College. McRae contributed to the public dialogue through his newspaper articles on classification of criminal types while Cunningham reviewed case studies and advised Akeroyd on specific prisoners, and Browne afforded Akeroyd the opportunity to address public forums to lecture both state and student teachers on prisoner management. Many sources within the criminal justice system also threw their support behind Akeroyd with the Honourable Samuel Maugher, Head of the Indeterminate Sentence Board, demonstrating strong support for a more empathetic and sympathetic approach to prisoner treatment. A primary issue for Akeroyd was prisoners serving an indeterminate sentence were prevented from accessing education programs, and as will be discussed later, Akeroyd was compelled to address the disadvantage.

In Akeroyd's middle and later phases, many of his allies came together at the Centre for Criminology at Melbourne University to plan, review, evaluate, and implement positivist views and practices.[260] It was through this agency, and particularly Akeroyd's connection with Anita Muhl, as a visiting lecturer in psychiatry and authority on criminology, that the discipline of criminology emerged as a prime tool for advising the government on criminal justice policy as well as generating community debate on criminal justice matters within Victoria. Muhl expressed great appreciation for Akeroyd's support in gathering a collection of case studies for her to analyse which she reported on extensively, particularly one specific prisoner A. E. Sodeman.[261] Muhl's book provided a collection of her lectures to Melbourne University in 1939 in which she covered wide-ranging topics from mental variations and different types of crimes through to methods for treating prisoners and preventing crime with many of her views resonating with those of Akeroyd. The resonance occurred within the themes of classifying criminals according to types of offences, tracing the causes of criminality back to family background, establishing parameters for case study development, identifying metrics in personality and IQ assessment, and developing treatment programs specific to criminal types. In a copy of her book held in the Victorian Department of Justice library, Akeroyd annotated the

---

[260] Finnane, 2006.

[261] Arnold Sodeman was executed for murder on 1 July 1936; Muhl, 1941.

book with underlining and comments.[262] Often Akeroyd underlined the text that he found important. It appeared that the sections on mental variation and sex crimes received more intense underlining attention than other sections of the book. Whilst the timing of these annotations could not be absolutely defined, it does appear that the timing of the release of the book in 1941 does coincide with Akeroyd's growing interest in the areas of mental deficiency and sex offenders. These comments indicated that Akeroyd did not provide alternative position to Muhl's, but it appeared to accept her perspectives and then reframe them based on his own experience and knowledge. At this point of Akeroyd's tenure, this is an important consideration because it demonstrated that Akeroyd drew upon Muhl's psychiatric background to further consolidate his education-based background. However, this is also notable because Akeroyd criticised the psychiatric perspectives about sex crimes and sexual offenders. His criticism appeared to be quite blunt in his rejection of psychiatric explanations on the reasons behind sexual offence behaviour that if this criticism was taken in isolation, it might give the impression that Akeroyd was quite dismissive of the role of psychiatry in providing a rationale to criminal behaviour. Put into the broader context of Akeroyd's interaction with the world of psychiatry, particularly through his engagement with Muhl, it does appear that either he did have a change of view or he may have had trouble with an individual's perspective. Whilst there is no real evidence available either way, Akeroyd's words reported in the press indicated he reversed his appreciation of the role of psychiatry in

---

[262] I am indebted to the assistance of Malcolm Feiner (Department of Justice Correctional Services Division library) for making this book available for me to peruse.

explaining the causality and treatment of criminality between his middle and later years.

Another key indication of Akeroyd's embracing of the positivist perspective was in the use of the word 'treatment' to reflect a therapeutic approach to dealing with prisoners. The use of the term 'treatment' in response to addressing individual prison needs provided solid evidence that Akeroyd was operating within the positivist perspective in framing his approach to the management of prisoners. Throughout the period of his appointment, Akeroyd extensively used the word 'treatment' referring to many aspects of prisoner management. In many instances, he was referring to the way prisoners were managed daily and often prefaced the word 'treatment' with the adjective 'humane'. Other times he used the word 'treatment' to reflect specific therapeutic programs introduced to respond to, or rectify, certain psychological or psychiatric issues that manifested prisons. However, Akeroyd largely linked the concept of treatment with education and prisoner training programs in general. While the word 'treatment' is often used broadly in Akeroyd's records, there is a clear direction toward dealing with issues of crime and criminality that manifests in prisoners as deficits which need to be rectified. This is clear in his 7 October 1925 papers on planning the approach to divest prisoners of their 'anti-social grudge' through 'a kindly treatment' program.[263]

In terms of applying treatment programs, Akeroyd linked the concept of treatment along with his evolving understanding of prisoner typologies or classification. It appeared that the link between the concepts of treatment and education remained constant throughout the period of his appointment. However, the relationship between treatment and punishment changes to the extent that, in

---

[263] VPRS 6603.

his later years, Akeroyd considered punishment to be a form of treatment. This will be explored in more detail later in this chapter. Conversely, it contrasts starkly to Akeroyd dismissing psychiatry as worthwhile treatment for specific sex offenders' classifications. It is difficult to draw definitive reasons from the available evidence to ascertain Akeroyd's reasons for singling out medical-based treatment rather than psychological-based treatment approaches for this criticism. However, the term 'treatment' was fundamental in Akeroyd's personal and public writing. It is the emergence of the concept of treatment aligned to the process of imprisonment which provided the hub of discussion and conjecture throughout Akeroyd's time.

Not only did he advocate for 'the way of the psychologist', he also introduced the way of education to tie together the means to identify needs and the means to address the needs through education-based programs.[264]

Akeroyd faced many battles to embed the concept of treatment into the prison management regime and consolidate the discipline of psychology as an authority in managing crime and criminality in Victoria at that time against the embedded classicist legal perspectives. The battle between emerged and prevailing perspectives is not new in public policy, and there are parallels well-articulated in Foucault's *Je Suis Pierre Riviere* where he provided insight into the battles between the medical profession and the legal profession in the French courts for the power or legitimacy to define normal and abnormal during the 1830s.[265] This publication offered insight into the battles between emerging and declining theoretical positioning and outlines, as Akeroyd witnessed, the difficulty to shift institutionalised practice

---

[264] Justice of the Peace, 1932.

[265] Foucault, *Je Suis Pierre Riviere*, 1975.

as well as the difficulty to sustain new and emerging practice in the face of established positions. Despite no direct evidence existing to confirm Akeroyd's specific reasoning, it remains evident that he drew a continuing connection between the treatment and education within prisons as well as his emerging awareness that education programs required tailoring for specific prisoner categories. Having examined the positivist underpinnings of his reform, it is now important to consider reform in the areas of education, punishment, sentencing, and classification.

While Akeroyd's reports and his reflective papers outlined his ideals and underlying principles, they also demonstrated the active development and deployment of education programs for staff and prisoners. Akeroyd made it noticeably clear that his education-inspired principles underpinned not only individual prisoner reform but also the professionalism he expected from his staff. In his early phase, Akeroyd's focus was on providing the platform for prisoner reform through education and training. Akeroyd's diary entry on 3 January 1924 specified the importance of introducing education and training programs to prisoners to enable them to develop 'marketable skills' and 'schooling . . . in trade work'. Following on from this commentary, Akeroyd followed up with the chief secretary to establish a schoolmaster at Castlemaine Prison. His early days also witnessed his connection with the Education Department of Victoria following his recommendation to establish a juvenile home at Janefield and have it managed by the Education Department.[266] These observations demonstrated that using his education background and experience to address deficiencies Akeroyd identified in prisoners and, from these

---

[266]   VPRS6604, 5 September 1924.

observations, he was able to clearly articulate his ideals of prison management built around the pillar of education for prisoners.[267]

Akeroyd continued his focus on the prison as an education institution throughout his middle years where he clearly enunciated his focus on dealing with the needs of individual prisoners rather than dealing with the prisoner group *en masse*. This provided a distinct change in direction from previous prison management regimes. It was in this time that the concept of the individual case plan was formed which Akeroyd instigated. In Akeroyd's words, this approach was to result in 'the complete investigation of each prisoner's personality and history, i.e., the preparation of a case history'.[268] This history would then provide the evidence to base the treatment program of which education or schooling was an integral component. However, the challenge of realizing his 7 October vision was starting to trouble him. Whereas his early years' statements about reforming individuals through education appeared to encompass all prisoners (even though he made special mention of focusing on young offenders), he started to differentiate prisoners who were 'reformable' and proceeded to focus on these prisoners.[269] This period also marks the strengthening of Akeroyd's approach to classification of prisoners regarding the capability to segregate the reformable from the unreformable.

Akeroyd's writings at this time focused on the importance of having educated and qualified staff to support the reforming of those reformable prisoners.[270] Akeroyd clearly noted the importance of good staff selection and training:

---

[267]   VPRS 6604, 7 October 1925.

[268]   VPRS 6603, undated.

[269]   VPRS 6603, 20 June 1935.

[270]   VPRS 6603, 1 June 1939.

The first necessity is good staff. The members of the staff must be men of good personality, interested in their work, upright men who rule more by force of character than by force of might — if I may put it so.

To this end they are carefully chosen. They must conform to a certain physical and mental standard — in the mental standard being judged by mental tests . . . After being placed on duty they are kept in temporary positions under supervision until they prove themselves, and are then placed on probation.

During the period of probation they are required to pass examinations . . . before being made permanent officers. Then before receiving promotion they must pass examinations in the principles and practices of prison Management and in the Laws & Regulations relating to penal establishments and goals.

Many of them will be able to compile histories of criminals, note the salient points of those histories and give the best methods of dealing with any particular person.[271]

Reflecting his expectations of teacher behaviours when he was an inspector of schools, Akeroyd set expectations about the professional approach of prison staff to meet his aspiration on the way they conduct themselves. Akeroyd adapted school-like structures to frame staff training, selection, and advancement processes within a prison setting. Under Akeroyd, the prison staff members needed to sit examinations, learn how to compile prisoner case histories, and pass mental testing to secure promotions. At all times, Akeroyd led by example. His diary and other records demonstrated his commitment

---

[271]   VPRS 6603, undated paper.

to maintaining extensive case study records of prisoners that detailed their IQ status and their social, cultural, and family backgrounds. His comprehensive record-keeping accorded with his expectations that his prison officers adopt a similar approach to prisoner management. It also proved he favoured modelling behaviours over punitive tactics to both monitor and manage prisoner behaviour within the prison system.

However, Akeroyd's approach to education for prisoners and prison staff met with opposition from within the prison office ranks and from some people in the community.

Akeroyd's approach to treating prisoners within a medical-like model (i.e. identify symptoms and then develop a treatment program or a treatment regime to remediate these symptoms) proved a significant challenge to prison staff given that the prison management approaches until the time of Akeroyd's appointment operated within a mixture of the classicist and conservatist punitive approaches. Staff operated under the expectation that prisoners were sentenced to prison by courts in accordance with the crimes for which they were convicted. The judiciary reflected the classicist perspectives that imposed not only prison sentences but also corporal and capital punishment sanctions. Further, prison staff and some public opinion reflected the conservatist perspectives that viewed that prisoners were incarcerated for punishment. Staff members' conflict occurred in response to Akeroyd's revolutionary approach to education-based reform as prison officers struggled to understand and reconcile the new prisoner–officer function and role as a case manager. The conflict manifested in letters of complaint, public comment via the press, and in early days through resistance of staff to undertake the duties expected of them. It became apparent to staff that not only had Akeroyd revolutionised the way he wanted prison officers to perform in their role, but he also changed the way that staff promotion was managed. These changes confronted the fundamental and accepted ways that prisons had been managed for those many years before Akeroyd's appointment as well as threatening the work practice comfort many staff members had been used to. Akeroyd directly dealt with many of these conflicts. He met with staff face to face, he confronted those he felt did not embrace the new approaches, and he continued to expound his position on the treatment approach through his public and private communications. It was apparent that Akeroyd's battles with changing staff member approaches to their role was a constant battle throughout his career.

At the same time, he was initiating these changes in staff practice as well establishing school-like structures within the prisons, Akeroyd was accumulating educational allies within the broader community. Akeroyd forged relationships with other educational agencies such as the ACER, Carlton Teachers' College, and Melbourne University's emerging Centre for Criminology. Akeroyd referred to such groups in his diaries and personal notes, but there was no record of him taking counsel from other possible criminal justice agencies such as the police service or even the judiciary. While he may have done so in practice, there is no documented evidence in his notes to demonstrate he actively sourced advice, support, or counsel from such bodies. The available evidence indicated that Akeroyd's educational background provided him the main links and frameworks for advice and directions he sought.

Whilst establishing education reform for staff and connecting education in prisons with educational allies in the community, establishing schools for prisoners within prisons remained a cornerstone of his prison reform agenda (including the reform schools at Janefield and Bayswater). This direction was complemented with appointing state schoolteachers to teach within the prisons. Appointing state schoolteachers to teach prisoners proved a significant breakthrough in prisoner reform under Akeroyd. It was engaging teachers to work in prisons and introducing a school-based curriculum into prisons that Akeroyd's unique legacy began to take shape.

In later years, Whatmore took the relationship between the state's prisons and education system to a higher level with prison schools being registered within the Victorian Education Department in 1954.[272] Regardless, Akeroyd's drive to embed education principles into penology created this major and enduring nexus in Victoria, and arguably the application of positivist theory enabled Akeroyd to create a neat connection between education and penology. Using Cohen's perspective of reform, Akeroyd was clear and transparent in introducing an education-inspired treatment approach to support the reform of individual prisoners. Akeroyd also revolutionized the role of prison staff in moving from the punitive function to supporting the treatment focus. While the Akeroyd-facilitated connection between penology and education laid the foundation for an enduring legacy, Akeroyd faced challenges in leading reform in the dimensions of punishment, sentencing, and classification where Akeroyd's positivist perspectives met with dispute from those whose views aligned with alternate major theoretical perspectives.

Sentencing and punishment processes in Victoria fell within the domain of the state judicial system in Akeroyd's time as it does now. The power of the judicial representation in both public and political debate challenged Akeroyd to reconsider his approach to providing a consolidated therapeutic approach to prison management. Akeroyd threw out his first judicial challenge in the dimension of punishment before focusing his attention on sentencing protocols. Akeroyd

---

[272] Blake, 1973; Semmens, 1999.

openly questioned the judiciary's role in punishing prisoners both in his private thoughts and in his public actions even though the judiciary had played a role alongside him in forming the Centre for Criminology.

In his early and middle phases, Akeroyd believed applying corporal punishment undermined his agenda to tailor reforms to individual prisoners. Akeroyd maintained his viewpoint despite recognising he was beholden to carry out court orders, many of which mandated corporal punishment and, to a lesser extent, capital punishment. The resulting clash between Akeroyd's positivist perspective and the judiciary's classicist perspectives challenged Akeroyd's concepts relating to the role and function of punishment.

In his essay written for the Honorary Justices' Association of Victoria, Akeroyd's clear challenge towards punishment protocols revealed this divergence of views. In the essay, Akeroyd reinforced his position on dealing with crime when he stated that crime

> *was not an isolated fact in a man's life . . . it is a mental symptom . . . that can generally be treated. It is not the investigation of an offence and the punishment of an offence . . . But an investigation of and the treatment of an offender.* [273]

His words not only challenged the prevailing classicist framework under which the judiciary had been working for many years but clearly stated his positivist position to both public and the judiciary. He reiterated his drive to replace the traditional concept of prison as a place of punishment with one of treatment in his reflections recorded in an undated paper submitted to the English and Scottish Committees of Inquiry into prison management. Akeroyd expressed

---

[273]   VPRS 6603, 1932.

his frustration at the challenges posed by changing prison management approaches from the punitive to the curative:

> *In the face of all this, they are asked to accept and incorporate*
> *into their in most being, so to speak, the idea that they are*
> *not held as punishment, or in any vindictive sense; and their*
> *anti — social tendencies are expected to be cured. I wonder!*[274]

In his early years, Akeroyd largely confined his railings against existing punishment protocols to his diaries and private documents, but the public debate on punishment in prisons gained momentum in the newspapers in 1931. In June 1931, a series of articles published in the *Herald* investigated whipping as a punishment and its various impacts on prisoners. Within days, subsequent reports in the *Herald* referred to ex-prison officials who argued that flogging was not a brutalising act and resulted in 'well under 7 per cent ever com(ing) back to the gaol'.[275] However, during this time of Akeroyd's early and middle years, the public debate evolved to argue the application of different types of punishment to be applied to different classifications of criminals. While Akeroyd was communicating his position on treatment in preference to corporal punishment at the time, it was unexpected that he adopted a strong pro punitive position leading into his later years.

The major landmark in identifying a shift in Akeroyd's thinking to accommodate the punitive aspects of a classicist sentencing perspective arose in his 1935 radio interview when he outlined the prevailing definitions of criminal as

---

[274]   VPRS 6603, undated, p. 17.

[275]   VPRS 6603, 17 June 1931.

a person who commits such acts such as render him liable to legal punishment such as fines, imprisonment, whippings and execution . . . the criminal is an immoral person . . . whose immorality finds expression in immoral acts . . . The ordinary citizen fashions his conduct according to these standards, the criminal does not.[276]

Whilst Akeroyd's words may well have used them to simply describe the prevailing judicial view, his following words served to challenge the radio audience with his own personal views:

So much for our definitions. Now of late years a very great change has come in our dealings with criminals. That change is by no means complete; but is gradually gathering impetus the world over. In the olden times only the crime was considered and punishment was meted out according to the gravity of the crime . . . Study your man, make an exhaustive analysis of all his reactions, the makeup of his mind, his heredity and the environment in which he lived. Then in the light of the knowledge so gained prescribe a remedy.[277]

While it is difficult to draw a particular inference from his choice of words 'so much for our definitions', it is apparent Akeroyd grasped the opportunity to consolidate and strengthen his preferred positivist perspective over other perspectives. Arguably, Akeroyd's radio presentation marked a turning point in his positivist pronouncements with, on the one hand, his speech appearing to strengthen his commitment to a positivist approach while, on the other, publicly recognising the popularity of the prevailing classicist position on

---

[276]   VPRS 6603, 20 June 1935.

[277]   VPRS 6603, 20 June 1935.

punishment. His acceptance was signalled in his 'Will punishment prevail?' radio speech.[278]

His statement can be interpreted in a couple of ways. It could be dismissing the role of punishment in favour of a treatment model. However, his words 'by itself no!' may also indicate Akeroyd's acknowledgement that punishment provides a beneficial result when administered in conjunction with education as a therapeutic tool. The question arises whether Akeroyd is consolidating his position on his education-led positivist approach as an elegant alternative perspective to other concurrent views or, conversely, whether his speech weakens the elegance of his positivist position by acknowledging the place of classicist perspectives on punishment. The key message from his words reveal Akeroyd now believed both punishment and education play a role in his prison and prisoner management planning perspectives.

In his later years, Akeroyd expressed growing unease towards using corporal punishment methods while publicly recognising that in his role of public service, he must comply with judiciary orders. In his foreword in Anita Muhl's book, Akeroyd expressed concern whether punishment facilitated or promoted constructive learning in the individual.[279] This provided significant insight into the way Akeroyd's thinking evolved in his later years as he increasingly drew on positivist perspectives of scientific theory and methodology to examine the 'cause and effect of criminal' behaviour. Simultaneously,

---

[278]   VPRS 6603, 1935.

[279]   1941, p. 2; VPRS 6603, 1938. There are two versions of the foreword he prepared for Anita Muhl's book. This version dated 1938 was the document in Akeroyd's closed papers. The other version was that published in Muhl's book. There was very little difference in both versions. The published version included an acknowledgement of the dean of the faculty of arts, Professor Boyce Gibson, as the auspicing agent; and it also included a recommendation that Muhl's book should be read by those 'whose daily life brings them into contact with crime' (Muhl, 1941, p. 10).

Muhl expressed her doubts that punishment served as an effective deterrent before arguing that the 'next sensible step is prevention' by addressing behaviour that contravened the criminal code rather than focusing on the concept that criminals are born criminals.[280] Muhl believed 'there is no such thing as a criminal type or born a criminal. Criminals are made because of early failure to develop adequate responses to life'.[281]

The extent to which Muhl's position influenced Akeroyd's thinking during his middle years and influenced his directions in his later years is subject to some conjecture. On the one hand, both share the consistent view denouncing punishment as an effective deterrent, but Muhl's acceptance of the role of criminal law validated the prevailing punitive perspective of the role of a prison within the criminal justice system. Muhl considered that the positivist treatment of individual's under-socialising factors, could coexist with the traditional classicist punitive sentencing position. Muhl never started her position on the punitive capacities available under the criminal law code and how this related to her position on punishment, but her recognition that the two seemingly different perspectives could coexist revealed her belief the divergent theoretical perspectives could operate concurrently. Whether Muhl's insight informed Akeroyd's understanding of the role of punishment within a treatment-oriented regime is unclear from the evidence available, but it is clear in his later years Akeroyd accepted punishment played a part in the prisoner treatment regime.

Over time, such a view became strongly embedded in Akeroyd's perspective as evidenced in the 1947 inquiry into corporal punishment

---

[280]   Muhl, 1941, p. 12.

[281]   Muhl, 1941, p. 13.

which was established to review the role of corporal punishment with prisons. Under questioning by the review panel, Akeroyd said,

> *I came to the conclusion that, generally speaking, whippings did good . . . I am referring to any sort of whipping. It did good in this way, that it made the prisoner realize his position fully and made him amenable to the subsequent teaching in the ideals of citizenship.*[282]

The press also reported Akeroyd's views on punishment when he stated that prisoners ought to be treated as follows:

- *Moral delinquents respond best to long imprisonment*
- *Whippings are a necessary evil. Only the birch or the cat-'o-nine tails can break through the resistance of the toughest, most degraded criminals.*[283]

His comments reflected a significant turnaround in Akeroyd's views from his early days and, arguably, revealed Akeroyd had advocated to the panel that using corporal punishment in some circumstances complemented his therapeutic education programs. There is little doubt, however, during the final years of his tenure that Akeroyd believed corporal punishment (i.e. flogging) was quite acceptable as a form of deterrence. His viewpoint turnaround raises the question as to whether Akeroyd had subsequently rationally accommodated the different criminological perspectives into his thinking, or he compromised his thoughts on the function of punishment to rationalise his concept of a psychology-based treatment model. This has left a somewhat perplexing position regarding Akeroyd's legacy in terms of his approach to punishment. In his early

---

[282] VPRS 6603, 1947, p. 6.

[283] *Sun*, 20 October 1947. Akeroyd used the dot points.

and middle years, Akeroyd expounded his strong commitment to the treatment approach and his philosophical rejection of punishment despite the requirement for him to carry out corporal and capital punishment. In his later years, his public position was in favour of corporal punishment but with the argument that punishment in itself was a form of treatment. This later-year position appears to be the legacy for which Akeroyd is associated in the minds of some contemporary Justice officials[284] and in the press of the time.[285] However, the enduring legacy appears to the introduction of the consideration of treatment programs within the sentencing process. The evidence is not definitive to make this legacy consideration a stronger statement. It is more than reasonable based on recorded history to believe that Akeroyd introduced the concept of addressing individual circumstances into sentencing consideration. Of further importance is the consideration of this battle that Akeroyd, as the senior prison management bureaucrat, faced in addressing the challenge, introducing a new approach into an existing and enduring conservative system. This moment is a critical point in the nexus of Akeroyd's private and public battles. As demonstrated in the quotes above, Akeroyd's own words over time reflect a diminution in aligning his earlier positivist approach to prisoner management and prison management, supporting a treatment approach in favour of accommodating elements of conflicting classicist and conservatist theory perspectives on punishment. It is this point which challenges whether Akeroyd's approach to punishment is one of reform, specifically opaque reform, or a complete compromise.

---

[284] An unnamed senior Department of Justice official commented to me that Akeroyd was best remembered for his pro punishment stance.

[285] *The Western Australian,* 1947

That Akeroyd came to regard corporal punishment as a form of treatment contradicted his early-days position on approaches to prisoner reform, specifically his belief that punishment was not consistent with prisoner rehabilitation. But it does appear that he viewed the application of corporal punishment in an altruistic way (i.e. for the benefit of the individual's reform) in his later years. This contradiction leads to the belief that he was challenged in his capacity to carry out his role within the educational values he held important. These challenges came from the long-standing authority of the courts to manage the judicial aspects of trial, sentencing, and meting out punishment. He was also challenged by the political authority of government in producing laws to support a safe society. Akeroyd, it is argued, realised it was that to do his job, he must accommodate the classicist and conservatist acts of corporal punishment within his education-based principles and talked about the benefits of corporal punishment as a form of treatment. Whilst this may not be considered a systemic reform as the act of corporal punishment was carried out in the many years before Akeroyd became inspector general, the change in the way that corporal punishment is viewed and talked about indicated that the approach to corporal punishment was an example of opaque reform. This is argued on the basis that there was a change in Akeroyd's s approach to corporal punishment and a change in the way he talked about corporal punishment, particularly in the way that he used positivist theory terms to explain the treatment benefits to individual prisoners.

This change in perspective regarding corporal punishment was not the only example of Akeroyd's changing theoretical perspectives. Another shift became apparent when Akeroyd considered the application of sentencing practice to those prisoners considered mentally deficient or acting without morality.

In the early days of his career, Akeroyd exhibited frustration with moves to exclude prisoners serving indeterminate sentences from education programs. The indeterminate sentence, which remained a viable sentencing option in Victoria between 1907 and 1955, enabled the detention of habitual criminals until such a time that the prisoners earned their release.[286] Akeroyd's attitude towards indeterminate sentence varied according to differing information sources. In the early days, Akeroyd was committed to reforming prisoners via education programs, and this direction received statements of support from members of the indeterminate board. In 1924, newspaper articles fielded commentary on the importance of introducing a 'human touch' into prisons to support prisoners' intellectual growth. Mr Maugher, a member of the Reformatory Prisons Board and head of the Indeterminate Sentences Board, weighed into the early debate by supporting education as a means of introducing a more humanist approach towards prison and prisoner management reforms. While Maugher's support may have provided some comfort to his aspirations for an education-led positivist approach, Akeroyd was concerned that those on indeterminate sentences and sent to reformatory prisons still faced restrictions to access reforming programs such as school and work. This restriction was contrary to the intent of the 1907 Indeterminate Sentencing Act which was constructed to provide education, work, training, and post-release support for habitual prisoners.[287] One of the underpinning concepts of the indeterminate sentence was its deterrent implication where prisoners needed to 'earn their way out of custody'.[288]

---

[286] Frieberg and Ross, 1999.

[287] Lynn and Armstrong, 1996.

[288] Freiberg and Ross, p. 14.

It appeared from Akeroyd's writings that the reformatory prisons were not meeting the expectation of the intent of the act and that indeterminate sentenced prisoners were not accessing the programs as expected. Further, Akeroyd expressed concerns about the membership of the board with reference to its capability to meet its functions. In an undated paper, Akeroyd wrote that membership of the Indeterminate Sentences Board

> *should be shrewd level headedmen of the world, of sterling character, not strayed by impulse but given to studying thoroughly each case and judging it on its merits . . . Members . . . should not all be of one type.*
>
> *I favour the following combination.*
>
> *(a) A medical officer who is also a psychiatrist.*
> *(b) A good practical educationalist who is also a man of the world and a good judge of men.*
> *(c) A hardnosed businessman*
>
> *I do not consider lawyers or ministers of religion suitable. Lawyers . . . are too apt to work by rules and regulations whilst ministers of religion are too apt to judge by feeling and emotion.*[289]

Inherent within this statement is Akeroyd's apparent perception of the shortfalls of the classicist and conservatist policy influences, and he represented this concern through his observations of those occupations aligned with the major theories. He expressed his confidence in the positivist perspectives provided through medical representation but derided the classicist (lawyer) input and the

---

[289] VPRS 6603, undated.

conservatist (minister of religion) input. Furthermore, he reiterated the importance of the educationalist perspectives to be able to provide a balanced and global view on understanding issues and strategies to redress these.

Akeroyd sought support from experts to help advise on matters of the effectiveness of both the Indeterminate Sentencing Act and the Indeterminate Sentences Board's management of prisoner management. Following his visit from Tasmania on Akeroyd's request, Dr Miller expressed his concerns in the media about a need to treat the mental defectives separately from other prisoners.[290] He also called for a review of the term 'indeterminate' to include prisoners on indeterminate sentences within the scope of reform. Miller's concern proved a starting point for extended public debate in the newspapers and official reports over the nature of indeterminate sentencing. Akeroyd had long voiced similar concerns that prisoners placed on indeterminate sentences and therefore housed in reformatory prisons were unable to access the education and training programs he planned. Akeroyd lacked the capacity to place prisoners in settings he felt more suitable for their treatment regime.

While the debate surrounding the appropriateness of the Indeterminate Sentencing Act and its associated practices continued for many years, Akeroyd's 1943 annual report best demonstrated his major concerns:

Nowadays, however, the prisoner has usually been an offender from an early age, and the problem becomes one of training him to live in accordance with the ethical standards of the community in which he resides. The problem is the same for gaols as for reformatory prisons despite the fact that the Parliament of Victoria has decreed a sharp distinction between the two.[291]

---

[290]   *Herald*, 8 January 1925.

[291]   Annual Report, 1943, p. 15.

Inadequate access to reformatory prisoners continued to play on Akeroyd's mind throughout his career amid the division between what reformatory means in theory compared with what happens in practice. Many of Akeroyd's reflections focused on the process involved in reforming individuals with, as his 1935 radio transcript demonstrated, a strong emphasis on the importance that education, training, and discipline played in reforming juvenile delinquent to correct the lifestyle of young offenders.[292] Yet it appeared that he was generally bemused by the restricted access to people incarcerated in a reformatory prison stymieing his ability to implement programs designed to reform them. In 1944, Akeroyd appeared to adopt a different perspective to applying indeterminate sentences as observed in his 1944 annual report:[293]

Apart from an efficient police force and despite any defects in administration it (the indeterminate sentence) is the most potent weapon this State has in its fight against crime.[294]

However, Akeroyd also advised that the indeterminate sentence proved a significant cause of unrest and 'rebellion' amongst the prisoner ranks.[295] The conflicting statements demonstrated Akeroyd's shifting views over time towards indeterminate sentences with his growing support suggesting acquiescence to the judicial position in the latter stage of his career.

The most remarkable statement from Akeroyd on indeterminate sentencing came with his public position that by using a treatment-based approach to prisoner management, the definite sentence

---

[292] VPRS, 6603, 1935.

[293] Freiberg and Ross, 1999.

[294] Annual Report, 1944, p. 15.

[295] Annual Report, 1944.

should be abolished.[296] Presumably this statement was made on the grounds that an indeterminate sentence may provide time for a treatment program to be fully realized rather than be cut short due to a prescribed sentence completion date.

His marked turnaround mirrors a similar backtracking in his position on the deterrent role punishment played in prisoner reform. In essence, Akeroyd was not able to influence the removal of the indeterminate sentence; and as is apparent in his approach to punishment, he appeared to accommodate the indeterminate sentence. Arguably, his acquiescence may have been symptomatic of a battle between conflicting perspectives with Akeroyd finding it somewhat difficult to influence the embedded strength of the prevailing judicial perspectives on this matter.

Whilst the issue surrounding indeterminate sentences appeared to be resolved in Whatmore's tenure after Akeroyd's appointment expired, the concurrent considerations of aligning the concepts of punishment and sentencing to the particular needs of specific prisoner groups continued throughout Akeroyd's years, and this is evident in his continued drive to identify the best treatment to reform individual criminal types.[297] It is in the area of defining particular types of criminal that Akeroyd devoted a lot of his consideration.

In his early personal diary notes, Akeroyd expressed the importance of classification of prisoners, and classification continued to be an important element of Akeroyd's positivist approach to prison and prisoner management. The use of the term 'classification' was not new to the prison system. As Hughes (1976) and Semmens (1999) noted, the concept of classification was evident in Maconochie's Norfolk Island days. The term 'classification' was used in the late

---

[296] VPRS 6603, undated.

[297] Freiberg and Ross, 1999.

1880s to separate young from old, the infirm from the healthy, and women from men. In the period prior to Akeroyd's appointment, the classification separated those on indeterminate sentences from others. The application of classification categories appeared blunt and functional based on broad prison population groupings.

Akeroyd took the classification dimension to a vastly different level. Throughout his career, he endeavoured to refine his understanding of individual prisoner treatment needs. He did this through his application of methodical case study notes and engaging in assessment dialogues with his professional colleagues.

Akeroyd's prisoner classification process involved correlating the personal attributes of a prisoner to the nature and frequency of crimes committed. From there, Akeroyd would devise the most suitable program for that particular prisoner class. His first words recorded in his first diary entry divided youngsters and reformatory men into separate classifications. Indeed, his early reflections and public presentations were primarily devoted to the lack of education and training available to young men in gaol. During his first month in his new role, Akeroyd's personal diary espoused his beliefs that young people in prison needed discipline, structure, and a learning environment. It was after his visits to the prison in Castlemaine on 9, 11, and 28 January 1924 that he flagged the need to align the three principles of penology with the three principles of education, namely 'classification, work of an interesting nature, and right ideals with living conditions conducive to self-respect'.[298] As discussed, the classification process in his early days started with the indeterminate/determined sentence classification, but he soon focused on the classification of the young offender.

---

[298]   VPRS 6604, 28 January 1924.

Consistent with his thoughts recorded in his private papers and personal diaries, in his early years, Akeroyd appeared to prioritise the needs of young offenders by focusing heavily on their rehabilitation. Concurrently, Akeroyd also broadened the focus on young offenders by challenging broader community perceptions via public debates in the late 1920s and early 1930s. Akeroyd's contemporaries also contributed to the debate. McRae's newspaper article in the *Herald* on 29 May 1926 was one of the first public comments within the Akeroyd period to draw public attention to risks young people face either offending or who had in fact already offended. The article attempted to engage readers to understand delinquency by arguing no singular cause existed but rather a range of contributing factors such as 'defective (*overly strict, or lax*)[299] discipline at home', a 'personal morbid complex', poverty, and/or 'excessive instincts'.[300] McRae proposed that while the causes are complex, they 'can be unravelled, and when the causes are found, it is well within human power to unravel them'.[301] The article was important in sparking community debate by drawing a link between crime, criminality, and personality as well as examining social causes. Whilst it is difficult to draw a direct link between McRae's article and Akeroyd's thinking, both shared a series of common threads in exploring concepts of mental defectiveness and moral defectiveness as well as an extensive investigation into juvenile delinquency. It was clear at this point in time that Akeroyd was extending the nature of the classification process from the practices of those inspectors general before him, and he was doing this through focusing on the behaviours and personality traits of offenders.

---

[299] McRae's italics.

[300] 29 May 1926.

[301] 29 May 1926.

From 1936 to 1939, Akeroyd concentrated his focus on young offenders and juvenile delinquency as evidenced by his key chapter published in his annual report to the government detailing specific programs for them. In an undated academic paper (thought to be around 1936), Akeroyd expressed his belief that it was crucial to identify and crack down on delinquency as it was a forerunner to criminality. Akeroyd wrote,

> *Delinquency, the forerunner of crime, is not now regarded by competent thinkers as naughtiness which must forthwith be punished, but as a symptom of some hidden, and often apparently unconnected cause.*[302]

This statement indicated that Akeroyd was starting to look at the causation links between criminality and juvenile delinquency in a different way from his predecessors and from the common thinking of the time. Befitting his inquiring mind, Akeroyd drew upon his positivist thinking and his colleagues to explore the matter of juvenile delinquency and classification of types of offenders in greater depth.

In drawing on the writings of contemporary academic and medical authorities to validate his views, Akeroyd reinforced his use of a positivist perspective to frame his reflections and planning. Akeroyd wrote a paper in June 1939 entitled 'A Reformatory School for Boys' proposing a school be established within the prison system that focused on the moral and vocational training of young boys 'thus enabling the boys when released to withstand temptation, live good moral lives and earn sufficient as farm laborers to keep them'.[303] The title proved an interesting choice in linking the word 'reformatory' to schooling given his ongoing battle with authorities to engage

---

[302] VPRS 6603, undated.

[303] VPRS 6603, 1939.

reformatory prisoners (including those on indeterminate sentences) in education and training programs.

Throughout his writings, Akeroyd regularly referred to the importance of the prison and prisoner management regimes to support prisoners to lead 'good moral lives'.[304] By linking the twin concepts of treating deficits while supporting prisoners to lead 'good moral lives' provided an insight that Akeroyd was influenced by two key theoretical frameworks, namely positivism and conservatism. The conservative theory informs that acts 'which offend morality as well as those which endanger persons or property' should be criminalised.[305] However, Akeroyd was continually challenging himself to gain a deeper understanding of the issue of moral deficiency to determine if any direct links existed between it and mental deficiency.

Akeroyd's reflections on issues surrounding moral deficiency and mental deficiency took on many twists and turns during his tenure. Initially he courted mental deficiency in his address to aspiring teachers in 1925 when he further refined the categories relating to the issue. He categorised mental deficiency in terms of 'idiots, imbeciles and feeble-minded persons' in an undated paper (thought to be around 1930). His intention was to seek more intensive tests to classify prisoners to implement better treatment programs as part of his broader prison management reforms. Through his connection with ACER, Akeroyd introduced the Simon Binet intelligence tests to create an initial psychological picture of the prisoner at the point of entry to the prison.

While his early focus had been on mental deficiency, he next raised the issue of moral deficiency in the public arena during his 1935 radio broadcast. Inexplicably, Akeroyd introduced the conservatist

---

[304] Akeroyd, VPRS 6603, 1939.

[305] Young, 1981, p. 277.

definitions of crime and criminality into the radio debate by reflecting on the criminal as an immoral person 'whose immorality finds expression in immoral acts'.[306] Rather than engage the audience with his views on mental deficiency, Akeroyd focused his presentation on the importance of treating and assisting the criminal to live a 'moral life'. His words marked an unorthodox diversion from his consistent line about the importance of understanding a prisoner's psychological attributes to which he returned in the foreword he wrote for Anita Muhl's book in 1938.

In his later years, Akeroyd's focus was drawn to the area of sexual offences. It appeared that this was a universal trend. Up until the 1930s and 1940s, sexual offenders and sexual offences were classified separately from other offences or offenders.[307] During this period, classifying sexual offenders in the United States followed a rise in the focus on offender treatment programs. Muhl devoted 29 pages of her book (the longest chapter) to issues surrounding the nature of sex crimes and the respective treatment practice. Muhl focused on the offender's underdeveloped sexual knowledge on the one hand and their feeblemindedness on the other. In each instance, Muhl maintained punishment was ineffective for sex offenders but strongly recommended treatment during their incarceration.

While no direct cause-and-effect relationship linking Akeroyd's and Muhl's positioning exists, it is evident that there was an increasing interest worldwide in examining the nature of sex offenders and the best means to deal with sex offenders.

In a twist of position toward the end of his tenure, Akeroyd differentiated his positivist perspective from others by arguing the science of psychiatry failed to reflect an understanding of people

---

[306] VPRS 6603, 20 June 1935.

[307] According to Hinds and Daly (2000).

convicted of sex crimes and dismissing psychiatric evidence as 'pure, unadulterated phooey'.[308] These remarks distance Akeroyd from the original position he adopted when he strongly supported Muhl's perspectives (as a psychiatrist) during her lecture four years earlier. It remains unclear what prompted Akeroyd to make such a statement publicly at that point in time, but it was evident that his words coincided with his increasing intense interest in prisoners in custody for sex-related offences. It is possible to conceive that Akeroyd had started thinking critically about positivist criminology and forming opinions about other theoretical approaches to prisoner treatment.

The legacy that Akeroyd and others created in discussions around linking prisoners' attributes to criminality laid the foundation for future debate and consideration. Most notably was their great interest in developing prison programs directly to identify criminogenic behaviours, an approach well embedded in the contemporary policy literature such as the Bearing Point Review (2003). However, the concept of classification within the Victorian prison system has changed markedly from Akeroyd's days. Where Akeroyd's and his contemporaries focus was on classifying behaviours and personality traits linked to offending behaviours, *The Law Handbook* explains that contemporary classification processes relate directly with a prisoner's security risk within the prison system and what risk their potential criminal behaviour presents to the public.[309] The level of risk is ascertained via court reports and internal assessments within the prison system. Regardless, Akeroyd's legacy remains intact regarding linking treatment programs to address specific prisoner attributes, but the term 'classification' has been somewhat modified in policy and practice to refer to a prisoner risk assessment and risk management.

---

[308]   *Sun*, 20 October 1947.

[309]   Fitzroy Legal Service, 2003.

There were some significant changes in prison and prisoner management practice throughout Akeroyd's period as inspector general. The first significant change was implementing a rigorous approach to planning and implementing prisoner reform compared to his predecessors. This was evident in Akeroyd's commitment to his education-inspired positivist approach to identify his understanding of deficiencies in the prisoner makeup and implementing treatment response to these identified deficiencies. Akeroyd investigated deficiencies such as lack of socialisation and poor educational skills leading into more refined assessments in his middle and later years of personality typologies linked to offences. These deficiencies were identified through a detailed assessment using the IQ testing, interviews, and extensive case notes on interview methodologies leading to individual case plans. These approaches were not evident in previous prison management regimes and highlighted the significant shift from dealing with the prisoner population en masse to dealing with prisoners as individuals. The practice of individual case plans, or in current terminology individual sentence management plans, continues in contemporary prison and prisoner management planning.

From these assessments and resultant plans, Akeroyd promoted a therapeutic program response to support the reform of individual prisoners. This was supported through his approach to formalise the schooling experience of prisoners whilst in custody. Through Akeroyd's contacts with the education sector and through his further association with formal education agencies in the community, the Akeroyd period witnessed the establishment of school-like practices within prisons. This included the use of schoolteachers to conduct school curricula with prisoner students in prison and other associated reformatory locations such as Janefield and Bayswater. Again, this practice was new to the prison system in Victoria at that time and has also continued through to contemporary times.

Akeroyd also recognised the importance of educated staff to enable the prison system to support the reform of individuals. Akeroyd's approach to initiate staff training programs and formalised education-based staff promotion structures was revolutionary in prison management practice up until Akeroyd's time. Eric Shade further formalised the prison officer training program in the 1970s, but again, the introduction of formal prison office training through education commenced in the Akeroyd period and continues through to current times.[310]

Through his positivist approach to prison and prisoner management, Akeroyd's interest in and commitment to further identifying criminal typologies through his classification processes contributed to his commitment to inform prisoner management practice, government policy, and community awareness. Akeroyd used varying means to engage with various community and government sectors including radio broadcasts, extensive discussion in his annual reports, and contributing to public awareness through newspaper reports. In addition, through his connection in the formation of the University of Melbourne Centre for Criminology, Akeroyd, along with his colleagues in the judiciary and education circles, found a means to strengthen the influence of criminological debate within community and government circles. Akeroyd used his education grounding to include and influence government and public opinion through his informative annual reports, radio interviews, presentations to community groups, and newspaper articles based on his insights arising from his learning.

---

[310] See O'Toole, 2006.

The most significant example of reform activity that resulted in an outcome contrary to his ideals expressed in his early and middle years related to Akeroyd's turnaround in his approach to corporal punishment. Akeroyd's strong opposition to corporal punishment at the commencement of his career was reversed by the end of his career where Akeroyd was recognised for his pro punishment stance. This turnaround provided insight into the challenges that Akeroyd faced in his role as inspector general. Despite his earlier position on corporal punishment, Akeroyd was compelled to implement the capital and corporal punishment for those found guilty of certain crimes as mandated by court. Through his private and public battles as expressed in his diary and his documentation, Akeroyd appeared to acknowledge that he did not have the capacity to fight against the prevailing conservatist and classicist perspectives regarding the application of corporal punishment. Despite his earlier protestations, he ended up advocating that corporal punishment does have a role in the criminal justice system. It was through his rationalizing that corporal punishment became a form of treatment that highlighted that he accommodated corporal punishment within his positivist perspectives and talked about corporal punishment in these terms that highlighted a disconnect between rhetoric and practice – an indicator of opaque reform. This highlighted the challenge Akeroyd faced introducing new approaches to the management of criminality in prisons in the face of well-established practices.

The other major area of turnaround for Akeroyd was his incapacity to overturn the indeterminate sentence. Akeroyd spent many of his early days trying to influence the government to overturn the indeterminate sentence as he felt the conditions of this sentence prevented certain classes of prisoner (those in reformatory prisons) from participating in education programs. Where Akeroyd was vocal in his challenges to the indeterminate sentence in his early days, his protestations became increasingly quieter, and he eventually became an advocate of the benefits of the indeterminate sentence. This was startlingly evidenced through his statement of ideals in his later years where he specified the number one ideal was the repeal of the definite sentence. The debate on the effectiveness of the indeterminate sentence continued beyond Akeroyd, and it was in Whatmore's time that the indeterminate sentence became repealed.[311]

Through his commitment to reform through education principles, Akeroyd introduced significant changes with his education–inspired positivist reform. The Akeroyd era witnessed the incorporation of school or study options for prisoner students as well as formalizing the educational capabilities of prison staff through education programs and career progression linked to educational attainment. Akeroyd's initiatives in prisoner education through his connections with the Education Department and his drive to establish formal schools paved the way for Whatmore's 1954 achievement in having each of the state's prisons becoming a school registered with the Victorian State Government. Akeroyd also introduced education programs for staff and built a staff promotion strategy around educational attainment that, whilst controversial and unpopular, was consistent with his positivist ideals. From these beginnings, Akeroyd laid the foundations for the formalized staff training program that Eric Shade was well recognised in the 1970s.

The elements of Akeroyd's education reform (such as vocational skill training and literacy and numeracy education) were also evident in Maconochie's Norfolk Island reform and at Point Puer in earlier times. Nowhere else was the strength of reform through

---

[311] As Freiberg and Ross identified in their book *"Sentencing Reform and Penal Change, 1999*

implementing and consolidating prisoner and prison staff education practice evident in Australia's history as in Akeroyd's time. It is the area of prison staff education that clearly separated Akeroyd's legacies from Maconochie's achievements.

Akeroyd introduced the formalization of individual case studies and case plans. Akeroyd's initiative was the first instance of this style of formalized recording of prisoner attributes and assessment of prisoner needs based on psychological profiles. This process was built on his approach to formally classify prisoners in terms of their offending behaviours. Whilst the classification practice today is driven through a prisoner security risk spectrum, the process of a rigorous classification of individual prisoners appeared to start in Akeroyd's time. Coinciding with classification was the evolution of individual case management plans. This also was the first of its kind in Victorian prison management history, and it is of interest that this practice evolved into contemporary sentence management plans and individual case management plans.

There is little acknowledgement in prison history texts of Akeroyd's impact on reforming prison and prisoner management in Victoria.[312] Indeed, Akeroyd's legacies are quite profound. It has already been stated that the next two inspectors general (Alex Whatmore and Eric Shade) were both educators who taught in the prison education system under Akeroyd, leaving a period of 52 years of educationalist-led prison management; and Whatmore, in particular (and has also been noted), was recognised for consolidating prison education within the state's education system. Whatmore was recognised for abolishing the indeterminate sentence. Akeroyd, on the other hand, was recognised more for his perceived pro punishment stance rather than his education-led reform.

---

[312] Apart from Lyn and Armstrong's reference to the term 'the Akeroyd era'.

There were significant achievements in prison and prisoner management reform within Akeroyd's period of tenure, many of which are attributed to Akeroyd's drive for reform. He maintained a steady and persistent focus on leading, developing, and implementing an education–led positivist–based reform. In doing so, Akeroyd faced significant challenges throughout his journey. Whilst these challenges emanated from differing political and theoretical positioning within government, judiciary, prison staffing, and, in some instance, community, one of the greatest challenges appeared to be private battles within the dimension of punishment.

CHAPTER 15

The Voice of the Prisoner

Throughout his career, Akeroyd maintained a focus on the reformation of individuals and held a belief in many individual inmate's capability to effectively participate in society given opportunities and support. Throughout his long career, Akeroyd provided personal support for many imprisoned individuals whilst recording the emotional and spiritual experiences of others facing corporal and capital punishments. Many of these experiences and insights are kept in his personal records.

On 18 November 1932, Akeroyd received a letter from an ex-prisoner, Joe Kelly. In this letter, Kelly shared his insights on Akeroyd's philosophical approach to penal reform and referred to practical illustrations where Akeroyd actively contributed to supporting individuals' reform programs. Further, this letter provided Akeroyd with articulate insights as expressed by ex-prisoners into the challenges faced by long-term prisoners trying to transition to community life following release. Akeroyd forwarded this letter to members of the Indeterminate Sentence Board not only to validate the reasons behind his education-led approach but also to inform others on the plight of long-term prisoners.

In support of Mr Akeroyd's ideas I shall endeavour with this humble pen of mine to draw some pictures that may prove of interest to those who may in time peruse them, word pictures of men whose records are written in scarlet and may be seen in the archives in both Russell St and Pentridge. Men, who without exception were considered to be beyond the pale — menaces to any who might come in contact with them, but who like that fabulous phoenix, have risen from their ashes to a new life, and who are entitled to every respect one can tender them; not because they have been severely punished for their past misdeeds. . . . But because the cause[313] has been removed by certain influential members of society who maintained the old methods were wrong entirely.[314]

Kelly went on to relate to stories on men, with the support of Akeroyd and others over time, who looked to the capabilities of these men and supported them into work.

Billings, a man who up to the age of forty . . . spent the greater part of his life in Pentridge . . . Inspector General placed him in a tile factory. . .. Billings worked his way from general rouseabout to foreman and from there to manager. Mr Akeroyd personally assisted another habitual criminal by the name of Thorpe to a position with (a picture magnate) a position he has held for some years. Mr Akeroyd is personally interested in the welfare of Watson, another who was supposed to be beyond consideration and who is at the present moment a valued employee of a certain firm in Broken Hill.[315]

Kelly went on to list four others, Brennan, Cohoun, Cotton, and Jackson, benefitting from the support of their benefactor,[316] who committed to live by a:

---

[313] Kelly constantly refers to the cause throughout his letter. I interpret this cause to reflect Akeroyd's words in his presentation to the 'Justice of the Peace' newsletter in 1932. Akeroyd wrote about societal hostile attitude to towards criminal arising from the perceived punitive function of prisons.

[314] VPRS 6603.

[315] VPRS 6603.

[316] Assume this is Akeroyd but maybe others as well.

grim determination not to let their benefactor down and a desire to leave the losing game behind, have become law abiding citizens, an under no circumstances would they return to a life of crime.'[317]

Kelly provided an important insight into the plight of prisoners transitioning from incarceration to community when he states that the point of transition and the management of that transition is a significant risk factor in successful return to community. Kelly wrote,

When a long sentence man obtains his release, primed with the best intentions and a few pounds in his pocket; he suddenly realizes, that the world has not been at a standstill, that there is a new order of things, a new Pharoah rules the land that knows not Joseph, his home town has been practically demolished and rebuilt, the old faces he knew have grown older, the friends he once possessed have new interests in life to occupy the leisure hours, and a sense of loneliness steals over him, the continual bustle of which goes on around him dazes him, and causes a feeling of helplessness to dominate him. The years of routine in Prison have told their tale. Years during which his very action has been ordered, his meals provided for him, he has not been required to think for himself or act on his own initiative hence his utter helplessness now.[318]

In a similar vein, Akeroyd received a letter from an unknown or unnamed prisoner in which the prisoner outlined several issues for him to consider in the reform of the prison system. This letter addressed issues with possible solutions for Akeroyd's consideration. Many of the suggested solutions arose from prisoners' experiences in

---

[317] VPRS 6603.

[318] VPRS 6603.

other jurisdictions. For example, the letter advised on the importance of supporting prisoner education with improved access to current books and magazines.

> *In order to provide funds for the support of library it is suggested that the kitchen refuse be sold, or that the full value be credited from the revenue of the piggery to the library for the purchase of needed literature . . .*

> *The lack of ventilation in cells of 'B' and especially 'C' Divisions is unquestionably detrimental [sic] to health. The suggested remedy is that opaque glass should either altogether be removed as is the case in the penal establishments of New South Wales, or, they placed on a pivot as is the case in similar establishments in South Australia . . . There are fully qualified tradesmen on the ground who have served sentences in the States referred to and who could carry out alterations at a very nominal cost.*[319]

This letter addresses issues and provides recommendations for the inspector general's consideration in the following areas: exercise, trafficking, discipline and punishment, and general searching.

According to Lynn and Armstrong, Joseph Akeroyd held a strong sense of justice. They both recorded an example of this when a prisoner was received at Pentridge in 1935 charged with the murder of several women in Melbourne. This prisoner claimed his innocence and advised the then deputy governor of Pentridge that he was in New South Wales at the times these murders were supposed to have occurred. This information was passed on to the police but was not followed up. On hearing this, Akeroyd and his colleague Clifford Book (later Judge Book) decided to investigate themselves and travelled to

---

[319]   VPRS 6603, undated.

New South Wales to validate this prisoner's claims. Both Akeroyd and Book duly confirmed the prisoner's claims, obtained affidavits, and presented these to the Victoria crown solicitor. The charges were consequently withdrawn. This action resulted in the police undertaking further investigation, resulting in the apprehension of Edward Cornelius who was duly tried, convicted, and executed for these crimes.[320] Interestingly, at the same time, the press reported on another instance of murder charges being withdrawn against Gordon Knights. Knights was charged with the murder of 12-year-old Ethel Belshaw in Inverloch and remanded in custody. Protesting his innocence, further evidence was provided to the police, resulting in a focus on Arnold Sodeman who was subsequently found guilty of murdering several young women. Knights was released and awarded compensation.[321] Sodeman and Cornelius shared exercise yards and regularly played draughts together awaiting their respective executions within three weeks of each other.[322]

Akeroyd kept personal records on many prisoners of interest to him. He did this in some instances to record his observations to gain insights into the reasons people commit crimes. In other instances, he recorded the ways prisoners responded to their incarceration; but in other cases, he recorded his concerns about those cases where he felt there was an injustice in sentencing.

Akeroyd's support for a reduced sentence for Herbert James Donovan is an example.

> *There is no doubt in my mind with the right handling he could be trained to be a decent citizen*

---

[320] Lynn and Armstrong 1996, p. 130.

[321] Shepparton Advertiser, 7 March 1936.

[322] *Weekly Times*, 6 June 1936.

He has the capacity and ability to do good work along certain lines.

(if he stayed at school outcomes may have been very different)

If his impairment is too long he will lose all initiative . . . Twenty years is too long and if I may suggest twelve years plus detention in prison in prison until the pleasure of his Excellency the Governor is known

A twelve year sentence would end in nine years. That would give ample time to train without robbing him of all strength of character.[323]

In the latter cases, Akeroyd was an advocate for those prisoners he felt served unjustly by the criminal justice system even though he was compelled to manage the implementation of those court-imposed sanctions. One such record was a query about the guilt of Harold Williams charged with robbery in 1932. Akeroyd's notes about Williams included his initial assessment, letters from others about Williams, and notes for interviews with Williams and other prisoners as follows:

12 April 1932. Letter from James Adams (alias E.G Lancaster) to Jim (Scott) regarding Williams' innocence and taking the fall for Scott.

'Send suitcase clothing etc. I thought you might have realised the position you have placed us and which you were fortunate to escape . . . However when the appeal fell through your absence was not unexpected neither will Stanways absence be unexpected on the 18th . . . The £60 which went astray

---

[323] VPRS 6603, 30 December 1930. Donovan's sentence was reduced to 15 years.

I would like you to devote to establishing the innocence of Willliams the fact of which you are well aware although I am not complaining about my harsh sentence — both Martin and I agree that it is most unjust that Williams should take your grief.

I hope you will look into my property and when Williams is taking your 15 strokes you will regret the position in which you have successfully placed him.'

20 April 1932. Harold Williams. Multum in Parvo Intelligence test. IQ 83

20th April James Adams (aka Lancaster). Multum in Parvo Intelligence test. 1Q 91

5 May 1932. Statement by Hugh Martin for the purpose of exonerating Harold Williams re Coles Robbery of 20 March 1931

5 May 1932 Letter from James Adams to Joseph Akeroyd re Coles robbery. 'Their [sic] has been no friendship between Williams and I, prior to my arrest I had only seen him once before that, but I must say he is an innocent man.'

1 June 1932. A Division, Report on corporal punishment meted out to Adams, Williams and Martin (15 strokes cat o nine tails).[324]

7 June 1932. Letter from Harold Williams (Henry) to Nellie

Nell I don't want you or your mother to worry over the punishment I received last week as it has done me more good

---

[324] The whipping was witnessed by Schoolmaster Mullins. Interesting that a teacher is nominated to witness such an event!

than harm as it has knocked into me what I was lacking so badly, that is a bit of sense. It will teach me in the future to regard whom [sic] I think are friends of mine to treat them as enemies of mine.

Akeroyd also kept detailed files on those executed whilst he was inspector general. These files included details of trials, letters received by the prisoner, offending history, general intelligence, and coroner's autopsy reports post-execution. Records were kept for Angus Murray (2 June 1924), Arnold Sodeman (18 January 1936), Edward Cornelius (17 April 1936), Thomas William Johnson (23 January 1939), George Green (17 April 1939), Alfred Bye (22 December 1941), and American serviceman Edward Leonski in 1942.

In Angus Murray's instance, Akeroyd kept copies of those letters sent to and by Murray in those days leading to Murray's execution.

To Angus Murray (April 7th)

Dear Mr Murray

With a deeply touched heart I pen these few lines and enclose these books, and I pray the authorities may allow to pass into your hands and a blessing to your precious soul may be the result.

I was a hell deserving sinner, but by his grace I am going to heaven, not by any merit of my own. I have done nothing toward my salvation. He did it all on the cross. He died for you and I and in his sight I was no better than you. I perhaps have not done what you have (not referring in any way to your position now) but I was a lost sinner and had to come the same way as you will to salvation. . . .

To Mr Albert Swan (7th April 1924)

Dear Sir

Your letter of the 3rd inst [sic] to hand; it is very good of you to be so thoughtful toward me in my present extremity and I am so deeply grateful that you should feel so concerned with regard to my eternal welfare. It is good to know there are some people who have other thoughts towards me than to hunt and kill as if I was a wild beast, as has seemed to be the case from when I left Geelong Prison, I am afraid that even you have a wrong impression of me to be a callous sort of an individual with no realisation between right and wrong . . .

Angus Murray

To Angus Murray (8th April)

Dear Mr Murray

I am taking the liberty of writing this note to you hoping you will grant me an interview as I would take it as a great honour to shake the hand with such a brave man who knows his fate is waiting for him on the 14th but remember where there is life there is hope and every cloud has a silver lining which we must all look for as wee in our own hearts believe you an innocent man so we must leave it in the hands of God . . .

Mrs A Annison

These examples of engaging with prisoners, listening to their stories, and recording their stories indicated the importance of engaging those most impacted by reforms to contribute their insights and advice into the reform discussion. Akeroyd used his educational principles to delve into the needs of offenders and seek to personally gain insights into the experiences of prisoners to learn more about lives. It appears that the inspectors general following Akeroyd found it more difficult to, or chose not to, focus on individual cases and actively engage the voice of the prisoner or to delve into the lives of individual prisoners to the extent Akeroyd did.

CHAPTER 16

My Story: MALWAYS

In 1998, the Melbourne-based community theatre company Somebody's Daughter[1] performed a play titled *MALWAYS* at the now-named Dame Phyllis Frost Corrections Centre (DPFC). This play was written by the women prisoners in concert with the prison education staff and Somebody's Daughter directors Maude Clark and Kharen Harper.

As is the intent of community theatre, there are many takeaway points of enlightenment, learning, and challenge for the participants and the audience to reflect on. For me, as general manager of a TAFE institute that managed all the education and training services for Melbourne metropolitan adult corrections and juvenile justice facilities at the time, the *MALWAYS* experience provided some of the most critical and enduring messages to all prison educators regarding the content and delivery challenges faced every day in these unique, and often bizarre, learning environments. As indeed intended through community theatre, the reflections and learnings are completely subjective – everyone takes their own meanings from the experience. However, the essential challenge, as T. S. Eliot dared us all, is to ensure we drive to gain our own meaning from our experiences.[2]

The *MALWAYS*[3] experience opened the door for the voice of some prisoners to articulate their understanding of their life journey to the point of ending in prison. This title was a deliberate play on words in which each of these women mapped their life and experiences onto a social map characterised by the Melbourne street directory known as *Melways*.[4] The women chose to replace the 'Mel' (for Melbourne) with the term 'mal', the French term for bad. The underpinning structure of the *Melways* street directory emerges as a grid overlaid on the streetscapes of Melbourne's inner- and outer-lying suburbs. The top axis of the grid is referenced by the alphabetic symbols ranging from A through to K whilst the vertical axis is represented by the numbers 1 through to 12. Each map connects with adjoining suburbs along the vertical and horizontal with, roughly, a suburb per page. Each map shows the interconnection of roads, streets, and lanes and also includes symbols for landmarks such as railway lines, stations, parks, reserves, and other significant local features.

Throughout the play, each woman expressed her individual journey to her point of incarceration in song, verse, and/or monologue. Whilst each journey was unique, this play produced a metaphorical map to illustrate the social and cultural parameters shaping the options available for life decisions they made along this journey. Without going into the intricacies of each woman's journey, the themes of the journeys could be paraphrased as follows.

In this play, the women likened their life as being symbolically bounded by the grid on this map. For illustration's sake, this grid is referred as the grid G5 on a particular page of the *Melways* road map. Emerging from the women's collective stories, each expressed a commonality, and that related to the limited scope for options they believed available for decision-making. This was symbolised by seeing that the boundaries of G5 encased and encompassed life as they knew it. All the options they believed were available for their decision-making were framed by the experiences they had in their G5. All their social contacts, their family contacts, their education (formal and informal), and their history were those bounded by the perceived walls surrounding this grid. There was not an appreciation or awareness there was a G6 or an H5 let alone another page in which there were other grids!

As bounded in their respective G5s, the women told the story that the features within their social map were interpreted along with their own experiences and as learnt by the experiences of others (family, friends, etc.). For example, one woman explained that the traffic lights on the edge of her G5 were always appeared red. She was not cognisant that the lights could be green nor associate with the licence that a green light afforded to go further. Hence, figuratively, she did not countenance the option of deciding to travel across this road. Another explained there was a railway station in her G5. To her, this railway station was a social meeting point. She knew that trains came through the station and that she could get on a train to go somewhere. However, she also did not consider that the train tracks connected with other train tracks further down the line, and these tracks led to alternate stations which linked with other tracks (i.e. other G5s on other pages of her *Melways*). The key message was that G5 symbolised the defined scope of life options available and the scope of behaviours available to them.

It was through engaging with writing this play that each of these women told her story that she came to a point in her life that she realised the symbols could also represent opportunities to do something else rather than reflecting a limited option bounded by the culture of G5. Each told her story, in her own way, which she started to realise that she had a choice to explore the various meanings behind the symbolic representations within their life grid and then seek to understand the opportunities presented through this expanded awareness. To each of them (as each explained), the exposure to education programs helped them to gain an alternate viewpoint of the awareness of the options and then an awareness of the capabilities to capitalise on these opportunities.

Whilst their exposure to alternate options available for their own decision-making emerged, the women also expressed further and alternate insights into options available. This alternate learning identified there were factors in our community which worked to ensure that those living in G5 stayed in G5. For example, some women related stories of previous releases from prison when they were subjected to extra scrutiny from police or justice agencies whilst on restrictive parole orders. Others broadened their perceptions to perceive that having offenders in our society served other, less obvious benefits to society. For example, one woman was able to see herself in a much broader social context when she expressed a critical perception that governments provided a substantial financial commitment to operating prisons, and prisons need prisoners to give them (i.e. prisons) meaning for existence. This raised the question of 'what does this insight meant to her?' to which she replied that she now had a broader context to understand the options in which she makes her decisions.

CHAPTER 17

Challenging Perspectives – A Reflection
on the Nature of Prison Reform

U p to this point, this book analysed Akeroyd's achievements and challenges in his quest to embed a therapeutic approach to prisoner management throughout Victoria's prison system in the mid–1920s through to the late 1940s. The clear and demonstrated changes implemented to prison and prisoner management policy and practice throughout the Akeroyd period were recorded along with outlining the many challenges Akeroyd faced whilst embarking on his reform. Whilst Akeroyd overcame some of these challenges with some others, he appeared overwhelmed. Analysis of Akeroyd's experiences by examining the influences of the criminological theories within policy positions provides insights into the challenges facing policymakers in prison education, prison management, and prisoner management policy and related programs through to contemporary times.

In terms of criminal justice reform, it is important to investigate and learn from the past to understand the practices of the present. Many of today's prison and prisoner management practices grew from those practices established in Akeroyd's time, and there are other practices embedded from earlier times. As Akeroyd wrote in his retrospective review of prison management practices in his 1933 annual report, it is valuable to apply the learnings of the present to retrospectively examine the practices in the past. Whilst Akeroyd recognised this as a challenge for him as the leading policy developer and implementer, this is also the challenge for contemporary policymakers and prison education practitioners. However, as the past practices are examined, we find whilst these practices may maintain similar names or descriptions to those of the past, the intent of the contemporary practices take on a different focus. It is in this examination that we explore the reasons for the changes and how these are communicated within and outside the prison environment.

The earlier chapters focused on Joseph Akeroyd's adoption of education-led principles for planning and implementing his reforms. His position on reforming the Victorian prison system was based on implementing a treatment-based therapeutic model which addressed those prisoner needs. These needs were ascertained from evidence gained through Akeroyd's application of a more rigorous scientific methodology compared to any practice in the years before him. This approach resulted in a more rigorous approach to gathering evidence to support policy directions. Akeroyd undertook this by writing, collating, collecting, and analysing prisoner case studies; applying IQ/psychological testing to individual prisoners; implementing education-based remediation programs to prisoners; and implementing an education-based approach to staff training and staff promotion. It would be easy to consider that Akeroyd's approach to prison and prisoner management in his early and middle year's actions was based in an almost entirely within a positivist framework underpinned by the application of scientific research methodologies and applying a science-based approach to arrive at policy and practice decisions. Like reformers in times before Akeroyd, the challenge faced by taking a clearly defined singular paradigmatic position into initiating and implementing reforms appeared important to break the cycle of incumbent and seemingly ineffective practices. By adopting a focused positivist perspective in the early phases of his incumbency,

Akeroyd, like earlier reformers such as Maconochie, was confronted with combative conflicting political and traditional community perspectives. He appeared to struggle with others' positions whilst attempting to establish a clear, coherent, yet unilateral and defensible position on ways to identify the psychological and social needs of prisoners and then set in place strategies and programs to treat these needs.

The first piece of evidence of Akeroyd's quest to address the issue of criminality lay in his initial strategies of designing a reform strategy informed by his educational origins. Akeroyd argued that implementing prison training programs was paramount in assisting individuals reach a meaningful existence upon their release. He saw the power of education and training as the vehicles for individual transformation and to achieve, in Akeroyd's terms, the elusive torch. This is reflective of Dewey's aspirational and liberation view of the role of education.[325] However, Akeroyd's focus on the importance of his concept of discipline brings forward a contentious reflection of the rationale behind Akeroyd's motivations at the time. The contention revolves around the application of Foucault's perception on the role of discipline in incarcerated environments which is to render the body docile therefore preparing the prisoner for easier management within the prison environment rather than to reforming the individual through educational enlightenment in preparation for life after prison. Whilst Akeroyd did not appear to fully appreciate this conflict in his early years it became his burden in later years.

In his 27 October 1924 paper, Akeroyd stated that discipline remained the fundamental key to achieving such success. Akeroyd embraced discipline as an important tool to initiate change or reform in the individual. He followed this up when he argued that discipline

---

[325] Dewey, 2008.

was essential from within the individual, and self-discipline was a critical consideration in setting the context for prisoner learning. Akeroyd wrote,

> *[Discipline] demands instant obedience and self discipline and helps to cleanse the foul minds that many of these youth have. This* <u>*discipline*</u>[326] *from above would be little use if it ended there. It must lead to* <u>*self discipline*</u>[327] *and opportunities must be created in prisons for responsibility so that they may have practice in bearing themselves worthily in the daily life of the prison.*[328]

Foucault challenged discipline's impact in the context of social control by arguing its chief function was to train the individual.[329] On the face of this statement, there appears similarity between Akeroyd's intent and Foucault's critique. Foucault argued that applying discipline, particularly through the legal structure, was critical to managing chapters within society. He argued that discipline:

> *'trains' the moving, confused, useless multitudes of bodies into a multiplicity of individual elements — small separate cells; organic autonomies; genetic identities; and continuities. Discipline 'makes' individuals; it is the specific instrument of a power that regards individuals both as objects and as instruments of its exercise.*[330]

In other words, Akeroyd saw developing discipline as a means of supporting individuals to realise their academic and career

---

[326] Akeroyd's underlining.

[327] Akeroyd's underlining.

[328] VPRS 6603, undated paper.

[329] Foucault, 1977, p. 170.

[330] Foucault, 1977, p. 170.

potential whereas Foucault felt that discipline applied in the prison environment subjugated individuals to enable mass management of incarcerated bodies. Whilst Foucault did not air his insights well after the Akeroyd period finished, the debate in the Akeroyd time showed these contrary arguments were present in public debate.

Akeroyd not only advocated the importance of discipline in prisoner reform but also promoted the importance of discipline among the prison officer ranks. With Akeroyd's intentions to ensure treatment programs and prisoner reform were managed rigorously, Akeroyd concentrated his efforts on training prison officers, among many other aspects of their roles, to observe and record prisoner behaviours. This approach resulted in some significant reform landmarked on his institution of formal training of prison officers and the promotion of staff based on educational achievement. There was marked conflict with staff members individually and as a group with this approach, and this conflict was also evidenced by the intervention of some leading political figures of the time (including John Cain Sr) on behalf of the prison officer group. In his later years, Akeroyd faced difficulties around maintaining his consistent approach to management of staff, and he was subjected to criticism from within the chief secretary's office regarding his apparent inconsistency.

Akeroyd's approach throughout his career was to change staff roles from punitive containment to more learned observers of prisoner behaviours to support reforming individuals through case planning and case management. Foucault's view that 'the exercise of discipline presupposes a mechanism that coerces observation' underpinned his exploration of the role of custodians and the function of the architecture to support observation.[331]

---

[331]   Foucault, 1977, p. 171.

The differing views on the observation role of the prison officer expressed by Foucault on the one hand and Akeroyd on the other provided insight into the challenge of reforming practices in a prison setting. Whereas Akeroyd was clear that he wanted prison officers trained to observe prisoners to obtain scientific evidence to understand their behaviours and therefore lead to a more rigorous approach to addressing these behaviours, Foucault and Cohen separately considered the traditional role of observation in prison to be more focused on maintaining the role of the prison as a place of 'containment and coercion'[332].

In the first instance, the Foucauldian perception presupposes that observation itself was a form of social control and is indeed integral in the process of normalisation whereas Akeroyd's stated intent to support, guide, and facilitate personal reform. This interpretation provides a view into the opaqueness of reform in the Akeroyd era where there were two distinct approaches to the role of a prison officer through one as an active conduit for rehabilitation through calculated observation and case planning and the other a custodian ensuring effective containment and coercion for easier mass management. The duplicity of this approach in the post-Akeroyd years was recognised through the experiences of Biles (1978), Gehring and Muth (1985), and Harris (1992) where they independently spoke of the parallel reform paths of prison management; and with the overt animosity between the two streams (prison management and prison education), it becomes clear that, for a period, the two streams operated independently albeit linked with a common language and commonly stated aspirations between prison management and education management but with differing applications of practices between the two disciplines. This provides an insight into the

---

[332]   Cohen, 1985, p. 108

opaqueness of prison management practices and reforms emanating from Akeroyd's era.

Akeroyd, using his educationalist background, regularly referred in his writings to the importance of delivery of programs in classrooms and wanted to create facilities for young offenders to learn education skills and trade skills. Whilst there was no direct evidence relating to the inability to resource suitable classroom facilities and training facilities in the industry areas, the effectiveness of Akeroyd's capacity to embed his reforms was hampered by the lack of resources, and this was particularly referenced to the inability to fund the capital works. Akeroyd's initiatives appear to have a clear altruism link between his ideological intent and his intended practice establishing schools in prison, or even seeing prison as a school and advancing the concept of educating prison officers in the ways of effectively managing prisoners whilst supporting individual prisoner case plans.

Akeroyd also focused on the concept of examination. To Akeroyd, examination was the study of the man to assess the achievement of certain skills in prison officers. According to Akeroyd, the examination of the man leading to the formation of formal case studies provided an insight into the prisoners' backgrounds, intellectual capabilities, and offending typologies. Again, Akeroyd instigated the process on examination with the benevolent intent to assist the prisoner reach the elusive torch and become a contributing citizen. This reform was revolutionary in Victoria's prison history and is considered a significant and influential reform.

Introducing a formalized education-based reform into Victoria's prison system was based on a clear alignment between Akeroyd's education ideals and his commitment to the principles of teaching. Akeroyd's reform in prisoner and prison staff education, setting up schools in prison to educate and train prisoners in response to individual needs, was clear in its ideological base and provided the platform for further development under the Whatmore and Shade regimes.

Whilst the education focus was the major dimension of Akeroyd's theoretical focus, it is in punishment which witnessed a stronger conflict between theoretical perspectives and hence stronger evidence on opaque reform.

In terms of his position on punishment, Akeroyd was primarily dealing with the clash of two distinct perspectives. The matter of punishment is central to all discussions on the rationale of the existence and the function of prisons, and the evidence gathered about Akeroyd's position to the concept and the implementation of punishment indicated areas of great concern to Akeroyd. This concern was compounded by the sole responsibility of the inspector general which mandated Akeroyd to implement the various disciplinary, especially corporal, and capital punishment measures imposed through court sanctions. Akeroyd struggled with the concept of punishment and its application within the Victorian prison system whilst being compelled to oversee corporal and capital punishment. Many of Akeroyd's early writings questioned the role of punishment in respect to its failure to encourage personal change. However, towards the end of his career, he advocated punishment as a valuable aid in the treatment program.

This marked turnaround was difficult to reconcile given his earlier fervent arguments against punishment. However, a reconciliation point may lie in the examples of the contradictory views he entertained in the private and public debates between the causation of crime and criminality and the ways to address those behaviours leading to criminal acts and the reflective processes to address the impacts on offenders and victims. Akeroyd's and other perspectives considered individuals' proclivity for offending through their under-socialisation or their psychological deficits against inequities in societal order as the stimulus for offending. This battle was an unwinnable position with the polarised views clearly institutionally embedded in the judicial, religious, and/ or political views of the time. Akeroyd's papers and presentations revealed he could no longer ignore alternative perspectives to his preferred position as he increasingly incorporated elements of these competing perspectives into his practice during his lengthy tenure in the prison system.

In his considerations of crime and criminality, Akeroyd and his contemporaries focused their efforts on examining the role and actions of the criminal in a bid to identify the underlying causes and solutions to combating crime within the community. They placed minimal emphasis on any relationship between social organisation and crime. Upon reflection, the major issues for Akeroyd appeared to be the constant challenges to his focused positivist stance of his early and middle years and his battles to respond to such challenges. It is notable that he responded to these challenges by placing every issue within the positivist frame of reference he most favoured. More likely, the greater challenge to him was his growing recognition of the complexity of identifying and addressing the causes and consequences of criminality within individuals that could not be explained by the singular theory he espoused.

Following the discussion about punishment, a further example of the competing theoretical perspectives emerged to become the first indication of a challenge to conservatist, classicist, and positivist thinking within Akeroyd's time. Some of the newspaper articles provided clues that many elements of the yet-to-be-articulated non-dominant sub-cultural or strain theory started to form in McRae's and Akeroyd's thinking. For example, Dr C. R. McRae's 1926 article in the *Herald* intended to argue a singularly positivist point of view, but his references to juvenile delinquent behaviour demonstrated elements of the yet-to-be-recognised strain theory. McRae reflected on a causal factor in delinquency as 'some morbid complex or unrealised wish rankling within the unconscious'.[333] McRae elaborated on his observation that some youth harboured aspirations to achieve and acquire possessions more so than others. Further, McRae stated 'still another cause (of delinquency) often found is poverty'.[334] McRae also made mention of other factors outside the realm of individual determinism that contributed to their behaviours. In fact, McRae stayed true to this belief that unrealistic aspiration and poverty could be overcome with the support of 'psychological clinics staffed with trained investigators capable of unravelling causes in the individual'.[335] It is at this stage of the Akeroyd era that the first inkling that alternate sociological perspectives which took hold much later in the world of criminological discourse started to emerge in Victoria in the late 1920s. These perspectives opened the focus on sociological factors impacting people's behaviours. In other words, the discussion moved from purely focusing on the so-called moral ineptitude to the psychological or under-socialised determinants within individuals resulting in criminal behaviour then to encompass consideration of the impact of individuals or groups of individuals responding to perceived social inequities. This was a landmark shift in criminological thinking at the time, and there did not seem to be any further development of this perspective in Victoria or Australia or overseas until the 1970s.

---

[333] McRae, 1926.

[334] VPRS 6603, 1926.

[335] VPRS 6603, 1926.

Whilst the Akeroyd era evidence is limited in relation to the subcultural causal links with criminality, the fact that McCrae started to draw a relationship between social disconnection and criminality was notable. McRae's position was a significant move from the focus on criminality being embedded in the individual which underpinned the positivist, conservatist, and classicist theories.[336] Whilst McRae's considerations may not have been explored in more depth at the time, Akeroyd did explore the causal links between the individual and criminality in more detail.

Juvenile delinquency appeared to be a key focus for Akeroyd during his career perhaps initially sparked by his teaching background before being further consolidated from working with young prisoners. In Akeroyd's (and McRae's) exploration into understanding juvenile delinquency, the categorising of sexual offenders, and identifying mental deficiency, it appeared that Akeroyd's writings encompassed what we now know, in broad terms, as hybrid combinations of positivist and strain theories.

Akeroyd's positioning as a benefactor in guiding prisoners, especially young prisoners, to develop the skills of good citizenship either by disciplining themselves or by external disciplinary actions raised questions about his view of prisoners and offenders. Like Muhl, Akeroyd viewed prisoners and young offenders as victims of their poor upbringing and under-socialisation. In this way, Akeroyd and Muhl's shared perspectives on the prisoner and young offender groups reflected Young's alert to the strategy of 'othering'. This highlights an emerging issue which contemporary criminological theorists could consider as an example of opaque reform. This is to say that introducing the strategy of classifying prisoners and groups of prisoners into certain categories may be used in ways that were

---

[336] See Young (1981) and Cohen (1985).

not intended by Akeroyd. Whilst this is not a criticism of Akeroyd, or of the ways that Akeroyd's reform has been used by others, the categorization of types of offenders can take a life of its own.

The nature of classification of prisoners within the custodial context serves a couple of purposes, one of which is utilitarian for ease of mass prisoner management, another for providing a rationale to marshal resources to address offending behaviours. Young wrote about the relationship between classification and the concept of 'othering'. Instead of grouping offenders with like needs or like presentations (such as offending behaviours), current classification processes group people with like security classifications based largely on the risk they provide for ease of management. This relates to risk presented to the public should the offender return to the community. This also incorporates the risk to the community of a detainee leaving the prison prematurely either by escape or by being trusted to manage his or her behaviours upon release.

It was equally evident in the early phase that Akeroyd either gravitated towards or engaged people of similar theoretical dispositions to complement his work. By attracting like minded thinkers, and often apparently influential like thinkers (such as ACER, Browne, Cunningham, Maugher, Muhl, and others), Akeroyd was able to establish an authoritative base to demonstrate that consistent and consolidated alternate methods that prison, and prisoner management could work. In this early phase, it was also significant that Akeroyd restructured the prison workforce to influence the deployment of his ideals. Recruiting more educated prison officers and implementing merit-based promotions based on qualifications and training rather than on time served also strengthened his ability to implement his devised strategies.

By consolidating an alternate approach to the prevailing practices and by building an authoritative ally base in his early phase, Akeroyd embarked on the next stage which was articulating his perspectives to reach a wider audience. Akeroyd's middle years witnessed his capacity to mount an elegant argument[337] strongly supported by a robust body of evidence – published initially in his annual reports and subsequently in the daily newspapers – strengthened his reform campaign through the newly formed Centre for Criminology and its subsequent emergence as a vehicle for policy advice to the government of the day, as well as legitimised the positivist position in the wider audience through its adherence to scientific methodology and rigour. His regular presence in newspaper reports and on public platforms such as the radio or to particular groups enabled Akeroyd to communicate the aspirations he harboured for an effective prison management system which used treatment programs to transform prisoners into effective citizens. It appeared that Akeroyd relied heavily on the media to engage community debate on his fresh perspectives to prison reform. The regular presentation of newspaper reports and letters to editors indicated the strong community feedback and buy-in to Akeroyd's initiatives. Using the concepts of syntactic simplicity and the number and complexity of arguments postulated,[338] Akeroyd provided elegant alternatives in terms of both the nature of his arguments about the causation of criminality and the treatment of criminals when compared to the prevailing

---

337

338   The *Stanford Encyclopaedia of Science* stated that the concept of elegance when analysing competing theories required a distinction between 'two senses of simplicity: "syntactic simplicity" (the number and complexity of hypotheses), and ontological simplicity (the number and complexity of things postulated). These two aspects of simplicity are often referred to as elegance and parsimony respectively' (http://plato.stanford.edu/entries/simplicity/).

punitive positioning. This was also enhanced by having the message reinforced in several venues and media by those allied to his position at the time. However, the challenge is to understand the extent to which Akeroyd's thoughts, aspirations, and initiatives subsumed and transcended the current theories.

The critical test rested in applying an appropriate punishment regime within the criminal justice prison system. Akeroyd made numerous definitive statements early in his role that punishment had no place in the world of treatment. The debate raged consistently throughout his incumbency culminating in the government inquiry into punishment in prisons in 1947. Analysing Akeroyd's reflections revealed a changing focus on the role of punishment as the years progressed, namely a growing accommodation that punishment was one means of treatment within the prison setting. His overall shift from refusing to accept punishment to acknowledging it as a legitimate component of prison operations indicated Akeroyd's inability to persuade his colleagues and antagonists to completely embrace the ideal treatment model he first envisioned. Indeed, it could be argued Akeroyd's influence proved no match for the powerful position the judiciary played in implementing sentences.

CHAPTER 18

My Story: The H Division Experience

As stated earlier, my direct experience teaching in maximum-security prisons spanned two phases: 1977–1981 was phase 1 whilst 1986–2010 was phase 2. In between these two, I went back to mainstream school teaching and spent three years working in a high-security youth justice facility in Melbourne. Why the break between the two phases?

Toward the end of phase 1, I had one of those epiphany moments that some people reflect on – a turning point. In fact, there were a couple of moments resulting in serious reflection!

The first was the H Division moment. H Division was the high-security facility in Pentridge Prison at the time. H Division was primarily a unit where the most dangerous prisoners were housed in a very restricted environment. By this I mean there was little or no contact with one another, short periods of activity time outside the cell, and often little activity time within the cell. However, I was able to conduct a physical education program in the small exercise yard for two separate groups of prisoners. These groups of prisoners were separated from one resulting from intense hatred for one another. In this small yard, I devised a modified circuit training program to assist maintaining physical and, by virtue of intense exercise, mental health. This program was well supported by the unit management because it did, I believe, provide cathartic release for the prisoners, thereby supporting a less confrontational management regime (as possible in this environment).

Each group consisted of eight prisoners give or take one on any day. Across the two groups, the roll call would constitute the top 20 most dangerous prisoners in the state if the press were to publish that list on any given day. Each session introduced exercises that could be done within the yard and any equipment (i.e. bolted bench seats), walls, and concrete floor within the yard. These exercises were designed to be performed in the cells when the session finished.

There were two unrelated incidents connected with this program. Both concerned the unpredictable nature of how programs in prisons can affect others (ostensibly me in these instances!)

The physical education programs were highly regarded in H Division for different reasons. The prison management saw the benefit of providing structure and motivation for prisoners to use their time whilst in a very confined punitive setting, thereby helping to possibly diffuse unwanted behaviours whist the prisoners saw the benefit of maintaining physical and mental health through exercise in small and very confined space.

In December 1978, Mark 'Chopper' Read, Jimmy Loughnan, and John Price were very active and committed members of one of my H Division physical education programs. I fronted up to work one day to find the northern prison (Pentridge A, J, and H Divisions) was in lockdown. Chopper, Jimmy, and John escaped from H Division and climbed onto the A Division portico roof to stage a protest. Read stood shirtless with his toes hanging over the edge of the portico whilst beating himself over the head with a plank of wood. He had slashed his chest and had blood oozing from his head and chest wounds whilst yelling protests to whomever was in sight whilst John rested in the shade of the division roof and Jimmy ran backwards and forwards between them.

At the time, I thought this would be the end of my physical education program as I imagined the authorities would connect this escape with the physical fitness gains made through the program, hence create a link between education and a risk to prison security. Surprisingly this wasn't to be! The H Division management was keen to see the programs operate as usual.

The second incident was more a stimulus for self-reflection. On this one day, I was demonstrating a modified press up to exercise a specific set of shoulder and abdominal muscles. I was face down demonstrating this exercise when I looked up as the faces so intently following my instructions when I had the epiphany. Here I was alone with 8 of the state's most dangerous prisoners, and the only guard was on a fenced-in walkway at least 6 metres above me. I felt vulnerable for the first time since I worked in the prison. Whilst I felt that I knew I was not at risk because the students were so intently engaged, my safety was not the triggering moment. The key observation that startled me was that whilst looking at these faces looking back at me, I noted there was not one intact ear amongst the lot of them! These prisoners cut off parts of their ears in a desperate attempt over time to get some timeout away from being in H Division.

It struck me that prison was a bizarre place; and I started to question why was I here doing this, for what and whose benefit? Concurrently my wife at the time constantly remarked on the foulness of my language. It dawned on me how I accommodated the prison lingo in my everyday communications. I was not sensitive to this, and once reality took hold that I swore like a trooper both in and out of the prison setting, I realised that I was in a weird place both mentally and physically. Even more concerning was that I was no different to many of my colleagues.

This insight led me to reflect that, in prison, everything fell to the lowest common denominator very quickly. Behaviours, language, expectations rapidly accepted the abnormal as normal; and this translated into life outside the prison. I reflected on the behaviours and language of many of my prison teaching colleagues at the time (remembering we were in this place as professional educators). I recognised that my behaviours and my language were reflective of many of the others. I made a commitment to myself that this was not acceptable to me as a person, as a teacher, as a comrade to my fellow staff members, to my family, and, particularly, to my students. I resolved to reorient myself away from the prison but with a commitment to never fall to the lowest common denominator again.

CHAPTER 19
Akeroyd – Legacies and Lessons

After a lengthy period of policy inactivity prior to 1924, the Akeroyd era witnessed an urgency of activity leading to significant reformatory actions in Victoria's prison and prisoner management policy and practice. Joseph Akeroyd explicitly implemented some of these reforms, and he was influential in other areas of reform. This investigation into Joseph Akeroyd's influence on reforming prison and prisoner management policy and practice unearthed his determined commitment to firstly explore and understand the causation links between crime and criminality in individuals in the Victorian community and secondly to implement therapeutic strategies to address these factors. Bringing his educationalist perspectives into prison management, Akeroyd faced conflict from staff and some sectors of the community over his approach to treat prisoners rather than punish them. There was overt conflict with staff over changes to staff roles and to staff promotion, and there was more subtle conflict with judiciary regarding the function of punishment of prisoners. Through his commitment as an educator as well as the prison management administrator, Akeroyd challenged himself, the government, his contemporaries, and the general community to understand and support the reform he was introducing. Whilst many of his practices were challenged at the time, it is also evident that initiatives he put in place in 1924 through to 1947 have left legacies which are still evident in contemporary practice in Victoria. Many of Akeroyd's legacies have been further developed or refined by others following in his footsteps, and his actual contribution in paving the way for significant reform in Victoria's prison management history may have been overshadowed by these subsequent developments. However, it is important to landmark Akeroyd's achievements and recognise his struggles in leading this era of significant reform at an exceedingly difficult economic time in the world's history. Indeed, it is important to recognise the private and public battles he faced in the early to mid-1900s are like the battles prison education and prison management face in contemporary times.

Access to Akeroyd's personal diaries and papers (including papers he wrote, official and private correspondence, and various reports) as well as access to the official government papers and newspaper articles of the time opened the opportunity to gain insights into his thoughts, actions, conversations, and reflections over the period of his tenure.

Before recording Akeroyd's achievements and his failures, it is important to recognise that reform within the criminal justice system is complex. Exploring the nature and impacts of reform requires an understanding of the conflicting viewpoints on the rationale underpinning the development and application of policy and strategy in prison and prisoner management.

The period of Akeroyd's appointment fell in the complex and unsettled period between the two world wars which also encompassed significant economic upheavals and was followed by the cold war. This period witnessed extraordinarily little reform in the areas of prison and prisoner management. In some cases, reform regressed in this period in Australia.[339] Whilst the literature argued there was truly little reform in the Akeroyd years, there was significant reform activity recorded in the years immediately after Akeroyd's retirement. These areas of reform in the Whatmore and Shade years

---

[339] See Gehring, 1990; Semmens, 1995; O'Toole, 2006.

included the formalization of prisoner education through registering each prison as school with teaching staff and resources funded by the Education Department, the formalization of prison staff training programs, and the repeal of the Indeterminate Sentencing Act.[340] Apart from Lynn and Armstrong's recording of the Akeroyd era and a high-level overview of developments in the Akeroyd era, there was very little recorded about the Akeroyd period. However, there were some key matters which raised questions about what reform may have occurred in the Akeroyd period but were not recognised in literature. Before exploring these reforms, it is important to register significant milestones in the relationship between education and prison management in Victoria in and around the Akeroyd era. Firstly, Akeroyd was appointed to his position directly from the teaching service, and he became the longest-serving inspector general in Victoria's history. Secondly, the next two inspectors general, Alexander Whatmore (1947–1971) and Eric Shade (1971–1976), were also educationalists resulting in a prison management regime spanning 52 years where the most senior prison bureaucrat was an educator prior to the inspector general appointment. Thirdly, Victorian prisons became registered schools in 1954. This administrative relationship between prison operations and education was unique in Australia and indeed through the Western world. This continued through to 1989 when each prison became a campus of a TAFE institute. This meant that until 2013[341] each prison education service was funded through the state funding body responsible for funding education

---

[340] Semmens, 1995; Freiberg and Ross, 1999; O'Toole, 2010.

[341] From 2013, the funding for prisoner education was transferred from the Department of Education and Early Childhood Development to the Department of Justice, the Department of Human Services, and the Department of Health to contract education and training services for the clients in custody.

and training to the broader community. As a state-based approach to prison management and prisoner education, these structures are unique to Victoria.[342] It is also recognised that the major reforms recorded in literature (such as the registration of prisons as schools and the formalization of prison officer training) occurred after the Akeroyd period. Given the lack of detailed information recorded about the Akeroyd era, this research determined to examine the nature and extent of prison management and prisoner management reform occurring in the Akeroyd era.

From the first day he assumed office as inspector general of Victoria's prisons, Akeroyd applied his experience and knowledge base as an educator to make sense of the world of crime, criminality, and prisons. Akeroyd's early diary recordings provided strong evidence that the principles of education underpinned his developing approach to the broader task of reforming the prison system. Using Akeroyd's words, it was clear that he believed the development of personal discipline was aided through the application of educational discipline. This understanding of and commitment to the discipline of education consistently provided Akeroyd with his theoretical and conceptual framework to address arising issues. Akeroyd's adherence to his principles of teaching, reinforced within a criminological positivist framework, provided a consistent and continuous point of reference for his reform agenda. Underpinning this emphasis on reform was Akeroyd's drive to establish the prison as an institution of education, not only for prisoners but also for staff and the wider community.

The first area of reform was the formalisation of education programs for prisoners. Akeroyd focused on identifying the educational, social, and employability needs of prisoners (particularly

---

[342] Semmens, 1995.

young prisoners) and introduced structured schooling experiences to help address these needs. Akeroyd's initiatives in prioritizing prisoner access to education and training programs within classroom settings as well as in the prison industry workplaces where he also ensured there was a focus on training aligned to prisoner case plans. Whilst there has been evidence in earlier periods in Victoria's penal history of incidental and ad hoc schooling practices taking place, Akeroyd's approach provided the first formalized approach to planning and implementing prisoner education programs based around evidence gathered about the needs of prisoners.

The second area of reform was the formalisation of education for prison staff. This initiative was driven by Akeroyd's strong desire to ensure that all resources within prison operations were focused on the prison as an educational institution. Within this goal, Akeroyd believed in the need to have educated prison staff to carry out the roles he wanted them to play in supporting prisoner reform. Whilst this drive to raise prison staff education standards provided conflict within staff and management relationships over the span of Akeroyd's appointment, it is evident that this is the first attempt within the Victorian prison system to formalize prison staff qualifications and set standards for promotion based around educational qualifications rather than on seniority.

Not only did he implement both prisoner and prison staff education reform, Akeroyd also directly led reform in a range of prison management practices. This was particularly evident in the introduction of prisoner case studies and prisoner classification. Following a lengthy period of inactivity within the state's prison policy and practice reform, it was noticeable that Akeroyd personally drove reformative practice, and he drove this practice through a positivist revolution. Akeroyd established and modelled the standards and practice of professional behaviour he expected others to employ. He modelled the practice of writing detailed case studies including formal psychological testing and structured recording observations of prisoners' behaviours to identify problems and map solutions to address these problems. Akeroyd regularly referred to what he considered to be the use of scientific methodologies to provide rigour in collecting and analysing data. To him, the application of the 'way of the psychologist' was the core to his approach to reform, and from this positivist perspective, this book demonstrated that Akeroyd introduced a change of prison and prisoner management policy and practice from a punitive to a treatment orientation.

Akeroyd clearly founded his approach upon his understanding of the principle of scientific inquiry and applied this methodology at every opportunity. He actively encouraged a rigorous approach to all components of treatment of prisoners, and he appeared to take every opportunity to learn from the experiences of prisoners' lives to give him clues to understanding the phenomenon of criminality. He exemplified this in his practice of personally interviewing prisoners at points in time throughout their sentences and for those inflicted with corporal punishment recording their reflections post the event. Akeroyd also interviewed some of the general prison population seeking their reflection after an execution took place. Akeroyd used these interview processes to enhance his understanding of the nature of criminal thinking as well as using these experiences as a test of prisoner and young offender learning from key events in prison life.[343] It was a key strategy for Akeroyd to fastidiously record notes

---

[343] An example of Akeroyd's methodology in collecting these stories is reflected in the bundles of papers he collected on each of the prisoners executed under his watch (except for Eddie Leonski, the US soldier hanged for murder). This research has not gone into detail into each of these particular bundles of papers apart from noting the existence and broad scope of these bundles

on many prisoners, and these notes ranged from detailed case study notes (including the baseline data provided through psychological testing) through to recorded detail of prisoner experiences as they progressed in their time in custody. Akeroyd used these notes to build his knowledge and evidence base on which he would plan to redress the causality of crime and criminality through what he considered effective programs.

In many of his reports and his presentations to various audiences, Akeroyd employed what he considered the strength of scientific facts to back up his various positions. He used this approach to challenge others to dispute the position he proposed. As discussed earlier, the establishment of individual case studies became a powerful tool for asserting an authority over the explanation of causal factors for criminal and aberrant behaviour. The accumulation of this evidence allowed Akeroyd to further explore causes of criminality in individuals, and Akeroyd's middle and later years witnessed his growing interest in classifying types of psychological attributes with specific criminal behaviours. The classification of the various behaviours gave an explanation to authorities, the public, and prisoners alike of the reason for individual behaviours and hence further reinforced Akeroyd's authority to assert treatment regimens to address these behaviours. In short, Akeroyd used the essence of positivist theory, through the application of scientific methodologies, to define the 'reality' of the situation, classify the reality in evidentiary terms that would provide for a meaningful approach to resolve the issues, and use the language of the classification to influence the implementation of his directions.

---

because these papers are worthy of detailed investigation on their own merits. Whilst the researcher found these bundles of papers compelling reading, the overall content was tangential from the key focus of this research.

Along with his education–led reform throughout the prison system, Akeroyd initiated strong engagement with Victoria's government education system to provide education (and later education and training) programs for prisoners. Whilst not fully implemented within his reign as inspector general in Victoria, Akeroyd worked on the key principle of involving the body responsible for providing education services to the broader community to provide the responsibility for delivery of education programs to those in prison. This strategy laid the foundation for consolidating the provision of education to prisoners as an integral component of prison and prisoner management. This was even further strengthened in 1954 when, under Whatmore's leadership, the Victorian Education Department formally recognized the education centres with the state's prisons as registered school, thereby allowing the state government to fund, staff, and manage the curriculum delivery to prisoner students. This connection between the prison services and the education services laid the foundation for a long-lasting relationship which appears unique throughout Australia, let alone the rest of the world, to this very day.

It was Akeroyd's commitment to his principles of teaching, his direct connections with the Education Department of Victoria, and his capacity to bring together like-minded people that led to significant areas of reform through his direct influence. It was also significant that Joseph Akeroyd indirectly contributed to other areas of reform especially through the consolidation of the discipline of criminology as a vehicle for informing and advising government policy. His achievements are significant in reforming prisoner education practices at the time, yet his indirect achievements provide insight into significant prison and prisoner management reform within the period of his appointment.

· The establishment of the Melbourne University Centre for Criminology was of important assistance to Akeroyd's initiatives at that time. This centre authenticated the development of the knowledge of crime, criminality, and penology and provided an authoritative vehicle for carrying the positivist message through academic, government policy, and public forums. The Centre for Criminology at Melbourne University was the first such institution in the world which devoted itself to the study of criminology.[344]

The consolidation of criminology as a vehicle for influencing policy was of great significance for two key reasons. Firstly, the mechanics of initiating and deploying such radical change appeared to be executed across disciplines and institutions (such as the judiciary as well as in prisons and the field of psychology). The drive to bring together academics, judiciary, and prison management practitioners supported by international criminological experts such as Anita Muhl indicated a unique collaborative approach to identifying and addressing the issues of the nature and cause of crime and criminal behaviours. Secondly, the emergence of this focus on criminological approaches to studying crime and criminality concurrently through the application of positivist theory supported Akeroyd's personal drive to implement and lead such significant change in prison and prisoner management strategies. Whilst the emergence of criminology as an influential policy vehicle could not be directly attributed to Akeroyd, it is evident that his involvement contributed to this initiative. For Akeroyd's involvement in supporting the way of the psychologist (as he would regularly write), the significance for him was the support for his single-minded commitment to the importance of using scientific reasoning and strategy. Akeroyd embodied positivist commitment, and this is evidenced not only in what he believed

---

[344] Finnane, 2006.

but also in the methodology and strategy used to implement his beliefs. This was happening at a point in time the rest of the world struggled with economic and social development. Akeroyd forged ahead through his strong belief in the ideology of scientific processes; and this was evidenced when he, along with others, provided a world-leading example of the implementation of scientific principles and assumptions to lead the government policy in prison and prisoner management.

Whilst it was evident that Akeroyd was one of many involved in the consolidation of criminology as an important policy advisory vehicle to the Victorian government at the time, it was also evident that Akeroyd was himself instrumental in connecting the wider community to the various criminological perspectives. He did this by bringing debate to the wider community through his annual reports, radio presentations, and public discussion in the newspapers. Of these communication channels, Akeroyd's use of the annual reports was a major vehicle to voice his growing confidence and strengthened commitment to his positivist approach to prison and prisoner management. As an educationalist, it appeared that Akeroyd used the annual reports to bring his own learning of criminological, psychological, and sociological issues to the attention of government with the express purpose to inform and educate. The issues he raised through these reports were also communicated to the public either directly or indirectly. Direct communication occurred through his radio broadcast or his lectures to education and community groups whilst the indirect approach occurred through the media, particularly newspaper reports. Perhaps Akeroyd's strategy was to indirectly influence policymakers, judiciary, and influential public servants through helping to sway public opinion. Regardless, it appears that Akeroyd was also keeping to his original calling as a schoolteacher by using every opportunity to educate not only his students and staff but also the whole community.

Akeroyd presented arguments and engaged allies to deploy his vision within the prison system. Whilst Akeroyd appeared to frame his arguments strategically, he also faced criticism from many quarters. In many cases, this criticism emanated from individuals and/or groups holding specific views based in different theories from that of Akeroyd. Akeroyd's drive to change work practices met with resistance at regular intervals from within the ranks as well as from his political masters.

Staff criticism of Akeroyd's practices emerged in three broad areas. Akeroyd's drive to change prisoner management approaches by requiring staff to develop case studies and record observations of prisoner behaviour in a rigorous manner elicited criticism from staff and unions. It appeared that this criticism evolved from staff concern firstly to changes in the prevailing or existing work practices such as being asked to do more (i.e. developing case studies and monitoring and implementing program plans) and secondly to work differently by moving from punishment and containment focus to encompassing a treatment focus. These issues received regular coverage in newspapers and internal reports over the time of Akeroyd's tenure.

The third area of criticism came from staff and from the bureaucracy related to changed staff recruitment and promotion practices. Akeroyd's initiatives to change staff recruitment by demanding greater focus on education achievement and to change staff promotion through education attainment rather than time served elicited continuous conflict from the existing prison staff. Whilst Akeroyd battled union perspectives and individual staff member complaints and grievances throughout his tenure, a most significant issue of conflict arose with the bureaucratic complaint regarding Akeroyd's inconsistent approach to staff selection in 1945. This issue was significant for this story as the way that Akeroyd dealt with the issue appeared out of character from the ways he dealt with conflicts regarding staff in his early and middle phases. In the early days, Akeroyd was consistent in stating his clear directions for the quality of staff members in terms of their approach to the job as well as their professionalism in their education for the job. Akeroyd did not appear to waver in his determination to drive change, and he appeared to maintain a strong commitment of consistency in the messages he conveyed and the way he conducted himself. He constantly provided comments of his positions and his disputes with the points made by the proponents, and these were evidenced by the annotations on various documents. However, in 1945, Akeroyd was criticized within his own bureaucratic department for inconsistency by not maintaining his long-term committed approach to staff promotion. It was notable that at that time, there were no apparent recorded notes of dispute or of alternative viewpoints expressed by Akeroyd within his personal or private records nor were there references made in memos of response to the claims made against him. Whilst it is entirely possible that some evidence of Akeroyd's response to these claims may have been made but not kept in his records, there well may be an explanation that Akeroyd may have chosen not to dispute the claims. However, it may have indicated that Akeroyd was coming to the end of his tenure and that he did not countenance undertaking a further battle. As stated, there is no evidence to indicate whether this was an aberration of judgement, whether this was a matter of not wanting to fight another battle, or whether this was an example of simply acquiescing to the constant challenge of an opposing perspective.

In broader terms, Akeroyd's drive to implement a treatment-based approach also received contradictory comments from interest groups through the public press, and the public press provided a constant medium to carry all sides of the debates. Akeroyd dealt with many of these conflicts by entering counter debates in the media and through reports, by leading by example, and by gaining a supportive alliance of like-minded professionals. Other areas of conflict related directly to the challenging theoretical perspectives surrounding fundamental elements of the criminal justice system such as sentencing and punishment. Akeroyd's attempts to address issues he saw in the application of the Indeterminate Sentencing Act continued throughout his career, and the issues he raised about the indeterminate sentence were not resolved until well after his retirement.

In all the areas of conflict, there was one area which provided a rich insight into the battles faced by Akeroyd and how he was able to deal with this conflict. This is in the dimension of punishment. This was best examined by reflecting on the challenges Akeroyd faced in opposing, seeking understanding, and then accommodating forms of punishment – particularly his consideration of the role of birching and whipping. In his early days, Akeroyd clearly held a position which supported a treatment approach to prisoner management rather than one which held the impost of punishment as the means to bring about conformity of law-abiding behaviour. Akeroyd wrote about his perspective on punishment in numerous public and private articles. He presented his position to public audiences, and he presented his position in the annual reports to the government. However, he recognised that corporal punishment was directed by the judiciary, and its implementation was mandated by the courts. Akeroyd therefore oversaw the carriage of this punishment, but of most interest was the way he followed up the whipping. Akeroyd followed up the whipping by constructing case studies in which he interviewed the affected prisoners to discover what they learnt from the experience. Hence, it is argued, Akeroyd turned to the theory in which he obtained most meaning to help him accommodate the act of corporal punishment. He turned the acts of punishment into a learning experience based on the gathering of data to assist in arriving at a scientific outcome of meaning for the experience.

It is at this point which evidenced a major turnaround in Akeroyd's position on corporal punishment. As time progressed and as evidenced by his interview to the state government punishment committee, Akeroyd appeared to become an advocate for the role of punishment as, in his terms, a means of treatment.

This latter-day Akeroyd position was in stark contrast to the early-day Akeroyd position. Whether these changes of position reflected a change in his philosophical thinking or this was a chosen compromise to a simple utilitarian position to enable himself to perform his role is a challenge to unravel. Some clues emerge indicating the latter was more likely. The first clue in this unravelling was revealed in his approach to corporal punishment. Despite his earlier protestations against the application of corporal punishment within his perception of the way treatment environment should operate (i.e. his positivist theory inclination) his actual approach deferred to the embedded strength of the judicial and political positions on the application of corporal (and capital) punishment. This deference demonstrated the embedded power of the classicist and conservatist theory perspectives prevailing against Akeroyd's emerging positivist ideals at that point of time.

Akeroyd never abandoned his desire to implement a treatment-focused prison system even though, on the face of it, he acquiesced his treatment focus to the punitive focus of the prevailing judicial and political focus of the time. Akeroyd's drive to use each punishment event as a learning experience both for the whipped prisoner and for those prisoners impacted by the hanging of a compatriot appeared to be Akeroyd's approach to translate a punitive experience into a learning experience.

Akeroyd's personal and formal reflections on the acts of the whipping, birching, and hanging including his personal anti-punitive position conflicting with his mandate to implement these acts then following up on the process of obtaining meaning arising from the act displayed an oscillation between his strong, almost unilateral commitment to a treatment approach and his accommodation of the punitive classicist perspective. It is unclear from his diary or from his notes whether it can be argued that Akeroyd placed so much of his thinking from a singular theoretical base that he was unable to accommodate other viewpoints which held currency within his world, and hence, he moderated his thinking to allow his singular view to envelop other perspectives but on the terms of his reference. Alternatively, it is unclear that his acceptance of the acts of punishment was his acquiescence to a position that he could not change. Hence, he embraced the act of punishment but only in a form he could accommodate within his clear positivist terms of reference.

This conundrum challenges those involved in forming and implementing public and social policy in contemporary times as much as it challenged Akeroyd. Akeroyd's approach to the accommodation of corporal punishment as a form of treatment is an example of opaque reform. Akeroyd used his positivist language and positivist theory to rationalize his position on corporal punishment. His accommodation of others' perspectives on corporal punishment allowed him to rationalise his position and give meaning to the area of punishment which had troubled him in terms he felt were palatable. It allowed him to continue with his rehabilitative perspective and accommodate alternate actions within his singular positivist perspective.

Obtaining meaning from Akeroyd's experiences requires some speculation. Given the timing of Akeroyd's accommodation of punishment as a treatment, it could well be speculated that Akeroyd may have considered that his time as inspector general was coming to an end and therefore chose not to dispute. Also, it could be speculated that the battle of his singular theoretical drive was worn down through the constant pressures of the opposing perspectives. Regardless of these speculations, it was most obvious from the evidence gathered that Akeroyd did not appear to dispute that he wavered from his earlier singular commitment to a consistent positivist approach to prison and prisoner management.

Whilst he implemented these changes, Akeroyd met a wide range of overt and subvert criticisms and oppositions. These criticisms came from those perspectives at the time which were embedded primarily in the conservatist and classicist theories. Akeroyd's experiences indicated that his drive to implement and embed practices clearly based within positivist theory met with continual overt and passive power exerted within the judiciary, political, and prison ranks as well as within a broader community sentiment. It is important to recognise that Joseph Akeroyd initiated policy directions which would influence the actions of the next two generations of inspectors general, and the resultant practices have become part of practice in contemporary Australian prison management. Indeed, it can be argued that Akeroyd set the foundation for his successors, particularly Whatmore, to implement the significant penal reforms in terms of removing the Indeterminate Sentencing Act, implementing juvenile justice settings, and overseeing legislative change to have each prison officially recognised as a registered school in Victoria's education system.[345]

The above discussion identified the achievements arising from contrary positions faced throughout Akeroyd's time. However, Akeroyd also faced challenges that he was unable to overcome. The press at and around Akeroyd's last days lamented his inability to embed his aspirational initiatives, particularly in the areas of capital and stock improvements, due to the lack of financial support. Whilst these limitations were, to some degree, out of his control, it must be regarded that, as a senior bureaucrat, he did have the responsibility to realistically ensure that his plans could be implemented. This may well be a harsh and unfair criticism, but the historical records do reflect that Akeroyd failed to implement the reforms to his satisfaction due to the poor facility stock. Another area of failure was his inability to overturn the indeterminate sentence practice. Again, calling this a failure may well be unfair as there were a range of other influential agencies connected with the sentencing process of which Akeroyd is one player. However, Akeroyd's successor, Alexander Whatmore, is credited with overturning the indeterminate sentence.[346]

Regardless of the significant challenges he faced, Akeroyd led a remarkable reform in the areas of prison and prisoner management in Victoria at a time which was ill suited to foster such reform. In the period 1924 through to 1947, we find the world between two major conflicts, suffering from a significant economic depression and leading into the cold war. There was little if any prisoner education reform recorded in the Western world throughout this time. Yet from the evidence accumulated, not only did Akeroyd lead a significant

---

[345] Freiberg and Ross, 1999; Semmens, 1999.

[346] As reported by Freiberg and Ross, 1999.

period of reform in these very adverse political and economic circumstances, but he also laid the foundation for a long-lasting reform in the management and practices, particularly of prisoner education in Victoria.

The examination of Akeroyd's influence in shaping prison and prisoner management reform in Victoria unearthed three key revelations. Within the general understanding there was little (if any at all) prison and prisoner management reform in the post–World War I through the post–World War II period, the first revelation is that there was significant reform activity in the Victorian prison system and that Joseph Akeroyd was pivotal in his role as inspector general at that time. The second revelation was that this period witnessed robust debate and positioning within seemingly conflicting major criminological theories seeking the authority to espouse the most appropriate ways to deal with crime and criminality. This debate witnessed the emergence of a clear positivist perspective (with Akeroyd as a lead protagonist) to challenge the incumbent classicist views of the judiciary and the conservatist views of the government. The uniqueness of the Akeroyd influence within the emergence of positivist theory was evidenced in his focus on the perceived treatment needs of individual prisoners gained from the introduction of a case study approach. The focus on individuals established a different approach to dealing with prisoner management which indicated that Akeroyd's achievements, using Young's terms, indicated the emergence of individualism within an exclusive society before this was recognised elsewhere in the world. A significant development in the emergence of positivist theory saw the establishment of the Centre for Criminology at Melbourne University as a policy advisory body for the government. The third revelation was the first hint of the emergence of the strain or sub-cultural theory which, unlike the three major theories, started to look beyond the individual for the cause of crime and criminality. Akeroyd's and McRae's words and ideas exemplifying the emergence of this sub-cultural theory emerged well before the published discussions of Matza and others in the USA and the UK in the 1970s.

These revelations certainly indicated that in Victoria, Australia, there was a highly active prison and prisoner management reform which laid the foundation for long-term legacies. Joseph Akeroyd played a role at the centre of this reform activity.

19.1   Akeroyd's Legacies

The two major areas of reform in Victoria's prison system, particularly in the education-led prison reform, occurred in Akeroyd's time. Much of his vision and many of his reforms were not embedded in his time however but were realised after his appointment ceased. In terms of education-led reforms, the third phase emerged post-Akeroyd when former teachers Alex Whatmore and later Eric Shade were appointed inspectors general of prisons. Prisoner education remained a priority under their stewardship while, as Gehring argued, prisoner education activity remained stagnant in the rest of the Western world during World War II and the cold war. Whatmore, appointed inspector general in 1947, built on the connections established by his predecessor, Akeroyd, by encouraging the formalisation of school operations within prisons which resulted in the state education authority assuming responsibility for education in prison settings. Semmens (1999) acknowledged Whatmore's era (the 1950s) as one of rehabilitation in Victoria's prison system.

In 1954, prison schools were established as special schools within the primary education sector. Whatmore appointed Eric Shade as the first chief education and training officer, and he would later take over the role as director of prisons (the successor role to inspector general). His succession cemented a period where the relationship between educationalists took a strong leadership in prison organisation and prison management. An era which witnessed a concerted focus on rehabilitation in prisons as well as the interplay between an emphasis on basic education skills on the one hand and an alternate focus on work skills on the other. The resulting competition witnessed many conflicts of priority within prison management decision-making from the 1950s until the 1990s.[347] In keeping with the directions commenced under Akeroyd, Biles reported that prisoners were administered a set of psychological tests upon arrival: 'This is in accord with the principle of not only satisfying the needs for education but in also helping to indicate the range of needs that exists in each man.'[348] However, not all parties appeared committed to the new directions or, at least, held widely differing views on how this accord would evolve. From 1925 until 1960s, a conflicted understanding of the various roles and functions emerged between education staff and custodial staff seemingly in response to ideological differences between their roles within the prison system. Indeed, many issues emanated from the second phase of correctional education reform which coincided with significant changes in prison management reform initiated under Akeroyd's tenure from 1924 until 1947.

It is noted that the Victorian approach to have each prison registered as a formal education institution and staffed and resourced through state education funds was unique in Australia.[349] In other Australian jurisdictions, teachers are generally seconded to the

---

[347] Biles, 1964.

[348] Biles, 1964, p. 205.

[349] Biles, 1977.

respective correction department to deliver programs in the various prisons. Biles provided an overview of different types of programs offered to prisoners (such as language, literacy, and numeracy and other academic pursuits; vocational skills; socio-leisure and recreation programs; and pre-release programs). He also provided an indirect reference which could indicate some criticism of the Victorian school-based approach at the time. Biles argued that it is important for prison education to be seen differently from school education on the basis that 'prison programs are not directly comparable to those provided for children in schools'.[350] Biles's sentiments were echoed in both the Collins Report (1984) and the Blackburn Report (1984) which recommended the move of responsibility and management of prisons education from the school's division of the Victorian Education Department to the adult education TAFE (Technical and Further Education) sector and marked the evolution of a fourth phase.

This fourth phase emerged after Blake's period of analysis. The fourth phase landmarked the importance of education in prisons by framing the prisoner's right to access education under the Corrections Act of 1986. Again, it appeared that Victoria held a unique position to all other states and territories of Australia by formalising prisoners' rights to access education under statute. The change also reflected a shift in focus from merely providing them basic skills to aligning the education and training needs of prisoners with the emerging labour market requirements of the contemporary Victorian and Australian economy. It resulted in shifting the responsibility for prison education and training from the state's school system to Victoria's TAFE system[351]. Whilst the structural alignment has remained consistent

---

[350]   Biles, 1977, p. 94.

[351]   Semmens, 1992; Simmons and Wilson, 1992; Penaluna, 1992; Wilson, 1995

until now, there were interesting shifts in focus on the purpose of providing education and training programs to addressing of prisoner criminogenic behaviours as a critical function as well as supporting employability skills for release[352].

Throughout his time, despite conflicting positions presented by contrary but influential theoretical perspectives, Joseph Akeroyd was committed to realizing his vision of the prison as a positivist institution which treated, schooled, skilled, and reformed prisoners into effective citizens. It is also recognised that this vision was not fully realized. According to Akeroyd, and to the press of the time, the economic circumstances of the time prevented the commitment of the resources required so desperately by Akeroyd to see his vision come to fruition. Whilst the impact of economic circumstances was no doubt influential in limiting Akeroyd's capacity to realise his aspirations, it is argued that Akeroyd's capacity to develop and implement reforming policy and practice was also impacted by the strength of the prevailing classicist and conservatist criminological thinking embedded in judicial and political practice at the time. Despite his vision not being fully realised, Akeroyd deserves recognition for the significant and long-lasting reforms he did achieve, and legacies built on the foundations he laid.

Akeroyd's impact on prison reform is likened to some extent to that of Maconochie. Whereas Maconochie's legacy in the ticket-of-leave initiative transformed into the current remission and parole provision, the impact of Akeroyd's positivist reforms led to continuing practices such as formalised education programs, case management, and classification processes becoming institutionalized practices through to current times. This analysis makes it clear that Akeroyd is by no means the only architect of the positivist reform to

---

[352] Bearing Point Review, 2000

prisoner management strategies in Victoria. Evidence from the early prison annual reports and from the enlightenment period advised that the birth of positivist thinking was in existence before Akeroyd assumed the key role as inspector general. However, until now Akeroyd's contribution to significant reforms through his education-led positivist approach has not been fully recognised. Access to his previously unreleased private papers allowed an awareness of and insight into Akeroyd's significant work in the developing policy and practice in implementing formalised education programs for prisoners and prison staff; introducing a rigorous approach to developing case studies and case plans for individual prisoners; professionalising prison officer training, recruitment, and promotion processes; establishing programs for youthful offenders; classifying individual prisoners in accordance with their social and psychological treatment needs; and promoting community dialogue about understanding crime and criminality through public and professional debates.

Whilst Akeroyd's successors have rightly received the accolades for embedding many of these reforms in institutional practice through legislation, it is important to recognise that many of these reforms were initiated in the Akeroyd era. Akeroyd epitomized the passion and fervour for a methodical science-based approach to prisoner management he believed was appropriate for Victoria at that time. Akeroyd's behaviours and initiatives also epitomized the essence of the positivist theoretical position for which he fought, and the evidence of his commitment and drive was recorded in his thoughts in his diaries, in articles in the newspapers, through his radio broadcasts and presentations to professional groups as well as his submissions to the government, and through formalized reports. Akeroyd brought his internal or personal debates to the public arena through his personal journals and notes. Through the medium of the annual reports, Akeroyd challenged authorities to accept his positioning. Akeroyd developed a network of like-minded individuals, people of some authority within public and intellectual standing such as McCrae, Muhl, Browne, and Cunningham to also contribute to the public debates. Yet it was over the issue of punishment that Akeroyd appeared to compromise his position in favour of the conservatist and classicist position of the judiciary. Such was his passion for prison reform through the application of his interpretation of scientific methodologies for therapeutic purposes that he struggled to accommodate conflicting perspectives unless he was able to fit these perspectives within the theoretical structure he felt most comfortable with. Akeroyd appeared to embody the conflicts that face contemporary prison managers and administrators to provide innovative program solutions within a complex political and social environment which harbours so many embedded and, in many instances, intangible, challenging perspectives.

It is appropriate that Joseph Akeroyd be now recognised for directly and indirectly leading an era of significant reform in prison and prisoner management practice, but as T. S. Eliot posed the question, the challenge is to glean the meaning from Akeroyd's and others' experiences.

CHAPTER 20

What Does This All Mean?

At the commencement of this book, Eliot's 'The Dry Salvages' proposed the challenge facing each of us as we progress through our personal and professional lives. This challenge was best expressed in the following excerpt from his famous poem:

> *We had the experience but missed the meaning. And approach*
> *to the meaning restores the experience in a different form.*[353]

My experiences working in prisoner education provided significant professional awakenings and shaped my approach to a long-varied education career. By exploring Akeroyd's achievements and challenges, this research helped me to restore my experiences and look at them in a different way. The experiences not only shaped my professional practice as a prison educator but also honed my insight into the relationship between education and crime and criminal justice issues. Through this chapter, I will reflect on and share my learnings as a prison education practitioner.

That first day working at Pentridge Prison indelibly enmeshed in my mind the curiosity of working out what a prison does and what it is supposed to do. The image of the recently released prisoner waiting outside the main gates and unable to cross the road was my first inkling of the daunting task that lie within the walls albeit I was unable to articulate that at the time. My first stint at working in a maximum-security prison lasted just four years. In that short period,

---

[353] Eliot, 2001.

I experienced so many events and insights I had not anticipated as I commenced this professional pathway. My relatively sheltered life as a teacher did not groom me for working in a prison. I saw tragedy of prisoners struggling to understand why they were in prison and trying to work out the emotional, social, and physical barriers keeping them in prison. Some merely succumbed and accepted the day-to-day existences of being told when to get up, when to work, when to eat, and when to go to bed. Others puffed their chests to confront and defy their keepers and/or fellow inmates with every day providing a battle to fight. I witnessed their feeling of importance in a world of belonging where for this brief period, they were with others who felt like them. A few decided this life was not for them, and consequently they either made a concerted effort to make changes or simply took their own lives. I heard stories of horror, and I inwardly (and sometimes overtly) recoiled with disbelief at what some people do to others in our society. As an educator, I found this intense microcosm compelling yet repelling. I felt the exhilaration of being in the middle of this underworld working with people whose names and faces graced the front pages of the popular press and were immortalised in film and drama, yet I felt the comfort of not belonging to it and being free to leave at the end of each day. Worst of all I experienced varying degrees of detachment from this grey, forbidding, insular, and bizarrely homogenous world of a maximum-security prison. I also witnessed the pain of families of victims struggling to reconcile with the tragic horror enforced on them and the shame and sorrow and, in some instances, the burden of feeling failure exhibited by parents and relatives visiting their sons and daughters in custody. This was a significant change for a primary school–trained teacher filled with the idealism of helping young children explore the world of learning to facing hardened, often institutionalised, offenders.

Like many of my colleagues, I took solace in deep black humour to cope with existing in a forbidding environment and be able to make sense of a world that did not make sense. I did not realise at the time how removed I was from understanding the lives of these prisoners or circumstances leading to their attendance in my prison classroom.

I realise now that I entered this world as a naïve 25-year-old with assumptions about who prisoners were and why they were in prison. Through this examination of Joseph Akeroyd's experiences and trying to make sense of my own, I realised I had extremely limited knowledge about the nature of crime and criminality within my own community which prepared me to effectively engage with prisoners as students. Even though I had undertaken special education qualifications, I believe that the content of that course did little to prepare my or others' understanding of the intricate nature of crime and criminality to become an effective educator in institutional settings such as prisons.

In those early days, my colleagues understood as little of our environment as I did. Now I can see how separate prison education was from prison management. The educators, with their assumptions of change through education, were isolated. The impact of this lack of preparation was professionally devastating. Unwittingly my language accommodated the prison lingo. Every sentence I spoke, either in the prison or, worse, outside, was punctuated with profanity; and it was natural to speak that way. I sought humour to deal with the tragedy happening all around me, and that even translated to the world outside the prison. I was not alone as these experiences were echoed in the lives of so many of my colleagues. We formed this image of the tough guys teaching tough guys in the tough world of a maximum-security prison. We accepted the atypical as typical; and now, much to my disgust, I realised that many of my colleagues adopted the unspoken approach that near enough was good enough because no one really cared about this group of people.

Small things hit home to prick my professional conscience. Ross,[354] a student of mine at Pentridge Prison, came up to me at Christmas 1980 and gave me a small bunch of lavender sprigs. Ross was a naïve university student unwittingly recruited to be a drug mule to get funds to continue his studies. He said he had nothing else to show his appreciation for the work I did to keep his studies progressing. The genuineness of Ross's gift and words hit home when I questioned whether I capably did help given my own spiral into institutionalisation. I knew I needed to take a break from prison education, restock, but ensure I arm myself with the capability to be a professional and capable prison educator. At that point, I committed myself to return to Pentridge Prison as a far more professional and committed educator with the personal, technical, and resilience skills to prevent me from falling to that lowest common level that my colleagues and I fell.

On reflection, I can see now that I did not have all the skills or tools to deal with working in this complex environment upon entering the role of prison educator. I did not have the comprehensive understanding of the nature of crime and criminality to provide insights into why a prisoner was in prison at that time, nor did I understand the theories about planning and implementing education programs appropriate to those individuals. Nor did I have insights into the discourse underpinning everyday decisions or the implications of long-term planning decisions on prison education service direction or developing and implementing effective individual prisoner education plans. I did not have those skills because of my lack of insight into those embedded and often unclear or opaque (yet very influential)

---

[354] Not his real name.

values driving assumptions on dealing with crime criminality within the aspirations of a cohesive society. Given this lack of theoretical and conceptual knowledge, I realise now that I did not have either the confidence or the language to articulate my concerns about existing practice. I was merely fitting into a world with so many competing values that it was easier not to consider values at all. Essentially, I was becoming institutionalised and felt the risk of being a cog in the process that prisons socialised prisoners to be prisoners.

Professional pride and my disgust that I had so easily let my personal values slide led to new resolve. I made a commitment to myself to consolidate and commit to those principles I was battling with an ability to articulate at the time. Those values were as follows: I should respect each individual prisoner who trusted me as their educator, that each prisoner had a unique story about his or her path to prison, that each prisoner was capable of making decisions about his or her actions, and that education was the most important means to connect prisoners with the world outside prisons.

I now see that I was attempting to develop an eclectic philosophical and theoretical position which weighted all factors equally in explaining criminality. The assumptions I made and the assumptions I questioned eventually led me to better understand my practice as an educator. By using the learnings of the past, particularly through Akeroyd's approach to the challenges he faced in planning, implementing, communicating, and evaluating prison reforms through an education lens, I learnt about different assumptions people make about causation and response to dealing with crime in our society. These assumptions emerge through high-level government and operational policy perspectives, through the language we talk about these with one another, and through the ways we put these policies into practice. Akeroyd's experiences and reflections helped me identify my position in the broad spectrum of embedded and emerging theories. Certainly, each theory contributes a particular unique perspective to prison management, and it is important for prison educators to ensure they understand what each can offer. The positivist, conservatist, and classicist theories of crime and criminality place flaws in individual behaviour at the centre of the cause of criminality. These theories not only underpin the assumptions built into the decision context in Akeroyd's time but are vastly evident in today's schema in the Western world. I can understand the political efficacy of adhering to these theories as they ignore complex social organisation issues by placing the responsibility for crime in the minds and bodies of individual offenders. The assumptions about contemporary prisons and prison education policy are still largely built around these major theories, but the policy considerations now need to consider the challenges and insights brought forward through the emergence of those critical criminological theories based on strain and Marxist perspectives. Modern policy must now consider the complex impact of social marginalisation of individuals through the imposition of laws and practices reflecting the power imbalance in our society. Akeroyd was before his time in starting the debates on these critical theories and for considering the implications of these critical criminological perspectives on prison and prisoner management long before these became formally recognised.

Planning for effective education programming and organising effective delivery strategies require well-grounded theoretical understanding of what a prison is, what it intends to achieve, and what it actually achieves. Using the knowledge of different theoretical perspectives about the functions of a prison, the prison educator recognises he or she is continually working and communicating with others who hold differing assumptions to undertake their respective roles. To fail to recognise this and to work in isolation from other agencies can only result in limited program offerings which may in turn further marginalise the most marginalised group in our community.

As I learnt more about Akeroyd, through his own words and those of others, I found his achievements inspirational. Like me, he came from a mainstream school system; but unlike me, he formed a clear vision from the very beginning of his time in prisons whereas I underwent many years of exposure to working in prisons before I could say I formed some concept about what a prison is and what the function of education in prison ought to be. Akeroyd pushed through barriers of resistance to embed his reforms with a steely resolve. He pioneered the merging of prison education and prison management in Victoria, and he did so by maintaining his vision of the educable prisoner being assisted to enter mainstream as a law-abiding society. I have the benefit of accessing many more years of research findings than Akeroyd had access to in his time, and I find myself amazed that many of Akeroyd's achievements were not recognised until now. It was through the examination of how Akeroyd's idealism translated to practice that I came to examine what form of meaning I gained from the experience.

I found Akeroyd's actions inspirational and reassuring but also unsettling. Akeroyd's single-minded and determined approach to reforming prison and prisoner management was awesome. I am grateful to him for institutionalising the value that education and educationalists can and do positively contribute to prisoners' lives whilst broadening community insights into the nature of crime and criminality. Commitment to his values shaped his drive to change those prison management approaches inherited from his predecessors. I greatly admired his determined and focused approach to plan and implement change and his capacity to take on detractors throughout his career. His capacity to build a core of colleagues and use his networks to broaden his sphere of influence was masterful and provided a blueprint on planning and implementing change.

Whilst I found Akeroyd's approach and actions inspiring, I also felt reassured there was consistency between Akeroyd's actions and my beliefs. I found Akeroyd's focus on the needs of individuals and his commitment to the importance of education to create an environment to facilitate change in individuals validated the core I gained through my experience working in adult and juvenile, male and female custodial settings. Akeroyd recognised that everyone had his or her own story, and he interviewed and recorded each individual's details. If he did not recognise the uniqueness of each person's journey, it is doubtful that he would have taken the effort to meticulously record these details. Through these individual dossiers, Akeroyd furthered his knowledge about groups and classifications of people, and this helped him to formulate strategies to treat or remediate individuals. Whilst Akeroyd's focus was based on the psychological and intellectual deficits of individuals, my focus on the importance of individual stories was fuelled through the *MALWAYS* experience examined earlier in this book. The prisoner voice from *MALWAYS* talked about individual experiences and demonstrated that people do make choices, and their decisions are based around the range of options they believe are available to them. This differentiates my perception from Akeroyd's on the appropriate focus of education. Whereas Akeroyd's focus was clearly on addressing assessed psychological and social deficits, my focus was to recognise that prisoners can and do make decisions but need to be challenged to expand their range of options to make the best decision available by challenging and extending the language used by individuals to tell and reflect on their personal stories.

Akeroyd's experiences also provided warnings where reform can fail. With the benefit of hindsight, the analysis of Akeroyd's public and private battles to clarify, articulate, and embed his reforms demonstrated his naivety in understanding the nature of crime and criminality. His assumptions on the causation of criminality sat strongly in one aspect of the theoretical spectrum outlined earlier. His positivist thinking dominated his focus on the causation of crime being embedded in the psychological and under-socialised deficits of individuals. Promoting systemic reform based largely on one specific theory or ideology without clearly understanding and acknowledging others leads to the risk of alienating or subverting practices which are held important by others operating within prison and other justice-related settings. As witnessed through Akeroyd's experience, this may result in overt conflict with staff, or it may also result in the opaque practice of rationalising practice to suit a theory.

The examination of Akeroyd's experiences were both reassuring and daunting when applied to the challenge of implementing change in a prison environment. Whilst Akeroyd was not able to implement all the changes he envisioned, his achievement in embedding education as an essential part of prison operations demonstrated that significant change in the complex environment of prisons is possible. But subsequent events show that this was not a final victory, despite many changes being embedded in legislation. Many times, I have witnessed the emergence of reforms only to see these recede and then re-emerge later badged in different words then recede once again. Akeroyd experienced the battle of leading and implementing reforms against the resistance of existing practices. However, Akeroyd's legacies realised a significant and long-lasting reform resulting in raising the profile of the important role of education in prisons. His legacy set Victoria apart from every other jurisdiction in Australia and indeed the world for over 80 years, when the provision of education in prisons and youth justice facilities was managed, staffed, and resourced by the relevant state education services, not by the prison services.

Although it is almost 100 years since Akeroyd commenced his role as inspector general of Victoria's prison system, the debates about crime and punishment today have a depressingly familiar tone. At the core of the debates are the polarised views on the causation of crime extending from individual culpability (primarily due to personal deficit theories) through to social dislocation. The range of competing perspectives between the mainstream and critical theorists explain the inconsistent application of the law to people's behaviours. The learning from critical criminology theorists showed some behaviours considered illegal in some settings yet the same behaviours are lauded in other areas. For example, as a society, we express starkly divergent views on particular behaviours. We encourage corporate brutality and bullying in the fight for economic success yet condemn bullying in any other social form; we fete those who kill in war but demonise those who kill in the community. As a society, we support the taking of drugs such as alcohol but criminalise the taking of other substances despite the extensive community harm of alcohol abuse. I am not saying that I advocate any of these activities. I simply make the point that in some instances, behaviours are criminal whilst in alternate settings, similar behaviours are tolerated or even celebrated. This means there are differential applications of law-and-order approaches to people's behaviours, and what is legal or not legal is not always clear cut in individuals' minds. By pointing this out, it is argued that our community is not harmonious and unified under a single set of values as some sectors of our community claim or at least our community has diverse perspectives of what the societal values actually are. Akeroyd and McCrae battled with this issue in trying to understand the drivers of sub-cultural group behaviours (particularly relating to juvenile offenders). However, the so-called subcultural issues occupy a lot of current news media space. Our community is made up of diverse groups some of which are considered to operate outside the law. Young questioned the reasons our society comprises groups of people, such as bikie groups; ethnic, religious, and regional-based cohorts; or gangs that work so hard to be a separate non-conforming subculture and why there are law authorities working so hard to maintain the alienation of these groups. As Young wrote, 'the enforcement of rules shape crimes and deviance and the existence of rules invites transgression'.[355] This is exemplified in recent and historical events where particular groups in our community are identified, isolated and marginalised. Examples of this in Australia (and in New Zealand) include the criminalisation of the bodgies and widgies of the 1950s, bikie gangs, the recent focus on young African male gangs, and the past focus on particular ethnic groups[356], [357]. Recent examples in the Western world include the moral panic escalation of outing black communities in Brixton leading to the now-infamous Brixton riots.[358] These riots precipitated the divisive law-and-order debate resulting in the election of the Thatcher conservative government. Again, I reiterate that I do not condone the behaviours of some of these groups but highlight that

---

[355] Young, 2011, p. 215.

[356] https://nzhistory.govt.nz/culture/the-1950s/overview.

[357] Keith Moore, Bodgies, Widgies and Rock and Roll – Teenage Rebellion and Moral Panic in Australia 1956–1959 (qut.edu.au).

[358] Scarman, Lord (1986), *The Scarman Report: The Brixton Disorders 10-12 April 1981*, Penguin Books, Harmondsworth.

increased focus of social control agencies, security agencies, and law enforcement on individuals or groups can be counterproductive.

The significant concerns of over-representation of indigenous people in custody and, especially, continuing indigenous deaths in custody were not overtly raised in Akeroyd's time. That is not to say that these matters were not apparent at that time, but it implies these matters were not openly on any political or social agenda. The Muirhead-led Royal Commission into Aboriginal Deaths in Custody in Australia (1987–1991) provided 339 recommendations to address significant improvements that were then needed within the criminal justice system and policing in relation to custody arrangements and support for Aboriginal and Torres Strait Islander individuals and communities that come into contact with the justice system. The commission also made recommendations highlighting broader community support strategies and focused education provision.

> *Aboriginal people now die in custody at a greater rate than before the RCIADIC with an average of 15.1 deaths per year between 1991 and 2018 compared to 10.5 deaths per year between 1980 and 1989. First Nations adults are 12.5 times more likely to be incarcerated(link is external) than non-Indigenous peoples and First Nations youth are 26 times more likely to be incarcerated(link is external). First Nations women continue to be the fastest growing prison population(link is external) in Australia.*

Whereas the education focus was integral in the Victorian prison management regimes of Akeroyd, Whatmore, and Shade, its influence waned in the times after Shade.[359] Prisoner education

---

[359] Both Biles (1978) and Harris (1992) intimated the relationship .between prison management and prisoner education followed parallel paths of reform but with overt animosity between both streams .

became a subordinate component of contemporary prison and prisoner management.[360] Prison educators felt undervalued in the prison, and education principles were subjected to overriding commercial, economic, and populist drivers. In many ways, contemporary prison education debates, particularly in Victoria, have not adequately presented a strong case for the value of education because the capacity to articulate its value has been lost in the polarised language of the dominant theories and the overarching government imperative for economic policy drivers.

Given the articulation of these perspectives, it now raises the question of clarifying the role of education in contemporary prisons in Victoria, whereas the current focus is on preparing prisoners with the vocational skills on the assumption that once prisoners gain skills, they will find work and that through work, they will derive the income to address other aspects such as accommodation, health, and family needs.[361] The assumption limiting the connection between the roles of education and training for work carries the significant risk that there are employment options available within the community and that work options within the prison are the same as those available in the community. If there is not a direct compatibility between the training options provided in prison and real work options, then the structure of education and training in prisons risks further marginalising those in prison. Worse still, if there is not a concerted approach to prepare and support prisoners to proactively develop the skills and ability to make their own decisions about life and work options, then token education and training provision is merely babysitting. The cheapening of education intent

---

[360]   See Biles and Harris.

[361]   http://www.corrections.vic.gov.au/home/prison/going+to+prison/work+education+and+training/.

to provide qualifications for non-existent work rails against the core Akeroyd principle of not further marginalising prisoners.

Akeroyd would be distraught with the current practice to commodify education in prisons to provide a service that is not arming prisoners with the capabilities for effective decision-making. Further, he would be concerned about the commercialisation of education provision in prisons leading to the practice of employing short-term contract and casual staff with limited capacity and knowledge to support a holistic approach to prisoners' education. This practice does not question whether practitioners have content capability but does question whether current prison education management policymakers ensure practitioners have well-grounded understanding of the environment into which they undertake education practice.

Contemporary prison populations are escalating, and prisoners present with more complex needs than in Akeroyd's time. This is evident through increasing levels of mental illness, continuing high representation rates of indigenous, and continuing high representation from lower socio-economic groups. The prison is the repository for the significantly marginalised people all of whom will return, at some point, to the broader community. Akeroyd demonstrated that education can be and needs to be an integral component of overall prison management to support prisoners to leave prison and become active citizens. Akeroyd's legacies challenge contemporary prison education practitioners to reflect on the purpose of their mission and arm themselves with the skills and knowledge necessary to fulfil this role effectively and professionally.

So many times, history witnessed the resurgence or re-emergence of the dominance of particular theories. Under the Dame Sally Coates review of education in prisons in the UK, the resurgence of the importance of the role of education as a critical aspect of prison and prisoner management practices is remerging.[362] I cannot help but think this is an indication the principles and practices originating within the Akeroyd reforms have not been lost but will come to the forefront of prison and prisoner management policy and practice once again.

---

362 Review puts education at heart of prison service - GOV.UK (www.gov.uk).

REFERENCES

Agnew, R. (2006). Foundation for a General Strain Theory of Crime and Delinquency. *Criminology.* Vol 30 Issue 1 February 2006 47–88.

Akeroyd, J. (1915–1941). Diary of J. Akeroyd. PROV, VA 2908, VPRS 6604.

Akeroyd, J. (1932). Case Histories of Prisoners. *The Justice of the Peace,* 22(11).

Akeroyd, J. (1899–1952). Personal Papers of J. Akeroyd. PROV, VA 2908, VPRS 6603 (closed papers).

Atkinson, L., and Gerull, S. (Eds.) (1993) *National Conference on Juvenile Detention: Proceedings of a Conference Held 10–13 August 1993.* Canberra, ACT: Australian Institute of Criminology.

Annual Report, Penal Establishments and Gaols, Inspector General of Penal Establishments (1910). Melbourne: Government Printer, Melbourne.

Annual Report, Penal Establishments and Gaols, Inspector General of Penal Establishments (1922). Melbourne: Government Printer, Melbourne.

Annual Report, Penal Establishments and Gaols, Inspector General of Penal Establishments (1924). Melbourne: Government Printer, Melbourne.

Annual Report, Penal Establishments and Gaols, Inspector General of Penal Establishments (1934). Melbourne: Government Printer, Melbourne.

Annual Report, Penal Establishments and Gaols, Inspector General of Penal Establishments (1935). Melbourne: Government Printer.

Annual Report, Penal Establishments and Gaols, Inspector General of Penal Establishments (1936). Melbourne: Government Printer.

Annual Report, Penal Establishments and Gaols, Inspector General of Penal Establishments (1938). Melbourne: Government Printer, Melbourne.

Annual Report, Penal Establishments and Gaols, Inspector General of Penal Establishments (1947). Melbourne: Government Printer, Melbourne.

Annual Report, Penal Establishments, Gaols, and Reformatory Prisons: Report and Statistical Tables for the Year 1949 (1950). Government Printer Victoria 1950/51 no. 6.

Annual Report, Penal Establishments, Gaols, and Reformatory Prisons: Report and Statistical Tables for the Year 1950 (1951). Government Printer Victoria 1950/51 no. 40.

Annual Report, Penal Establishments, Gaols, and Reformatory Prisons: Report and Statistical Tables for the Year 1951 (1952). Government Printer Victoria 1951/52 no. 24.

Annual Report, Penal Establishments, Gaols, and Reformatory Prisons: Report and Statistical Tables for the Year 1952 (1953). Government Printer Victoria 1952/53 no. 18.

Annual Report, Penal Establishments, Gaols, and Reformatory Prisons: Report and Statistical Tables for the Year 1953 (1954). Government Printer Victoria 1954/55 no. 18.

Annual Report, Penal Establishments, Gaols, and Reformatory Prisons: Report and Statistical Tables for the Year 1954 (1955). Government Printer Victoria 1955/56 no. 2.

Annual Report, Penal Establishments, Gaols, and Reformatory Prisons: Report and Statistical tables for the Year 1955 (1956). Government Printer Victoria 1956/58 no. 11.

Annual Report, Penal Department: Report and Statistical Tables for the Year 1956 (1957). Government Printer Victoria 1956/58 no. 35.

Armstrong, J. (1980). The History of Victorian Prisons. *The Bridge*, 4(1), 1–4.

Ashforth, B., and Mael, F. (1989) Social Identity Theory and the Organisation. *The Academy of Management Review*, Vol 1 Jan 1989, 20–39.

Bearing Point (2003). *Education and Training Provision in Victorian Prisons – The Way Forward,* discussion paper, Office of Correctional Services Commissioner: Melbourne.

Bean, P. (1981). *Punishment*. London: Oxford.

Bessant, J., Watts, R., Dalton, T., and Smyth, P. (2006). *Talking Policy: How Social Policy Is Made*. Australia: Allen and Unwin.

Biles, D. (1977). *Crime and Justice in Australia*. Canberra: Australian Institute of Criminology.

Biles, D. (1978). Punishment: A Personal View. *Educational Magazine*, 35(1), 12–15.

Birgden, A. (2004). *Reducing Offending Framework*. Melbourne: Corrections Victoria.

Blackburn, M. (1984). Ministerial Review of Post-compulsory Schooling. Melbourne: Department of Education.

Blake, L. (1973). *Vision and Realisation: The History of State Education* (L Blake Ed. Vol. 1). Melbourne: Education Department of Victoria.

Braithwaite, J. (1999). *Crime in a Convict Republic*. Paper presented at the History of Crime, Policing and Punishment, Adelaide: Australian Institute of Criminology.

Browne, G. (1924). Experiment in Citizen Making: How Detroit Prevents Crime. *Herald*.

Campbell, N. (1931). Prisoners Today and Yesterday: Men and Methods Are Changing. *Herald* (10 June 1931).

Clinard, M. (2008). *Anomie and Deviant Behaviour* (13th edition). USA: Thompson Learning.

Cohen, S. (1985). *Visions of Social Control*. New York: Picador.

Collins, M. (1984). *Report of the Ministerial Review of Educational Services for the Disabled*. Melbourne: Ministry of Education.

Cote, S. (2002). *Criminological Theories. Bridging the Past to the Future*. California: Sage Publications.

Crotty, M. (1996). Doing Phenomenology. In P. Willis and B. Neville (Eds.) *Qualitative Research Practice in Adult Education*. Melbourne: David Lovell Publishing.

Crotty, M. (1998). *The Foundations of Social Research – Meaning and Perspective in Research Processes*. London: Sage Publications.

De Kretser, H. (2012). Time for Prison Reform across Australian States, retrieved from *World Today,* www.abc.net.au/worldtoday/content/2012/s3511023.htm.

Dewey, J. (2008). *Moral Principles in Education.* Project Gutenberg e-book.

Doll, E. (1924). Classification of Prisoners for Purposes of Training Work and Parole, 14 *J. Am. Inst. Crim. L. & Criminology* 110 (May 1923 to February 1924).

Eggleston, C. (1998). *The Need and Value of Correctional Education: Why Is It Important?* Paper presented at the International Forum for Education in Corrections Systems (Australasia), Brisbane, Australia: IFECSA.

Eggleston, C., and Gehring, T. (1986). Correctional Education Paradigms in the United States and Canada. *Journal of Correctional Education,* 37(2), 86–92.

Eliot, T. S. (2001). *Four Quartets.* London: Faber and Faber.

Elliott, A. (1999). *Contemporary Social Theory* (Elliott A Ed.) Massachusetts, USA: Blackwell Publishers.

Einstadter, W., and Henry, S. (2006). *Criminological Theory: An Analysis of Underlying Assumptions* (2nd edition). Lanham, MD: Rowman and Littlefield.

Eysenck, H. (1969). The Technology of Consent. *New Scientist* (June), 26.

Eysenck, H. (1977). *Crime and Personality.* New York: Paladin.

Fairclough, N. (2005). Critical Discourse Analysis. *Marges Linguistiques,* 9(2005), 76–94. Retrieved from www.ling.lancs.ac.uk/profiles/263.

Fairclough, N. (2005). Critical Discourse Analysis in Transdisciplinary Research on Social Change: Transition, Rescaling, Poverty and Inclusion. *Lodz papers in pragmatics,* 7(2005). Retrieved from www.ling.lancs.ac.uk/profiles/263.

Finlay. L. (2008). *Introducing Phenomenological Research.* Retrieved 19 April 2012 from www.linda.finlay.com/introducingphenomenological reserach.doc.

Finnane, M. (2004). *The Difficulties of My Position: The Diaries of Prison Governor John Buckley Castieu 7855–7884.*Canberra: National Library of Australia.

Finnane, M. (2006). The ABC of Criminology, Anita Muhl, J V Barry, Norval Morris, and the Making of Discipline. *British Journal of Criminology,* 46(3), 399–422.

Finnane, M. (2008). Retrieved from www.emelbourne.net.au/blogs/EMO1210b.htm.

Fitzgerald, M. (1981). *Crime and Society* (M. Fitzgerald Ed.). London: Open University Press.

Fitzroy Legal Service (2003). *The Law Handbook.* Melbourne: Fitzroy Legal Service Inc.

Foucault, M. (1977). *Discipline and Punish: The Birth of the Prison.* London: Allen Lane.

Foucault, M. (1980). Prison Talk. In C. Gordon (Ed.), *Michel Foucault, Power/Knowledge: Selected Interviews and Other Writings 7972–7977.* Brighton: Harvester Press.

Foucault, M. (1989). I, Pierre Reviere. In S. Lotringer (Ed.), *Foucault Live: Interviews 7966–84*. New York: Semiotext(e).

Foucault, M. (1994). *Aesthetics, Methods and Epistemology (Essential Works of Foucault 7954–7984)* (J. Faubion Ed. Vol. 2). Penguin Books: London.

Freiberg, A., and Ross, S. (1999). *Sentencing Reform and Penal Change*. Sydney: Federation Press.

Garland, D., and Sparks, R. (Eds.) (2000). *Criminology and Social Theory*. UK: Oxford University Press.

Gehring, T. (1993). Plain Talk about Correctional Education. In R. Semmens (Ed.), *Yearbook of Correctional Education*. Maryland: Correctional Education Association.

Gehring, T., and Eggleston, C. (2007). *Teaching within Prison Walls: A Thematic History*. San Bernardino: California State University.

Gehring, T., and Muth, W. R. (1985). The Correctional Education *I* Prison Reform Link: Part 1. *Journal of Correctional Education,* 36(4), 140–146.

Gehring, T., and. Wright, R. (2003). Three Ways of Summarising Correctional Educational Progress Trends. *Journal of Correctional Education,* 54(1), 5–14.

Giles, M., Le A., Allan, M., Lees, C., Larsen, A., and Bennett, L. (2004). *To Train or Not to Train: The Role of Education and Training in Prison to Work Transition*. Australia: NCVER.

Graham, L. (2005). *Discourse Analysis and the Critical Use of Foucault*. Paper presented at the

Australian Association for Research in Education Annual Conference, Sydney.

Guba, E., and Lincoln, Y. (1994). Competing Paradigms in Qualitative Research. In N. Denzin and Y. Lincoln (Eds.), *Handbook of Qualitative Research*. California: Sage Publications.

Harris, I. (1992). *Corrections Education in Victoria: Reflections of an Experienced Practitioner*. Paper presented at The Way Out: The role of Employment, Education, and Training for Offenders in the Criminal Justice Systems. Perth, Western Australia: Outcare.

Heseltine, K. (2011). *Prison-based Correctional Rehabilitation: An Overview of Intensive Interventions for Moderate to High-Risk Offenders*. Canberra: Australian Institute of Criminology.

Hinds, L., and Daly, K. (2001). War on Sex Offenders: Community Notification in Perspective. *Australian and New Zealand Journal of Criminology*, December 2001 vol 34, no 3, 256–276.

Holloway, D. (2000). *The Inspectors: An Account of the Inspectorate of the State Schools of Victoria 1851–1983*. South Melbourne: Rossco Print.

Howells, K. Heseltine, K., Sarre, R., Davey, L., and Day, A. (2004). *Correctional Offender Rehabilitation Programs: The National Picture in Australia*. Canberra: Australian Institute of Criminology.

Hughes, R. (1986). *The Fatal Shore: The Epic of Australia's Founding*. New York: Vintage Books.

Ignatieff, M. (1981). The Ideological Origins of the Penitentiary. In M. Fitzgerald, G., and Pawson, J. (Eds.). *Crime and Society* (pp. 37–59). Great Britain: Routledge and Keegan Paul.

Ignatieff, M. (1983). *State, Civil Society and Total Institutions: A Critique of Recent Social Histories of Punishment (Vol 3).* Chicago: University of Chicago.

Inspector General of Penal Establishments (1921). *Pentridge – Special Report* (Parliamentary Papers). Melbourne: Public Records of Victoria.

Johnson, R., Onwuegbuzu, A., and Turner, L. (2007). Towards a Definition of Mixed Methods Research. *Journal of mixed methods research,* Vol 2, 112–133.

Keating, J. (1999). *Public Education Redefined: Education and the State in Victoria.* Paper presented to the AARE annual conference, Melbourne.

Kinesh, S. (undated). *Paradigms, Methodology and Methods.* Retrieved from www.bond.edu.au/ prodext/groups public/@pub-tls-gen/documents/genericwebdocument/bd3 _012336.PDF.

Knight, T. (1980). *Education and Detained Youth: Curriculum for Youth Competence and Community Linkage.* Melbourne: La Trobe University.

Lloyd, S., and Sreedhar, S. (2013). *Hobbes' Moral and Political Philosophy. Stanford Encyclopedia of Philosophy* (Summer 2013 Edition), Edward N. Zalta (editor). Retrieved from http://plato.stanford.edu/archives/sum2013/entries/hobbes-moral/.

Lynn, P., and Armstrong, J. (1996). *From Pentonville to Pentridge: A History of Prisons in Victoria.* Melbourne: State Library of Victoria.

Martinson, R. (1974). What Works? Questions and Answers about Prison Reform. *The Public Interest,* 35, 22–54.

Matza, D. (1969). *Becoming Deviant*. Eaglewood Cliffs: Prentice Hall.

McRae, C. (1926, 29 May 1926). Youngsters Who Make a Bad Start. *Herald*.

Melossi, D., and Pavarini, M. (1981). *The Prison and the Factory: Origins of the Penitentiary System* (G. Cousin, Trans). London: The Macmillan Press.

Merton, R. (1964). Anomie, Anomia and Social Interaction. In M. Clinard (Ed.). *Anomie and Deviant Behaviour*. New York: Free Press.

Merton, R. (1966). Social Problems and Sociological Theory. In Merton, R., and R. Nisbet (Eds.). *Contemporary Social Problems* (2nd edition). New York: Harcourt, Brace & World.

Muhl, A. (1941). *The ABC of Criminology*. Melbourne: Australian Council of Educational Research University Press.

Muth, W. R., and Gehring, T. (1986). The Correctional Education / Prison Reform Link: 1913–1940 and Conclusion (Part 2). *Journal of Correctional Education*, 37(1), 14–17.

Nisbet, R. (1970). *The Sociological Tradition*. London: Heinemann.

O'Toole, S. (Ed.) (2002). *Corrections in Australia*. Australia: Butterworth.

O'Toole, S. (2006). *The History of Australian Corrections*. Sydney: UNSW Press.

O'Toole, S., and Eyland, S. (2012). *Corrections Criminology*. Sydney: Hawkins Press.

Oxford Dictionary. www.oed.com.

Paterson, H. (1989). *History of Prison Education,* unpublished thesis. Melbourne: LaTrobe University.

Penaluna, K. (1992). Integrating Employment and Training in Prison. In Sirr, P. (Ed.). *The Role of Employment, Education and Training for Offenders in the Criminal Justice System: Conference Proceedings.* Perth: Outcare.

Petrow, S. (1995). Better Than the Streets: Juvenile Reformatories in Tasmania 1860–1896. In Semmens (Ed.). *What Works for Whom in Corrections? Policies, Practices and Practicalities.* Conference proceedings. Hobart: Printing Authority of Tasmania.

Report of the Inspector-General of Penal Establishments on Developments in Penal Science in the United Kingdom, Europe, and the United States of America: Together with Recommendations Relation to Victorian Penal Administration Published 1952. Government Printer Victoria 1951/52 no. 25.

Report of Director of Penal Services for the Year 1957. Published 1959. Government Printer Victoria 1958/59 no. 26.

Report of Director of Penal Services for the Year 1958. Published 1960. Government Printer Victoria 1959/60 no. 23.

Reports of Director of Penal Services for the Year 1959 and Half Year Ending 30 June 1960.

Published 1960. Government Printer Victoria 1960/61 no. 20.

Rhodes, G. (2014). *Inmate Culture: Newgate Prison.* Retrieved from www.prisonvoices.com/?p90.

Rothman, D. (1971). *The Discovery of the Asylum: Social Order and Disorder in the New Republic*. Boston and Toronto: Little, Brown and Company.

Ruche, G., and Kirschheimer, O. (2009). *Punishment and Social Structure*. New Jersey: Transaction Publishers.

Sarre, R. (1999). *Beyond What Works? A 25-Year Jubilee Retrospective of Robert Martinson*. Paper presented at the History of Crime, Policing and Punishment Conference. Canberra: Australian Institute of Criminology.

Schutt, R. (2006). *Investigating the Social World: The Process and Practice of Research*. London: Sage Publications.

Semmens, R. (1992). Offender Employment, Education and Training: Current/Future Realities. In

Sirr, P. (Ed.). *The Role of Employment, Education and Training for Offenders in the Criminal Justice System*. Conference proceedings. Perth: Outcare.

Semmens, R. (Ed.) (1993). *Yearbook of Correctional Education 1993*. San Bernardino: CEA and CSU.

Semmens, R. (1995). *International Forum on Education in Penal Settings*. Paper presented at the What Works for Whom in Corrections? Tasmania: IFEPS.

Semmens, R. (1999). *The Track Record of Correctional Education*. Paper presented at the International Forum on Education in Penal Systems Conference. Fremantle: IFEPS.

Semmens, R., and Oldfield, J. (1999). Vocational Education and Training in Australian Correctional Institutions. Adelaide: National Centre for Vocational Education Research.

Simmons, V., and Wilson, R. (1992). *Victorian TAFE Approach to Delivery of Education and Training in Prisons.* In Sirr, P. (Ed.). *The Role of Employment, Education and Training for Offenders in the Criminal Justice System.* Conference proceedings. Perth: Outcare.

Sirr, P. (1992). *The Way Out: The Role of Employment, Education and Training for Offenders in the Criminal Justice System.* In Sirr, P. (Ed.). *The Role of Employment, Education and Training for Offenders in the Criminal Justice System.* Conference proceedings. Perth: Outcare.

Social Welfare Department: Annual Report Year Ended 30 June 1963 (1964). Government Printer Victoria 1963/64 no. 33.

Social Welfare Department: Annual Report Year Ended 30 June 1962 (1963). Government Printer Victoria 1963/64 no. 4.

Social Welfare Department: Annual Report Year Ended 30 June 1965 (1966). Government Printer Victoria 1966/67 no. 2.

Social Welfare Department: Annual Report Year Ended 30 June 1966 (1967). Government Printer Victoria 1967/68 no. 8

Social Welfare Department: Annual Report Year Ended 30 June 1968 (1969). Government Printer Victoria 1968/69 no. 38

Social Welfare Department: Annual Report Year Ended 30 June 1967 (1968). Government Printer Victoria 1968/69 no. 4.

Social Welfare Department: Annual Report Year Ended 30 June 1970 (1970). Government Printer Victoria 1970/71 no. 23.

Social Welfare Department: Annual Report Year Ended 30 June 1971 (1971). Government Printer Victoria 1971/72 no. 13.

Sreedharan, E. (2007). *A Manual of Historical Research Methodology.* India: Centre for South Indian Studies.

Taylor, I., Walton, P., and Young, J. (1973). *The New Criminology.* London: Keegan Paul.

Unknown. (1924, 14 March 1924). Crime and Criminals: Address by Hon. Samuel Maugher. *Warrnambool Chronicle.*

Unknown. (1924, 29 November 1924). A Human Touch for Our prisons. Editorial. *Herald.*

Unknown. (1924, 2 December 1924). Human Touch in Prisons – Model Reformatory System. *Herald.* Melbourne.

Unknown. (1924, 18 August 1924). Penal System: Extensive Changes Proposed. *Argus.* Melbourne.

Unknown. (1924). Pentridge! Life within Its Urbane Walls. *Sun.* Melbourne.

Unknown. (1924, 16 June 1924). Prison Education. Letter to the Editor. *Argus.* Melbourne.

Unknown. (1924, 18 August 1924). Prison Management. Letter to the Editor. *Argus.* Melbourne.

Unknown. (1924, 16 August 1924). Reforming Criminals: How Not to Do It. *Age.* Melbourne.

Unknown. (1924, 18 August 1924). Reforming Criminals: The Government's Proposals. *Age.* Melbourne.

Unknown. (1924, 19 March 1924). Schools of Crime: Contaminating Evils of Prison System. *Herald.* Melbourne.

Unknown. (1925, 31 October 1925). The Curing of the Criminal. *Age*. Melbourne.

Unknown. (1925, 8 September 1925). Mental Defectives: Special Schools Advocated. *Age*. Melbourne.

Unknown. (1925, 17 June 1925). Penal Warders: Better Conditions Sought. *Argus*. Melbourne.

Unknown. (1925, 8 January 1925). Prison Reform: Visiting Expert's View. More Specialists Needed. *Herald*. Melbourne.

Unknown. (1925, 17 June 1925). Prison Warders: Claim for Improved Conditions. *Age*. Melbourne.

Unknown. (1926, 31 July 1926). Study of Crime: Is the Criminal Responsible for His Actions? *Age*. Melbourne.

Unknown. (1931, 16 June 1931). Flogging Deters Criminals. *Herald*. Melbourne.

Unknown. (1931, 20 June 1926). Flogging Not a Deterrent. *Herald*. Melbourne.

Unknown. (1931, 6 January 1931). Further Cases Revealed: Attorney General's Action. *Argus*. Melbourne.

Unknown. (1940, 6 July 1940). Gaol Smuggling Does Not Worry Authorities Here. *Argus*. Melbourne.

Unknown. (1947, 20 October 1947). Curing Crime the Old Way. *Herald*. Melbourne.

Unknown. (1947, 18 October 1947). Psychiatric Evidence Hooey Says Gaol Head. *Herald*. Melbourne.

Unknown. (1948). Prison Terms suggested for Sex Offenders. *Melbourne Truth*. Melbourne.

Unknown. (1950). Whipping as Legal Punishment. *West Australian (1879–1954)*. Perth.

Victorian Department of Education. (1924). *Education Gazette*. Melbourne: Victorian Government.

Victorian Sentencing Committee (1988). *Victorian Sentencing Report*. Melbourne: Victorian Attorney General's Department.

Vinson, T. (1998). *Pentridge Prison Unlocked: Victoria's Prisons from Solitude to Sociability*. Melbourne: Jesuit Social Services.

Walter, M. (Ed.). (2006). *Social Research Methods: An Australian Perspective*. Melbourne: Oxford University Press.

Watts, R., Bessant, J., and Hil, R. (2008). *International Criminology: A Critical Introduction*. Oxen: Routledge.

White, O. (1947, 12 August 1947). How Can Crime Best Be Prevented? *Herald*.

Wicharaya, T. (1995). *Simple Theory, Hard Reality: The Impact of Sentencing Reforms on Courts, Prisons and Crime*. Albany, NY: State University of New York Press.

Wilson, R. (1993). *Vocational Education and Training in Victoria's Youth Training Centres*. In Atkinson, L., and Gerull, S. (Eds.) (1993). *National Conference on Juvenile Detention*. Canberra, ACT: Australian Institute of Criminology.

Young, J. (1981). Thinking Seriously about Crime: Some Models of Criminology. In Fitzgerald, M., and Pawson, J. (Eds.). *Crime and Society: Readings in History and Theory* (pp. 248–309). London: Routledge and Kegan Paul.

Young, J. (1999). *The Exclusive Society*. London: Macmillan.

Young, J. (2007). *The Vertigo of Late Modernity*. London: Sage.

Young, J. (2011). *The Criminological Imagination*. Cambridge: Polity.